CONTEMPORARY LANDMARK TELEVISION

LIFE ON MARS

CONTEMPORARY LANDMARK TELEVISION

LIFE ON MARS
FROM MANCHESTER TO NEW YORK

Edited by Stephen Lacey and Ruth McElroy

UNIVERSITY OF WALES PRESS
CARDIFF
2012

www.uwp.co.uk

British Library Cataloguing-in-Publication Data
A catalogue record for this book is available from the British Library.

ISBN 978-0-7083-2359-5
e-ISBN 978-0-7083-2360-1

The right of the contributors to be identified as author of this work has been asserted in accordance with sections 77 and 79 of the Copyright, Designs and Patents Act 1988.

Designed and typeset by Chris Bell
Printed by CPI Antony Rowe, Chippenham, Wiltshire

CONTENTS

SERIES EDITORS' PREFACE

THERE IS NO DOUBT that the landscape of broadcasting has been transformed in recent years, and the pace of change shows no sign of slowing. Technological change (satellite and digital television, the rise of the Internet), the internationalisation of television formats and programmes, the availability of the DVD box sets, new technologies for recording and time-shifting viewing, the proliferation of TV channels and the segmentation of the TV audience – these have all ensured that television, once dubbed 'ephemeral', is now a major cultural commodity in a global marketplace. The discipline of television studies, although a relative newcomer to the field of cultural and media studies, has grown confident in its ability to confront and debate the challenges that the new ecology of broadcasting poses.

Contemporary Landmark Television focuses on one corner of the wider picture in recognition of its continuing significance for both home and overseas audiences. The series offers scholars and lecturers timely investigations of current broadcasting, especially in the UK context, through a focus upon television's prime output: programmes. By being responsive to the contemporary television landscape, the series recognises that television scholarship benefits from engaging with the current viewing experience of scholars and students. For us, one of the enduring values of television as a mass medium lies in its contemporaneity with its audience: television exists in the moment – even when that 'moment' is lengthened by new technologies of recording and distribution – and in so doing, enjoys a privileged position as a creative source of artistic and social intervention in the world of its viewers.

The choice to engage with programmes themselves is recognition of the turn towards television aesthetics in recent scholarship, and of the now-contentious nature of some of the accepted categories. The term 'landmark' is used cautiously in the series title to denote programmes that may be significant to a variety of people – audiences, critics, programme makers – in a number of contexts. However, we recognise that landmark, and its synonyms such as 'classic' or 'quality', cannot be assumed but must be debated, and a reflection on key terms is an important aspect of the series' approach. Also, broadcasters such as the BBC and Channel 4 in the UK have sought to meet the challenge of digitalisation by exploiting online programme assemblages (the chat room, forum, and programme games and quizzes), and these have become staples of British television drama, in the process significantly extending our understanding of what constitutes a television programme. Therefore, an important emphasis of the series is the treatment of individual programmes or series 'in the round' – in their production and reception contexts, and where relevant in their different iterations. It also draws on, where possible, the perspectives of practitioners and television professionals themselves. Programmes – even long-running series – exist in a wider context of other programmes, and the series will occasionally consider clusters of programmes linked by a common theme.

Although aimed primarily at students and scholars of television, Contemporary Landmark Television intends to be accessible to the general reader with an interest in how television programmes have been commissioned, produced, debated and enjoyed, as well as to professional broadcasters. Whoever the reader, we hope that he or she will be both stimulated and challenged by the experience.

NOTES ON CONTRIBUTORS

Joseba Bonaut is currently an instructor and researcher at San Jorge University (Spain). He obtained his PhD on television and sport at the University of Navarra (Spain). His research interests are sport and the media and Spanish cinema and television history, and he has published on these topics in both Spanish and English. He is a member of the European Network for Cinema and Media Studies (NECS) and the European Communication Research and Education Organization (ECREA).

John R. Cook is Reader in Media at Glasgow Caledonian University. He has written numerous articles on television drama and its contexts of production for journals such as the *Historical Journal of Film, Radio and Television*, the *Journal of British Cinema and Television* and *Critical Studies in Television*. He has recently completed an edited collection with Peter Wright, *Critical Essays on Star Wars* (I. B. Tauris, forthcoming).

John Curzon recently completed his doctoral thesis at the University of Warwick on the representation of the spaces of post-industrial northern England in film and television drama.

Nichola Dobson completed her doctoral dissertation on the animated situation comedy genre and has since taught at Queen Margaret University, Edinburgh and Glasgow Caledonian University where she was also research assistant on 'Television fiction, society and identity: Catalonia and Scotland' with Universitat Rovira i Virgili Tarragona, Catalonia. She has a guest column in *Flow*, the online television journal.

Matt Hills is Reader in Media and Cultural Studies at Cardiff University. He is the author of *Fan Cultures* (Routledge, 2002), *The Pleasures of Horror* (Continuum, 2005) and *Doing Things with Cultural Theory* (Hodder-Arnold, 2005) and is currently completing a monograph on the BBC series *Torchwood*.

Mary Irwin is currently a research fellow at the University of Warwick on an AHRC-funded project, 'A history of television for women 1947–1989', and has research interests in television and film documentary and television drama.

Peter Hughes Jachimiak is Senior Lecturer in Communication, Cultural and Media Studies at the University of Glamorgan. He has published on a range of cultural texts from the 1970s and 1980s, including the acclaimed comic strip *Charley's War* and the simulation war game *Fulda Gap: The First Battle of the Next War*. Currently writing a monograph that employs a self-reflexive, auto-ethnographic approach, Jachimiak's research into the 'otherness' of childhood and Britain in the 1970s provides insight into the relationship between media-informed memories and identity construction.

Stephen Lacey is Professor of Drama, Film and Television at the University of Glamorgan. He is the author of the monograph *Tony Garnett* (Manchester University Press, 2007), and is co-editor of two key volumes in television study, *Popular Television Drama: Critical Perspectives* (Manchester University Press, 2005) and *Television Drama: Past, Present and Future* (Palgrave, 2000). He is a founding editor of the journal *Critical Studies in Television*, and is co-director of an AHRC-funded research project (with Universities of Reading and Leicester) entitled 'Spaces of television drama: production, site and style'.

David Lavery is Professor of English at Middle Tennessee State University and the author/editor/co-editor of numerous essays and books, including *The Essential Cult Televison Reader* (University Press of Kentucky, 2010) and volumes on such television series as *Twin Peaks*, *The X-Files*, *Buffy the Vampire Slayer*, *The Sopranos*, *Lost*, *Deadwood*, *Seinfeld*, *My So-Called Life*, *Heroes*, and *Battlestar Galactica*. He co-edits the e-journal *Slayage: The Online International Journal of Buffy Studies* and is one of the founding editors of *Series/Season/Show* and *Critical Studies in Television*. He has lectured around the world on the subject of television.

Ruth McElroy is Principal Lecturer in Communication, Cultural and Media Studies at the University of Glamorgan. Her research examines television and cultural identity in distinct national contexts and with an emphasis on history, place and gender. She has published in journals such as *Critical Studies in Television*, *Media History*, *Television and New Media* and the *European Journal of Cultural Studies* for which she is book reviews editor. Ruth contributes to the work of BAFTA in Wales as a committee member and chair of selective award juries. With Steve Blandford, Stephen Lacey and Rebecca Williams, she recently produced a research report, *Screening the Nation: Wales and Landmark Drama* (2010) for BBC Audience Council Wales.

Brett Mills is Head of the School of Film and Television Studies at the University of East Anglia. He is author of *Television Sitcom* (BFI, 2005) and *The Sitcom* (Edinburgh University Press, 2009), has published numerous chapters in edited collections and has articles appearing in journals such as *Screen* and the *International Journal of Cultural Studies*, including 'My house was on *Torchwood*!: media, place and identity' (IJCS, 2008).

Robin Nelson is Director of Research at University of London, Central School of Speech and Drama and an emeritus Professor of Theatre and TV Drama at Manchester Metropolitan University. His most recent book is *Stephen Poliakoff on Stage and Screen* (Methuen Drama, 2011) and he is also the author of the landmark volumes, *State of Play: Contemporary 'High-end' TV Drama* (Manchester University Press, 2007) and *TV Drama in Transition* (Macmillan, 1997). He has published widely on practice-as-research in the performing arts and is a founding editor of the journal *Critical Studies in Television*.

Teresa Ojer is currently a lecturer and researcher at San Jorge University (Spain). She obtained her PhD 'The BBC as a model of corporate governance, funding system and quality contents' at the University of Navarra. Her main research interests are the study of European public television, quality television and media management and has published widely on these topics, and in particular on the BBC, in Spanish and English. Teresa is a member of the European Network for Cinema and Media Studies (NECS), of the European Media Management Education Association (EMMA) and European Communication Research and Education Organization (ECREA).

Rob Smith is Senior Lecturer in Music at the University of Glamorgan. He regularly performs and improvises live jazz and is currently undertaking a doctorate in community music performance.

Andy Willis is Reader in Film Studies at the University of Salford. He is the co-author of *The Cinema of Alex de la Iglesia* (Manchester University Press, 2007) with Peter Buse and Nuria Triana Toribio and *Media Studies: Texts, Institutions and Audiences* (Blackwell, 1999) with Lisa Taylor. He also edited *Film Stars: Hollywood and Beyond* (Manchester University Press, 2004) and co-edited *Spanish Popular Cinema* (Manchester University Press, 2004) with Antonio Lazaro Reboll and *Defining Cult Movies: The Cultural Politics of Oppositional Taste* (Manchester University Press, 2003) with Mark Jancovich, Antonio Lazaro Reboll and Julian Stringer.

INTRODUCTION

Stephen Lacey and Ruth McElroy

LIFE ON MARS: CONTEXTS OF RECEPTION

LANDMARK TELEVISION DRAMA is shaped by the contexts of its production and reception. Only by attending to these contexts can we fully grasp television drama's role in our everyday lives and in the wider mediated society of which it is a part. Programmes have a provenance; they come from somewhere and with stories about how and why it is they look as they do. Many of these stories are themselves highly mediated, appearing in the form of actor interviews, press and fan reviews, and DVD box-set extras, so that a television programme's genealogy includes the stories told about it by its makers and its audiences.

Life on Mars drew widespread attention from UK audiences and reviewers when it was first transmitted on BBC 1, Monday, 9 January 2006. Achieving figures of around 7.5 million, the show was ranked sixth in BBC 1's top thirty programmes for that week, sandwiched between the medical dramas, *Casualty* (1986–) and *Holby City* (1999–), behind the regular soap opera, *Eastenders* (1985–) and ahead of staples such as the *Six O'Clock News* and the legal drama *Judge John Deed* (2001–7). In the same week, *Lost* (ABC 2004–10) gained Channel 4 just over 5 million viewers whilst ITV's Sunday evening wartime detective drama, *Foyle's War* (2002–), was viewed by over 8 million. For the BBC, *Life on Mars* was to prove both a ratings success and also a critical success and was yet another hit for both BBC Wales and Julie Gardner, its then Head of Drama. Three years earlier, this same creative team had led the successful revival in Cardiff of *Doctor Who*, a much-loved science fiction show that had run on the BBC from 1963 to 1989.

Life on Mars won numerous awards, including two International Emmy Awards in 2006 and 2008, the audience-voted Pioneer Award at BAFTA in 2007, and Best Drama Series and Best Writer Awards in the 2007 Broadcasting Press Guild Awards. Despite being described as 'a dead cert for drama series' in the 2007 BAFTAs by *Observer* TV critic, Katherine Flett, *Life On*

Mars lost out to Jimmy McGovern's *The Street* (BBC, 2006–9), a replay of what had happened earlier in the year at the Royal Television Awards.

Professional reviewers and television industry figures paid considerable attention to *Life on Mars*, largely because most liked the show and regarded it as stylish and innovative. *The Independent*'s Robert Hanks, for example, described it as 'one of the most original and intriguing dramas British television has produced in years' (11 April 2007). *Life on Mars*'s generic hybridity – its combination of realism and fantasy, of science fiction time travel and traditional cop show – required some explanation, but it also allowed the show to earn its reputation for originality, including from some of its writers' most highly respected peers. The writer and director, Stephen Poliakoff, for example, put it thus:

> What do audiences want? In all areas of television they hunger for surprise. Every hit from *Life on Mars* to *Monty Python* has dramatic surprises . . . They want television to enrich their lives and let them see the world afresh, not just fill a space in their evening. If you commission it, the viewers do turn up. ('What is television for?', *The Guardian*, 26 November 2007)

The BBC's press office played no small part in achieving such coverage. Pre-transmission publicity has become a characteristic feature of contemporary television and, in this case, included numerous press releases and stories such as Alice Fowler's interview with John Simm (*Daily Mail* Weekend section, 7 January 2006), which was published the Saturday before the show's Monday transmission. Here, Simm was presented as a serious actor from the north of England, who had previously excelled in dramas such as *Cracker* and *State of Play*:

> 'I like the madness of it,' Simm declares. 'It's *Back To The Future* meets *The Sweeney* – and that's really mouthwatering. When I first read the script, it was so insane I thought, "You must be joking." For me, the hardest thing was to make it real.' As one might expect from the team behind *Hustle* and the award-winning *Spooks*, realism is in big supply.

Both actor and producer credentials (*Life on Mars*'s producers, Kudos, also made *Hustle* (BBC, 2004–) and *Spooks* (BBC, 2002–11)) were used as brand introductions to a series whose time-travelling conceit, when used in a cop show, may have appeared bizarre to an unprepared audience. Billboard and on-screen advertising also played an important part in publicising *Life on Mars*. In the multi-channel age of fragmented television, sometimes known as TV III, such promotional techniques help to ensure that viewers select specific programmes from the general flow of content so that high-cost drama series, such as *Life on Mars*, find an audience.

By the time the second series of *Life on Mars* was about to be aired in February 2007, the BBC had undergone a re-launch of its channel idents and it took the opportunity to produce a seventies-style ident specifically for use in conjunction with the series' transmission, offering viewers a nostalgic version of the BBC itself before running with the show. Such playful innovations not only suture the high-production values of quality drama to the specific broadcaster, they also wrap around programmes a wider experiential invitation to watch and participate, prompting on- and offline discussion with other viewers. Breaking the conventions of old-style idents was just one of the ways in which *Life on Mars* entered the public consciousness even when individual episodes, and the series itself, had ceased airing.

From the middlebrow *Daily Mail* to the populist *Daily Star*, from the right-wing *Express* to the left-wing *Observer*, praise was heaped on *Life on Mars* from the UK press with critics frequently listing the show in their daily and weekly TV guides. Mike Ward told *Daily Star* readers, 'If you reckon cop shows have run out of fresh ideas, take a look tonight at BBC 1's new series *Life on Mars* (BBC 1, 9 p.m.). It might sound like a David Attenborough documentary set on a far-flung planet but this is actually one of the most inventive police dramas in years' (9 January 2006). Meanwhile, *The Independent* was amongst the first to speculate about the series' export potential. Writing just one month after it first aired in the UK, Ian Herbert announced that 'BBC drama *Life on Mars* is about to cross the Atlantic to the United States'. He continued:

> BBC Worldwide is in discussions with US networks about the series ahead of its 'Showcase' event in Brighton later this month, where it is expected to be one of the hottest properties for the assembled ranks of 500 of the world's top television executives . . . The global appetite for the Manchester-based drama is extraordinary, considering the number of commissioning editors who turned it down before the head of drama at BBC Wales finally accepted the script. ('American TV networks go in search of *Life on Mars*', *The Independent*, 9 February 2006)

Two features of this story are worth noting. First, it provides a good example of a common trope in British television production, namely the battle for discovery between gifted writers with a script, and television executives who fail to spot a winner. The final heroic discovery brings praise on BBC Wales and, though not named here, on Julie Gardner; it also bolsters the programme's cultural value as exceptional and therefore distinct from mainstream, everyday television. This sense of being different from staple television is one hallmark of how quality television may be made (see Akass and McCabe 2007). Secondly, this story points to how the deregulation of British television, implemented most notably under the then BBC Director-General John Birt in the nineties, has led to an increasingly marketised model of television as writers pitch their wares to diverse channels who, in turn, are concerned to maintain and improve their market position through their commissions. Critics of deregulation contrast this with the long-term creative relationships established between writers and producers in an earlier age of British television drama. There is some truth here, though it was precisely Julie Gardner's reputation for working closely with writers that helped to smooth *Life on Mars*'s progress from script to screen. Still, that such a BBC hit was not produced by the BBC itself but by the independent production company Kudos is the result of the earlier deregulation which required the corporation to source 25 per cent of its output from outside the organisation. In *Life on Mars*, then, we have a programme commissioned in Wales, set and filmed in Manchester, made by a London production company, transmitted on the UK network and marketed globally by BBC Worldwide.

Not all of the discussion of *Life on Mars* was light-hearted, however. The series' ebullient, bloke-ish discourse was itself the subject of debate. In a *Guardian* comment published on 17 April 2006 ('Language and liberty: over-zealous officers don't change the fact that political correctness has improved the world') the former deputy leader of the Labour Party, Roy Hattersley, wrote how:

> *Life on Mars*, the story of a detective inspector transported by time-machine back to 1973, bases most of its jokes on the rejection, in a more robust age, of effete modern preoccupations. The renewed assault on careful use of language is not surprising . . . The campaign for what has come, derisively, to be called political correctness is essential to a civilised society.

In April 2007, the National Association of Schoolmasters/Union of Women Teachers (NASUWT) criticised the programme for the potential effect that its abusive language and bullying tone might have on impressionable schoolchildren. Whilst not calling for the programme to be taken off air, Chris Keates argued thus:

> If you've got abusive terms like 'fairy boy', that is particularly worrying in a context where our evidence is showing that one of the factors which causes young people to consider suicide is the fact that in schools they are subject to homophobic bullying. (Laura Clark, 'Teachers blame *Life on Mars* for homophobic bullying', *Daily Mail*, 13 April 2007)

Keates casts a rather different light on the seventies from those nostalgic reviewers who lauded the series when she described it as a period when 'women couldn't get jobs, they couldn't get promotion. People who were gay were being verbally abused . . . life was extremely unpleasant for a large number of people.'

Life on Mars entered the public discourse of viewers and non-viewers alike by eliciting debate over what the seventies signified for contemporary British society and how the history of that decade – in relation to policing and equal rights, in particular – might be told. It offers an excellent example of how television drama can do more than merely represent social issues in narrative form; it can instead become a dynamic catalyst for social debate, a vehicle for contests over meanings and values. Seen from this angle, the middlebrow and right-wing press' fondness for the show is perhaps unsurprising, for it allowed them to return to their long-standing critiques of the social gains which pre-dated *Life on Mars*. James Delingpole's tribute to the series ('Oh for the 70s, when real men ruled and political correctness was unknown', *Daily Mail*, 15 February 2007) provides a good example of how *Life on Mars*'s reconstruction of seventies policing was read by some as a lament for conservative social values:

> We don't want our police forces run by lily-livered sociology graduates, banging on about 'institutional racism' and pretending crime is 'society's fault'. . . . What we want is the sort of old-fashioned, no-nonsense rozzer who solves the crime quickly, gets another bad guy, any bad guy, it doesn't matter which – off the streets, and enables us to sleep that little bit more safely in our beds at night. What we want, in fact, is someone like DCI Gene Hunt. The problem with DCI Hunt, unfortunately, is that he doesn't exist.

For some viewers, Hunt became a nostalgic fantasy figure, dramatised both through the scipted one liners and structurally though his classic position in the cop show genre's binary structure. Nonetheless, the show's dramatic revival of abusive language and macho behaviour could unsettle its most admiring, conservative fans. If it is Sam Tyler's repeated question, 'Am I mad, in a coma or back in time?', that structures *Life on Mars*, the question haunting many reviewers, and some fans, was why viewers in the noughties were so deeply enamoured of such an unappealing figure as DCI Gene Hunt (Philip Glenister). Glenda Cooper sought to explain Hunt's nostalgic appeal as:

> [T]he triumphant return of unreconstructed man. He is meant to show us what's bad about 1973 but he also shows us the shortcomings of 2007 . . . In a world of short-term contracts, job insecurity and portfolio careers, Hunt's undying loyalty to his squad (even while rabidly insulting them) makes us wistful for a time gone by when you had a job (and colleagues) for life. ('Why women love DCI Hunt', *Daily Telegraph*, 13 April 2007)

Television nostalgia is framed here as a longing for social stability and coherence. In contrast, Trudie Goodwin, the actress who for twenty-four years played Sergeant June Ackland in *The Bill* (ITV), reflected on her own role and how those of police officers have changed, 'The women police officers I talked to . . . were still desperate to be treated the same as the men, who outnumbered them nearly tenfold . . . It all reeked of a male-dominated, chauvinistic force, the like of which we're now seeing in DCI Gene Hunt in *Life on Mars*' ('Cops and clobber', *The Guardian*, 8 March 2007).

STRUCTURE OF THE BOOK

We have chosen to introduce this volume with a discussion of the contexts of reception of *Life on Mars* and have considered some of the main ways in which it has become a familiar point of reference in cultural discourses beyond television. Some of the themes identified above are returned to, inevitably, in more detail in individual contributions. The book opens in Part I, however, with consideration of aesthetics, in particular the question of *Life on Mars*'s relationship to genre, which establishes an agenda that runs through subsequent chapters.

Parts II and III are devoted to the complex question of how *Life on Mars*, and to a lesser extent *Ashes to Ashes*, engages with history, memory and cultural identity. Part IV deals with two attempts to remake *Life on Mars* in new national contexts (the USA and Spain), a testimony both to the success of the series beyond the UK and evidence of an accelerating trend towards the internationalisation of drama series. Part V aims to balance the emphasis on reception contexts in this Introduction with a consideration of the contexts of production. It consists of an edited transcript of an interview, plus question and answer session, with Julie Gardner, ex-Head of Drama at BBC Wales and executive producer of *Life on Mars* and now Senior Vice President, Scripted BBC Worldwide Productions, and Claire Parker, producer of the series for Kudos, held at a symposium on *Life on Mars* at the Cardiff School of Creative and Cultural Industries in November 2007.

Life on Mars exemplifies an increasing tendency towards generic hybridisation, the self-conscious mixing of dramatic genres. Several chapters in this volume comment on this process, and Dobson addresses it directly. For her, hybridisation is a means to innovate within an industry that is increasingly reliant on familiar genres as a way of capitalising on niche audiences; with both being a vehicle for securing increased viewing figures. However, it is salutary to note that the key generic features noted by critics are not always present for producers. Gardner and Parker caused some puzzlement at the Cardiff symposium when they maintained that the series' basic premise, that Sam Tyler was in a coma, meant that it could *not* be science fiction. This contention closes down one option that the series seemed to want to keep open – that Tyler had indeed 'gone back in time' – and may be disappointing to some readers of this book. For Claire Parker, the issue was how to make Tyler's predicament 'real' at the level of his emotional response and psychological dislocation, and this therefore precluded 'science fiction'. However, as

Gardner later conceded, the fact that parts of the audience wished to engage with the *Life on Mars* as if it were science fiction was evidence of a particular kind of investment and opened up interesting lines of interpretation that had not occurred to the series' makers and did not contradict the kind of realism for which Parker and her colleagues had worked. In this way, *Life on Mars* is a case study of the ways in which a programme becomes transformed through the engagement of its viewers.

It is no accident that many of the examples Dobson cites come from the USA – *The X Files* (Fox, 1993–2002), for example – since *Life in Mars* marks a moment in the 'Americanisation' of British television drama. This is particularly true of the modes of storytelling, of narrative construction, that are employed by the series. Julie Gardner (see Chapter 13) dates this process, or this stage of a more long-term process, from the early noughties, where it was particularly evident in a new wave of series drama, some of it also made by Kudos. The key example for her is *Spooks* (Kudos/BBC, 2002–11), which brought a new narrative energy to television drama, which she characterised as 'quite American, in the good ways, that kind of pace the wit of the story-telling, the clear definition of a genre', and which ran counter to an inherited literary/dramatic tradition. The degree to which this tradition still dominated UK drama in the early noughties is open to debate, but the thrust of the argument is persuasive.

Of course, even if the debt of *Life on Mars* to the hybridised generic narratives of much American series drama is accepted, the series' content is resolutely British. *Life on Mars*'s 'Britishness', particularly its depiction of the UK in the seventies, is evident in the texture and detail of its *mise en scène*, and runs through much of the press and audience comment already discussed. This aspect of *Life on Mars* is, inevitably, central to many of the essays in this book, although contributors approach the issues from different angles. Cook and Irwin place the series' representation of the seventies in the context of an outbreak of nostalgia for the decade, previously regarded as a hiatus between the sixties and the eighties, as seen in the numerous forms of 'memorialisation' that populate the schedules – programmes such as *I Love the 1970s* (BBC, 2000). Noting that such programming feeds on novelty, they argue that although *Life on Mars* may benefit from the discourses of nostalgia, particularly in the characterisation of Gene Hunt, the specific narratives ask for a different kind of response. Hunt may have the fast car, but Tyler often has the last word. Reflecting both the positive and negative aspects of the series' seventies portrayals, this chapter sees *Life on Mars* as a kind of 'moonage daydream' of received cultural memory, oscillating between the values of past and present. The argument is developed in relation to the first series of *Ashes to Ashes*, which the authors argue has a problematic relationship with the past.

One of the main discourses that anchor *Life on Mars* in a particular time and place is that around the music that provides a consistent and evocative soundtrack to the series. Smith explores how both the popular music of the early seventies and the more abstract electronic soundscapes and musical sequences of the recent past (2006 – Tyler's present) are combined, juxtaposed and contrasted in *Life on Mars* to support the narrative conceit that the world was a brighter, messier and more exciting place in 1973 than in 2006. It also addresses the issue of how electronic and mediatised sounds act as a portal to the world from which Tyler is exiled and are deployed to create differentiated responses to the worlds of 2006 and 1973.

Willis offers a different take on *Life on Mars*'s re-imagining of the seventies. He argues that the series looks at the decade through a lens that does not fully acknowledge its turbulent and polarised politics, but rather offers a more generalised, 2006-friendly version of the events, organisations and issues. The series' view of the Manchester police of the 1970s, he observes, and of the police force of the era more generally, reflects and comments upon attitudes to the policing of Britain in the twenty-first century much more than it does the actual police force of the decade, owing much to *The Sweeney* (ITV/ Euston Films, 1975–8) in its rough-and-ready, blokeish and very influential version of seventies policing. A different, though not necessarily contradictory view of *Life on Mars*'s relationship to the fictional seventies was offered at the Cardiff symposium, where both Julie Gardner and Claire Parker observed that many of the production team (as distinct from the writers) had no first-hand memories of the decade, and the references to iconic texts came during shooting, and were introduced by the first series director, Bharat Nalluri, as a way of establishing a 'tone' and a consistent approach to setting, design, lighting and the *mise en scène*.

The interplay of past and present is constituted as a 'then' and 'now', a 'BC' and 'AD', by John Curzon, who takes a single episode (1.3) as a starting point for an exploration of the way that *Life on Mars* re-tells a recurrent narrative of post-war culture: the transformation of the north from an industrial to a post-industrial economy. In Curzon's opinion the years in question, 2006 and 1973, are not innocent choices, but carry particular significance as moments of transition from the north as a place of place of production to one of consumption. In this episode, to which other contributors also refer, the squad are called to solve a murder in a factory that, in 2006, has been converted into flats, one of which is lived in by Sam Tyler. Drawing on sociological analyses of post-industrial living, Curzon argues that Tyler is positioned as a 'comer-in', an interloper into both the gentrified landscape of 2006 and its industrial predecessor, 1973.

Curzon places *Life on Mars* not in the expected lineage of science fiction or seventies police drama series, but in relation to other texts that negotiate the economic and cultural transformation of the north, such as British New Wave cinema of the early sixties, the popular sitcom, *The Likely Lads* (BBC, 1964–6) and its successor, *Whatever Happened to the Likely Lads* (BBC, 1973–4). Looking elsewhere, Nelson also finds unexpected connections to television's refashioning of recent history. Using the long-running but formulaic sixties-set series *Heartbeat* (ITV, 1992–2010) for comparison, he notes contemporary television's disposition to bring together, in hybrid forms, different strands of television's past. Arguing that *Life on Mars* avoids the tropes of formulaic generic drama, he draws upon a small-scale study of viewer interest to investigate the way that the series offers a range of appeals to different segments of the audience, and proposes that when ingredients are mixed creatively something truly innovative may emerge.

Life on Mars was the beneficiary of much online discussion. Analysing threads from one of the most popular online fan fora at the point that the US remake was being planned, Mills traces the ways in which 'British-ness' is defined by fans in relation to the series. He notes that many posters voice an anxiety that this essential characteristic of *Life on Mars* (specifically, its northern Englishness) will be compromised during its journey across the Atlantic. 'British-ness' is couched in debates about audiences, location, performance and casting, and demonstrates significant assumptions about what defines British television. The concerns about these changes not only suggest a worry about a favoured programme being 'ruined', but also demonstrate perceptions about the relationship between Britain and America, and the value of 'British-ness' as a televisual representational strategy. Even the move to London called for by *Ashes to Ashes* is seen by some posters as a kind of betrayal of the original's working-class roots.

Generally, it is the view of those writers who consider it that the translation of *Life on Mars* into other national-televisual contexts has not been successful. Lavery regards *Life on Mars US* (ABC, 2008–9) as a disaster, arguing that it fell victim to the Writers' Guild of America strike of 2007–8 from which it never recovered. Comparing it to the successful ABC series *Lost* (2004–10), under whose wing it sheltered in the schedules for a time, Lavery argues that the series did not display the confidence of its essential premise, and did not understand what had made the original distinctive. A similar problem beset the Spanish version, according to Bonera and Ojer, whose analysis of the reworking of *Life on Mars*, *La chica de ayer* ('The Yesterday Girl', Antena 3, 2009) situates the series in the context of developments in the Spanish broadcasting industry and other, more successful adaptations. Noting key differences and similarities between the ways in which some of the key themes and motifs were translated from the UK context, the authors compare UK and Spanish media contexts and examine how *La chica de ayer* renegotiates the ambiguities of the original series. Like *Life on Mars US*, which they also consider briefly, the Spanish version misreads the importance of the original's precise cultural references (the new title gives an indication of this) and does not, in their view, find Spanish equivalents.

Like Brett Mills, Ruth McElroy also looks at online fan responses to both *Life on Mars* and *Ashes to Ashes*, but her main concern is gender and its representation. McElroy sees both series as sites for the making of retrosexualities, understood as depoliticising, performative interventions in contemporary consumer culture. A great deal was made in the press of the supposedly ironic retrosexism of Gene Hunt and the apparent ease with which the show's producers felt able to play with the politics of gender, often in contrast with the anxious care taken in dealing with matters of race and ethnicity. The responses of fans, however, were more complex, and McElroy focuses on one instance of online fandom, a 'live' collective viewing of 1.8 (the series' finale) of *Ashes to Ashes*. Such an instance of 'live' reviewing and viewing is becoming an increasingly prominent element in the consumption of contemporary television, she argues, and provides evidence of how the sexual identities of fans and fictional characters are constructed by recourse to memory, history and politics.

There is another dimension to the series' central conceit that is not easily assimilated into the discourses of either genre or realism, to which notions of the 'uncanny' have relevance and which give rise to the way that *Life on Mars* reflects on television itself. Jachimiak draws on studies of science fiction and Freudian notions of the uncanny to explore how the series negotiates one of the most disturbing tropes of time-travelling fiction, the possibility of the traveller meeting his or her younger self. The uncanny is also important to Matt Hills, who argues that one of the distinctive features of *Life on Mars* is the manner in which it represents television itself. Noting that the series' makers were clear about its self-referentiality with regard to television, Hills explores the role of the television image within its diegesis as a central narrative and thematic strand (something which Jachimiak also discusses). The television set in *Life on Mars* becomes not just a 'monstrous' entity problematising Tyler's reality; it is ultimately represented as a 'portal' to the narrative present day, and hence as a perfectly individualised and interactive medium. *Life on Mars* utilises icons of seventies television not just within a nostalgic, denotatively 'old media' *mise en scène* (television and its test card as 'historical' objects) but also connotatively to code this television as a fantastical version of 'new media' which, in cultural discourses of the twenty-first century, promises immersion, interactivity and individuation.

ASHES TO ASHES

As we noted earlier, this book is primarily about *Life on Mars* and its contributors did not have the opportunity to comment on much more than the first series of *Ashes to Ashes*. However, even though it strays beyond the remit of an Introduction proper, it would be wilful not to say something about the successor series now that it has reached its conclusion. Indeed, the final episode of series three of *Ashes to Ashes*, broadcast on 21 May 2010, provided a resolution to the remaining enigmas of *Life on Mars* itself – or possibly a reworking of the programme's basic premise, depending on one's point of view. Certainly, *Ashes to Ashes* was more than simply a continuation of *Life on Mars* under a different title. Although the essential conceit of both shows was the same – that the narrative followed the attempts of a contemporary police detective, catapulted back in time by a serious accident, to return to their familiar world – much had changed. The central character of the earlier series, Sam Tyler, was swopped for DI Alex Drake (Keeley Hawes), London replaced Manchester as the prime setting and 1981 substituted for 1973 as the year into which each programme's protagonist had been unwillingly dumped. Only Gene Hunt and his team, DS Ray Carling (Dean Andrews) and DC Chris Skelton (Marshall Lancaster), remained, having decamped to the capital in search of new opportunities.

According to the series' co-creators and main writers, Matthew Graham and Ashley Pharoah, *Ashes to Ashes* was conceived at a relatively early point, and plotted in outline as a three-series show sometime before *Life on Mars* had reached its conclusion.[1] *Life on Mars* was eight years in the making, but Graham and Pharoah had written only two scripts of *Ashes to Ashes* when filming started on the first episode, and the writers maintain that this gave them the chance to adapt and develop characters and situations across each series (Wylie 2010).

Ashes to Ashes achieved and maintained a popular audience in the UK that was similar to that for *Life on Mars*: the last episode was watched by 6.45 million people, compared with 7 million for the last episode of *Life on Mars*, but the series' averages were broadly comparable. The critical response to series one, however, was mixed. As McElroy and Cook and Irwin argue in this volume, the problem of Alex Drake's gender – in particular the way it is constructed in the first episode of the first series – was a major difficulty. In addition, the possibility of romance between its two protagonists was introduced as a source of dramatic tension, which altered the central dynamic of their relationship. Though clearly intended to be playful and ironic, it was in danger of being read as merely reactionary, particularly when placed in the context of a televisual and broader cultural history, as McElroy reminds us. Series one was also conservative in other ways. Lord Scarman, a High Court judge known for his integrity, liberal views and support for constitutional and police reform, appears in episode 1.8. He is represented as an inept and interfering figure, removed from the 'reality' of eighties policing, and is the butt of a Gene Hunt tirade in defence of his team with which the audience are intended to concur. In choosing to celebrate Hunt and all he stands for in an overtly political context, the makers of *Ashes to Ashes* resolved much of the tension between valorising Hunt's values and critiquing them that critics – and the contributors in this volume – found so productive in *Life on Mars*. Graham and Pharoah observed that they were persuaded by their producers to make the first series lighter in tone than *Life on Mars*, more 'camp', brightly coloured and self-conscious.[2] Interviewed after the airing of all three series, Graham reflected that 'we'd had a bit of a kicking on the first series from some areas and . . . we wondered whether we'd overplayed the lightness' (Wylie 2010). Series two was always planned to be darker – metaphorically and literally – with series three closer to the tone of *Life on Mars*.

One of the main differences between *Life on Mars* and *Ashes to Ashes* is the role played by Gene Hunt. Pharoah noted that Hunt was not a major character in the early drafts of the former: it was clearly Sam Tyler's show. However, the critical and popular response to Hunt caused the writers to give him a more central place in the local narratives of each episode, and by the end of series two *Life on Mars* was as interested in what happened to Hunt as it was in Tyler. There is no doubt, however, whose show *Ashes to Ashes* is. From his first appearance in episode 1.1, when he emerges from the Quattro complete with cowboy boots, Hunt is reconfigured as a sheriff from a classic western, and the generic reference is clear and self-referential throughout all three series. (Interestingly, Smith notes how musical references to Morricone's scores for Sergio Leone's 'spaghetti westerns' are threaded through the soundscape of *Life on Mars*.) Graham likened Hunt to 'an old, grizzly sheriff now in a town that the railroad is approaching, like one of those westerns where the railway is coming and bringing modern ideas' (Graham 2008). The comment invests Hunt with an essential integrity, a moral and physical authority that derives from the generic character type, and also signals that inevitable progress will challenge that authority. In the face of an investigation into police corruption, Hunt instructs his team: 'I'm the sheriff. I say we keep it squeaky clean.' It also indicates a new tension in all three series, which is particularly apparent in the third, between Hunt's inherited, seventies-style retro-reaction and a moral sensibility that is demonstrated in his relationship with his team, the full complexity of which will be revealed in the denouement (as Drake says, 'you made us feel safe').

However, initially Hunt is portrayed as representative of a particular set of broadly reactionary values. Having discovered a character who, for good or ill, resonated across the culture, the makers of the series were determined to make the most of him, and this was reflected in the way in which *Ashes to Ashes* was promoted. For example, when *Life on Mars* was first launched the influential UK listings magazine, the *Radio Times*, carried a picture of John Simm and Philip Glenister leaning on the bonnet of the Ford Cortina (7–13 January 2006): however, in this instance Simm is in the foreground. The appearance of *Ashes to Ashes* also made it to the front cover (2–8 February 2008), but this time Glenister was prominent, and there was no visual reference to Keeley Hawes at all. The magazine greeted series three with a full-face mid-shot of Glenister above the caption 'Gene Genius' (27 March–2 April 2010). The issue contained a lengthy interview with the actor and 'Gene Hunt's manifesto for Britain', a spoof tirade written by Ashley Pharoah in mock-Churchillian rhetoric which derides environmental activism, Nelson Mandela and the Italian manager of the English football team, and reassures the reader that when social protest arrives he will be there to contain it: 'Take heart, my friends', the manifesto concludes 'The Gene Genie will always be with you' (ibid.: 16). Hunt's cartoon prejudices are offered ironically, perhaps, but there is an implicit assumption that they are what make him 'attractive' to a significant part of the audience.

We have already noted how Gene Hunt had become a point of reference in wider social and cultural discourses. In 2010, he also entered the domain of national electoral politics when he and his car, the Audi Quattro, appeared in a poster in support of the Labour Party. The poster, launched on 2 April 2010, the day on which the first episode of series three was transmitted, was chosen as the result of a competition and reproduced a publicity still of Hunt sitting on the bonnet of the Quattro, his faced replaced by that of the leader of the Conservative Party and soon-to-be prime minister, David Cameron. The slogan used was 'Don't let him take Britain back to the 1980s'. The poster elicited a mixed response, mostly because, as was pointed out by several commentators, it was by no means certain that the public would see the connection between Hunt and Cameron as a negative one. The Conservative Party responded by claiming Hunt's robust approach to policing as their own, judging that this would resonate with an uncommitted electorate. A report in the *Daily Telegraph* on 3 April 2010 caught the tone: 'The Conservative leader said: "I think there will be thousands of people, millions of people, in the country who wish it was the 1980s and that police were out there feeling collars and nicking people instead of filling in forms."' The Conservatives hurriedly produced a different version, identical but with a new slogan: 'Fire up the Quattro, it's time for change'. Back to the future indeed.

The crucial role assigned to Hunt is, of course, most apparent in the denouement of series three, which resolved Sam Tyler's central predicament: 'Am I mad, in a coma or back in time?' Sam – along with Alex Drake, Ray Carling, Chris Skelton and Shaz Granger (Montserrat Lombard) – have all been in a coma of sorts, as has Gene Hunt himself, which is presented as a form of purgatory for the dying or the dead who cannot quite let go of life. Hunt has become, of his own volition rather than by nomination, a gatekeeper between purgatory and the afterlife proper, easing people on their passage from one state to the next. Heaven, into which the team, including Alex, disappears, is the Railway Arms, and Nelson, the barman from *Life on Mars*, is the ferryman. Graham explained the conceit thus:

> The place that Alex finds herself in is the same place that Sam found himself in and it is a plane between a Heaven and Earth, really. When we discussed the philosophy behind it we decided that, seeing as how the cosmos was infinite, everybody who dies can afford to go to some kind of purgatory plane that is relevant and significant to them. So we just liked the idea, it tickled us, the idea that coppers with issues would go to a place designed for coppers. And a coppers' paradise surely has to be *The Sweeney*, or *The French Connection* if you're an American. And so we thought, 'Well, OK, that's the place where you've got all the freedoms and therefore you've got all the chances to make all the big mistakes that could lead you to Hell but all the good decisions that would lead you to Heaven . . . That was kind of right back from the beginning, right back from *Life On Mars*.

And what we decided was – we do imagine that a coma patient hangs between life and death. So it felt OK and not breaking the rules of that kind of logic to have Sam, who is in a coma, and Alex, who has been in a coma up until the beginning of series three, in that place. (Wylie 2010)

This way of resolving the enigmas of both series was decided before *Life on Mars* had finished airing, although it was planned in detail during the development of *Ashes to Ashes*. The process by which the detailed decision making occurred is illustrative of the complex ways in which digital media are having an impact on the relationship between the writers of long-running series and their fans. Matthew Graham has said (on 'Dust to dust') that he and Ashley Pharoah 'dropped into' online fan forums to get a sense of how committed viewers were speculating on the series' resolution. Noting that many were getting close to their initial intentions, the writers decided to 'go beyond' them, without losing touch with viewers' developing expectations. A number of possibilities were considered, including some that would have located the series firmly inside a self-referential postmodern sensibility that would have appeared very radical in the context of the prevailing illusionism of British television drama:

Gene was going to smash all the doors down and knock the walls down . . . and you would be able to see film lights behind, like the Truman Show. He was just going to kick it all to pieces and he was going to say, 'Look, it's not even a real police station. It's just all pretend.' And we all really liked it but then we thought, actually that might be a post-modern step too far. (Wylie 2010)

No doubt fans of both *Life on Mars* and *Ashes to Ashes* will have their own views on the ending. Certainly, unlike the ending of *Lost*, the long-running US series that reached the end of its life at about the same time, it attempts to provide a resolution that makes sense of the narrative. In this, the consensus in the press and online would suggest that it was successful, although the resolution of any long-running series cannot hope to account for all the pleasures each episode offers, even if it manages to tidy up loose ends. Certainly, it does not invalidate the analyses of *Life on Mars* that are contained in this book. The series has its own identity and internal logic; its enigmas are its own, inviting a response that recognises the meanings in play at the moment of viewing and re-viewing, without the retrospective certainty of how it will eventually be resolved.

The series' makers opted for an ending that framed the narrative in a religious schema, although it does not adopt a religious sensibility. That is, incidents and events in the narrative are made sense of within a religious, specifically Christian, framework, although the moral and philosophical positioning of the characters remains within the broadly humanist values of comradeship and loyalty that have been in evidence throughout. Even Keats, who is clearly the devil, is not allowed to disturb this. *Ashes to Ashes* has become, at its conclusion, much less about the interplay of past and present, about the playful invocation of a version of Britain in the eighties, and more about the 'universal' themes that writers in this volume have noted in relation to *Life on Mars* – of loss, grief and acceptance. Certainly, as Graham noted, 'it's not even a pastiche of *The Sweeney* now' (Wylie 2010). However satisfying the resolution is as a resolution, it may be that the journey through both *Life on Mars* and *Ashes to Ashes* was more interesting than the arrival.

NOTES

1   For a brief discussion of the early planning stages of *Ashes to Ashes*, see *http:// blogs.menmedia.co.uk/ianwylie/2008/04/mars-to-ashes-the-writers-talk/*.
2   Unless otherwise stated, all quotations from Pharoah and Graham are from 'Dust to dust', on the DVD extras on *Ashes to Ashes: Series 3*, BBC Worldwide/ Contender Home Entertainment, 2010.

REFERENCES

Akass, K. and McCabe, J. (eds) (2007), *Quality TV: Contemporary American TV and Beyond*, London, I. B. Tauris.

Graham, M. (2010), 'Dust to dust', DVD extras on *Ashes to Ashes: Series 3*, BBC Worldwide/Contender Home Entertainment.

Wylie, I. (2010), 'Interview with Matthew Graham', *http://lifeofwylie.com/2010/ 05/23/ashes-to-ashes-the-answers/*, accessed 8 August 2010.

PART I | QUALITY TV
FORM AND AESTHETICS

1 *LIFE ON MARS*

HYBRIDITY AND INNOVATION IN A BRITISH TELEVISION CONTEXT

Robin Nelson

'Just your regular run-of-the-mill time-travelling cop show'.
(Matthew Graham)

N THE RECENT PAST, both in the academy and in broader culture, much emphasis has been placed upon 'American Quality TV' (shows such as *Sex and the City* (HBO, 1998–2004), *Six Feet Under* (HBO, 2001–5), *The Sopranos* (HBO, 1999–2007) and *The Wire* (HBO, 2002–8)), so it's good once again to have an opportunity to celebrate a British TV drama success. *Life on Mars* (Kudos for BBC Wales, 2006–7) is the case in point. Indeed, so success-ful was the series in Britain that an American version, based on the UK format, has subsequently been made and screened in the USA (see Lavery, Mills, and Bonaut and Ojer below). This chapter, however, focuses on the British original and argues that much of its appeal lay in a specifically British context in its evo-cation of Britain in the seventies and, specifically, the police series, *The Sweeney* (ITV/Euston Films, 1975–8).

Though many people enjoy overseas imports as part of their television diet, audiences worldwide are known to want some programming with local resonances. In today's global marketplace for television, such home-grown product is increasingly becoming a rarity, as producers have one eye on trans-national sales potential. In the first instance, however, *Life on Mars* came into production after a number of false starts to fill a slot in the UK schedules.[1] Thus the final production team's focus was on finding success in a UK context, and local resonances of Britain in the seventies increasingly informed the details of the realisation of the script. Format sales to America were only an afterthought. Accordingly, this chapter unpacks and celebrates textual aspects of *Life on Mars* as a distinctive and innovative product but located in British television traditions.

It is well known that some of those aspects of *Life on Mars* which have become highly significant to viewers were not part of the original production concept. Most notably, the possibility that DCI Sam Tyler (John Simm) is a coma victim, and that the entire series is a fiction constructed by his unconscious mind, was not part of the primary concept. Indeed Matthew Graham has acknowledged that initially, 'there was no coma angle at all'. In his words, borrowed for the epigraph for this chapter, *Life on Mars* was conceived as 'just your regular run-of-the-mill time-travelling cop show' (Graham 2008).

In an industry context where producers are always seeking to replicate successful programmes, albeit with that all-important twist, it is unlikely to have escaped the notice of the creators of *Life on Mars* that another 'regular run-of-the-mill time-travelling cop show' has achieved considerable success in the British television schedules. The reference, of course, is to *Heartbeat* (ITV, 1991–2010) which, having moved from its original Friday night slot in 1991 to Sunday night in 1993, sustained substantial audiences for seventeen years. For readers unfamiliar with the series, *Heartbeat* is set in the sixties and centred on the police station in the rural North Yorkshire village of Aidensfield, with the first episode being set in 1964 and the most recently broadacast set in 1969 (time evidently travels very slowly in Aidensfield). *Heartbeat* is not strictly time-travelling between one time zone and another, though its loose representation of the sixties in music and clothes draws also upon a nineties postmodern retro fashion interest in the sixties. In summary, *Heartbeat* is a police series, set in the past in a regional UK location, with a soundtrack that draws upon popular music tracks of the time and thus resonates with the idea of 'your regular run-of-the-mill time-travelling cop show'. Moreover, *Heartbeat* claims (in terms of audience numbers) to be the most enduring and successful British TV drama series of all time (see Nelson 1997).

Whether or not the creators of *Life on Mars* had *Heartbeat* specifically in mind when dreaming up a new police series, the earlier police series is evoked here as a benchmark in differentiating a 'quality' British TV drama, *Life on Mars*, from *Heartbeat*, which may be seen as a popular, but formulaic and sentimentally nostalgic, drama. In making the comparison, attention will be drawn to how treatments of a standard television genre, the police series, can differ markedly in their use of hybrid generic mixes to afford a new twist. The more creative treatment, in *Life on Mars*, produces a text which is thought-provoking and, albeit to a limited extent, culturally challenging, although it remains entertaining to a broad audience. In contrast, the more sentimental treatment in *Heartbeat* invites indulgence in a vision of a mythologised past which may well attract a substantial British audience on a Sunday night after *Songs of Praise* and the *Antiques Roadshow*,[2] but eschews any invitation to critical engagement or 'complex seeing' which is integral to 'quality' drama.[3]

To start with some basic characteristics, most contemporary TV drama combines genres, or aspects of genre, partly in the hope of attracting a broad audience made up of different target market groups. Focus group research on *Heartbeat*, for example, yielded three such groups – Green Mums, EastEnd Girls and Lager Lads – which led respectively to the foregrounding of soft social

issues, a romance narrative and police detection stories featuring classic vehicles – all set to the refrains of sixties pop music tracks (see Nelson 1997: 79–85).
As noted, *Heartbeat* is not strictly time-travelling between the 1960s and the
present, certainly not in the way that *Life on Mars* affords in its very structure a double cross-perspective between the seventies and the early noughties.
 Particularly among the forty-five-plus age-group, as we shall see, *Life on Mars*
has a special appeal in evoking remembrances of times past. However, unlike
Heartbeat, the element of nostalgia is not sentimentalised. Where *Heartbeat*,
partly because of its rural location in the north York moors, is very loosely
located in the sixties – evoking more, perhaps, the *Dixon of Dock Green* (BBC,
1955–76) television policing ethos of the fifties[4] – *Life on Mars* is time-specific
both in its evocation of the seventies police series, *The Sweeney*, and in the
accuracy of production detail (a few anachronisms notwithstanding).

 Heartbeat is something of a TV drama by numbers to serve the perceived
needs of its focus-group-identified target markets (see Nelson 1997: 73). *Life
on Mars*, though it is much less mechanical in its approach, also affords a
range of appeals to different sectors of a potential audience (as indicated by
a small audience research project conducted by the author).[5] It has varied
appeals to different viewers because it is a hybrid mix of a police-detective
series (with action-adventure overtones of *The Sweeney*), a telefantasy (from
the stable adjacent to *Dr Who* (BBC Wales, revived 2005) and *Torchwood*
(BBC Wales 2006–)), with aspects of documentary realism (in the seventies
domestic setting), and a touch of romance (in the possibility that DI Sam Tyler
and WPC Annie Cartwright (Liz White) might get together). The dual time
frame, moreover, gives rise to consideration of issues of cultural change such
as gender, race, social policy and policing. It is also funny.

 Indeed the humour of the series is part of the subtle mix that gives *Life
on Mars* its distinctive feel. Most notable, perhaps, are DCI Hunt's (Philip
Glenister) apothegms and epithets, his well-turned – though definitely not PC
– summaries of the situation: 'You so much as belch out of line and I'll have
your scrotum on a barbed wire plate' or 'We're looking for a short skinny bird,
wears a big coat lots of gob' and the almost prophetic, 'There will never be a
woman prime minister as long as I have a hole in my arse.' Reflecting a macho
culture, one that was already in fact in question by the seventies, Hunt gets to
say what some men used to say – and possibly what some still wish they could
say – about women, sex, life's frustrations and social pressures in general.

 But Hunt does not have the monopoly on humour: in their size 14
approach to police procedurals DS Roy Carling (Dean Andrews) and Chris
Skelton (Marshall Lancaster) afford some Keystone Cops action. In a telling
sequence (in episode 2.7), they chase Hunt through an old warehouse building, having announced that they are obliged to arrest him. He eludes them
by simply donning shades and then swapping his camel overcoat and shades
with a friend. As he remarks when Carling and Skelton chase the decoy,
'I can't believe they fell for the same trick twice: they really are stupid.' There

is visual humour, too, in the car chases in *Life on Mars*, the direction under-cutting Hunt's driving style and macho swagger. In a famous sequence, Hunt's progress is obstructed by a brass band, so he takes a shortcut through the back alleys, mowing down washing lines, and almost some local women, in his recklessness. Some of the characterisation in the set-piece comic sequences is two-dimensional, and the action almost slapstick. Carling falls in behind his DCI with flailing fists and a blind loyalty, whilst young Skelton's failure with women is matched only by his lethargy and incompetence in policing. But the performances, built on glimpses of backstory, breathes life into what would otherwise be caricatures.

Besides their intrinsic entertainment value, the comic capers of Carling and Skelton serve as foils to DCI Gene Hunt whose swaggering, swearing, unreconstructed character captured the popular imagination. Though 'Gene' is an unlikely name for the 1970s, it seems highly appropriate for Hunt, evok-ing something of the cowboys illustrated in the posters on his office wall (Gene Autrey, possibly) and something of the rock and roller (Gene Vincent), which, chronologically, might have informed the choice of name. However, Hunt's image and his 'hit out first and ask questions later' approach to polic-ing most strongly references DI Jack Regan (John Thaw) of *The Sweeney*.

An overt intertextual play between *Life on Mars* and *The Sweeney*, fore-grounded in the imagery of the signature camel overcoat and the Roman bronze Ford, is matched in the self-consciously comic dialogue. As Anthony Clark has remarked:

> [D]ialogue was as important to *The Sweeney* as action and many of Regan's best lines, often delivered through gritted teeth, have become famous. 'Get your trousers on, you're nicked' and 'Shut it!' have both passed into popular usage, while quotes such as 'We're the Sweeney, son, and we've haven't had any dinner yet, so unless you want a kickin' . . . ' . . . demonstrate how the show blended humour into the action. (*http://www.screenonline.org.uk/tv/id/473709/index.html*)

The same summary of linguistic attractions might be made of *Life on Mars*, except that, from a twenty-first-century perspective, the character of Hunt is placed almost in inverted commas, in its parodic formulation. The intertextual play with *The Sweeney* keeps modern, media-savvy viewers aware that *Life on Mars* is a detective series situated in the tradition of British police-detective series. But the parodic pleasure is not available to all. The intertextual play works fully only if viewers saw *The Sweeney* in the seventies and feel the res-onances, which is why the fifty-somethings in my audience survey locate *Life on Mars* in traditions of both British television and British cultural life. For those who recall the earlier police series and its popularity, a '*Sweeney* aware-ness' heightens the pleasure in Hunt's more elaborately forced expostulations. He even outdoes Regan, with phrases such as 'She's as nervous as a very small nun at a penguin shoot.' But played with conviction by the excellent Philip Glenister, the character of Hunt is simultaneously grounded, giving maximum impact to the tension between the double vantage points of the series.

The initially two-dimensional character of Hunt is fleshed out, almost literally, by the charisma of Glenister's swaggering but motivated performance such that, in the penultimate episode, Hunt's near-alcoholism as a metaphor of his conflicted personality is explained by his sense of failure at being unable to find – and save the life of – his brother. In retrospect, this backstory might be seen to inform his attitude both to life and to policing. Like his *Sweeney* predecessors, Hunt is constructed initially as a flawed, but basically honest, police officer, doing a dirty job against the odds. His rage at 'the scumbags of the world polluting his city' is palpable and indicates a moral purpose, however misguided his methods might be. Hunt's crude but direct form of justice has had popular appeal in British drama since the consolidated state agencies outlawed direct revenge under the reign of Elizabeth I. A line can be drawn all the way from *Hamlet* (1601) and *The Revenger's Tragedy* (1607) through to television's *Trial and Retribution* (ITV, 1997–2009). But the popular trope is ultimately enriched in *Life on Mars* in the rounding of a familiar, stock figure with a deepening of character motive to produce the memorable icon that Hunt has become. But DCI Hunt represents more than a character with viewer appeal. From a twenty-first-century point of view, Hunt's behaviour is unacceptable. Thus any attraction to him emotionally is offset by an awareness of today's cultural standards and the distance marked by the evident change in social attitudes between the seventies and the present day. It is the simultaneous offering of such multiple perspectives which invites from viewers a mixed response encapsulated in the phrase, 'complex seeing'.

John Simm might equally be applauded for the quality of his performance as Sam Tyler, his vulnerable thoughtfulness in marked contrast with Hunt's brash aggression. However, Tyler is not quite the 'Dorothy' of Hunt's construction, since he holds his own in the action sequences and in many direct confrontations with Hunt, both physical and mental. Though their policing methods are poles apart, a mutual respect between the two detectives grows throughout the series, building up to the penultimate episode of series two when Sam helps get Gene out of a very sticky situation. Because of his position between two time zones, however, the character of Sam Tyler was always destined to be an even more complex figure than Hunt. Over and above finding himself on another planet in respect of policing methods and other aspects of culture (the lack of mobile phones, computers, databases), Sam Tyler is suffering the anguish of not knowing how he got to be where he is and whether he will 'get back home' to the twenty-first century.

One motivation for a possible amnesiac trauma is the abandonment of Sam by his father who, if we are to believe the final episode of series one, runs away, having become involved in some minor criminality. The significance of the loss of a father is prefigured in episode 1.5 where a Manchester United fan is killed by a supposed fellow fan in order to incite a battle with Manchester City supporters (the two football teams being legendary rivals). Sam identifies strongly with the bereaved boy, ultimately finding his father's killer and giving the boy the match ticket he has taken from the guilty fan. The repeated appearance to Sam of people from his former life – he meets his mother and father, his Auntie Heather, and the mother of his girlfriend, Maya, not to mention the little girl in the red dress with the clown from the seventies BBC test card – makes family loss the prime suspect in the search for the cause of Sam's predicament. However, to add another layer of character and plot complexity, the 'coma angle' emerges to offer an increasingly viable alternative explanation. John Simm's ability to convey internal emotional turmoil allows these various possibilities credibility and keeps them in play.

Tyler's twenty-first-century 'new man' attitude to women also draws from Simm a sensitivity to the romance element of the programme, ably supported by Liz White who plays Annie Cartwright. The construction of WPC Cartwright in part as a homely and old-fashioned young woman, but one who also has a degree in psychology, is in marked contrast to the 'babes' who typically figure in American Quality TV. It is another feature marking *Life on Mars* as a British quality vehicle that the overt sex appeal of a starlet is avoided in the portrayal of Annie, who only reveals a hint of sexuality in the line of duty (episodes 1.5 and 2.2). This restraint lends the 'Will-they-won't-they?' device a quaint charm based on Sam's sharing with Annie his dilemma about being in two places at once. Such understatement is also a feature of the deft use of pop music tracks contemporary with the action. The quite extensive use of David Bowie's 'Life on Mars' in the first episode introduces the device in picking up on Tyler's sense that he's 'landed on a different planet' in seventies Manchester. Connections between the song lyrics and the action thereafter are left for viewers to make and, increasingly as the series developed, short refrains of a song sustain the feel of radio as a soundtrack to contemporary life (particularly for those who lived through the seventies) as well as serving other functions (as discussed more fully by Rob Smith below).

The use of popular music in this way, besides the specific seventies resonances, makes a broader contribution to the mix of genres and dramatic modes in *Life on Mars* and finds a parallel in its narrative form. Like many contemporary TV dramas, *Life on Mars* is a mix of serial and series forms, or a 'flexi-narrative' (Nelson 1997: 10–49), the dominant narrative mode of contemporary television drama. What is exceptional about *Life on Mars*'s dramatic structure, however, is the increasing complexity, as the show developed, of its long-form narrative dimension. Umberto Eco (1981) insightfully suggests that, as viewers, we take 'inferential walks' through long-form narrative. In respect of mysteries, we don't know what will happen but we know that we *will* know what will happen. We enjoy the uncertainty and speculation because the prospect of the satisfaction of closure is assured. Indeed, the more familiar, and thus predictable, the vehicle, the greater the assurance of the outcome. What makes *Life on Mars* distinctive in this respect is that, because of its unusual treatment of the police series' form, the resolution of the enigma is not at all assured.

As we have seen, the romance strand is understated with just the possibility that Tyler might get to kiss WPC Annie Cartwright. Her old-fashioned homeliness, coupled with the fact that Tyler is distracted by a love in his previous life, however, creates a distinctive tension in the 'Will-they-won't-they?' drive of this otherwise regular narrative device. Another core tension, overtly brought to a head in the final episode of series two, concerns whose side Tyler is on. In a world where tribal bonding is all-important for the Manchester police force, Tyler's outsider status and his antagonistic critique of what he sees as Hunt's outmoded police methods creates a running narrative tension throughout the series. This tension is allowed to simmer until brought to the boil in the final episodes when Tyler prepares to shop Hunt, gathering the evidence on his misdemeanours for DCI Frank Morgan from Hyde, another Manchester police station.

The most puzzling serial narrative enigma of all, however, is the one developed as the series got underway: 'the sunken dream', the mystery of where DI Sam Tyler has come from and whether, and how, he will 'get home'. In the titles refrain, is Tyler 'mad, in a coma, or back in time'? As the story unfolds, none of these narrative meta-arcs affords an easy inferential walk. Indeed each story strand opens up on to another narrative prospect. Even in the denouement, the writers have fun with the possibilities. In the final episode, Sam is led by Frank Morgan to his parents' supposed graves in the name of Walker, but, insisting he knew Vic and Ruth Tyler and that his surname is indeed Tyler not Walker, Sam spots nearby gravestones bearing the Tyler name. But these graves turn out to be dated from the 1880s and Morgan's explanation that Sam is amnesiac, having lost his memory in a road accident, suddenly seems not only plausible but corroborated: Sam Tyler (formerly Walker) is a detective from Hyde whose identity has been changed to allow him to go undercover in Manchester's A-Division in order to root out highly questionable policing methods. But, just as everything seems to be making sense, Sam's pointed accusation that Frank himself is a figment of the imagination, flips us back to the narrative possibility that Sam is in a coma from which he is slowly awakening. Indeed, we see him coming round to see Frank Morgan as smug surgeon, congratulating himself on his success. So the supposed 'reality' of *Life on Mars* was all a dream and Hunt merely an imago based on the anti-hero of a bygone TV series: 'somewhere over the rainbow' indeed.

To confirm it, Sam is a DCI in A-Division, but bored out of his mind discussing the ethics of policing policy with the suits. As he tells his mother, he has literally lost that feeling which dreadlocked barman, Nelson (Tony Marshall), has told him distinguishes life from its alternative. And life with Hunt, however procedurally and ethically flawed, was at least vibrant. Sam offers his apologies to his colleagues around the meeting table, makes for the office-block roof and takes a running jump. With Sam suspended in slo-mo in mid-air and a fade to black as he disappears from shot, we are momentarily left dangling on whichever narrative hook we have chosen to cling to. But scarcely have we had time to mutter 'It's a cop-out leaving future options open' than we land back in the 1970s reality of the train heist and Sam is in yet another time frame, namely 'make-your-mind-up' time. Will he sacrifice his colleagues to 'get home' once and for all, or will he forsake his personal salvation to save them? Sam fires his pistol, shoots the villain dead and saves the day. And, following the inevitable pub celebration, Sam is even finally rewarded with that Annie Cartwright kiss. But, in the context of *Life on Mars*, a tinkling, romantic piano can scarcely avoid carrying an ironic overtone and, when Hunt arrives to transport the posse off for another battle with the scumbags of Manchester, the car radio is still speaking to Sam from 2006, though the contact is fading. Sam changes channel and Bowie is belting out 'Is there life on Mars?' Though Sam appears to have opted squarely for the vibrancy of life in the seventies (confirmed in the sequel, *Ashes to Ashes* (BBC, 2007–10)), the narrative closure remains incomplete.

Some viewers no doubt settle comfortably for the generic romantic trope, but others are allowed to sustain a 'perpetuated hermeneutic' and 'hyperdiegesis' as Matt Hills dubs the characteristics of a fantasy text with cult propensities. The perpetuated hermeneutic involves 'a central mystery that repeats familiar characteristics but whose resolution is endlessly deferred' whilst the hyperdiegesis involves 'an internally logical, stable, yet "unfinished" fictional world' (Hills, cited in Johnson 2005: 2). *Life on Mars* illustrates both such features of telefantasy. Indeed, in one segment of the audience, the time-travelling aspect of *Life on Mars* afforded a predominant pleasure. These viewers made that unusually strong investment in negotiating the text typically associated with cult fandom. The sense of a TV drama carrying cult resonances for viewers often arises from the more cosmic or philosophical layers of textual significance, and *Life on Mars* affords this in the coma and time-travel angles. But the series also had a different cult appeal to the forty- and fifty-somethings for whom it involved negotiation of the recollections of their formative years with their experience of culture today. The small details of seventies domestic life lay a trail for them imaginatively to follow. For those others who were caught up in the time-travel possibilities, the series offered encouragement through small but telling details: the hospital ward in which Sam comes round is named Hyde ward and the room number is 2612. If this means nothing to you, you are not in this cult viewer segment, so phone a friend on Hyde 2612.

In the contemporary world – in which the axioms of Newtonian physics have been challenged by quantum mechanics, relativity, complexity theory and so forth – time travel has captured the popular imagination. Besides the bending of time, the expansion of perception is also a possibility to be pondered, if not indulged. This might suggest embarkation on a fantasy journey of one's own, but consider the following poser from a correspondent to Matthew Graham cited on the show's website. The viewer asks of the *Life on Mars*'s production team:

> Are you drawing from Zen Buddhism, advaita Vedanta, dzogchen, non-dual philosophy? Is this detective his true self? To wake up to who he really is? To 'cheat' death by realising he is the One who was never born and will never die. (Graham 2008)

Matthew Graham advises that the correspondent should 'stop eating the foam from inside [his] sofa'. But the point remains that a number of (notably younger) viewers, as my own audience research suggests, were most gripped by the enigma of Tyler's predicament. *Heartbeat*, being anchored at least in a myth of the north York moors, evokes no such cosmic readings (none that have surfaced, at least). In respect of narrative form and cult viewing, *Life on Mars* further exploits the flexibility of contemporary flexi-narrative in its risky refusal, even in drawing the narrative to an end, to close down any of the many possibilities. In other words, *Life on Mars* sustains the polysemy of the fluid, multi-narrative textual play and intertextuality it has mobilised. Matthew Graham might suggest refraining from eating sofa foam but it is the playful-ness of the text with genre, with narrative form, with intertextual referencing, which makes it a 'quality' TV drama. However, *Life on Mars* remains popular in addition, for some, to being cult television.

Life on Mars is popular in that it draws upon the generically popular form of the police-detective series and retains its pleasures of swift action. It locates itself in the domain of popular culture in using seventies music tracks. It is cartoon-like in that it creates a larger-than-life, parodic anti-hero in Gene Hunt, and it is in other aspects inclined to slapstick humour, as noted ear-lier. But, at the same time, *Life on Mars*'s appeal rested in part on its quite accurate evocation of seventies domesticity. In the viewing undertaken as part of my small qualitative audience research with a group of forty- and fifty-somethings, individuals exclaimed whilst watching an episode, 'I recognise that cocoa tin', 'We used to have wallpaper like that', 'Me dad used to walk round like that with the TV aerial trying to get a better picture'. We had quite a discussion about Sam Tyler's striped shirts. It was agreed that there was indeed a fashion for men's striped shirts in the seventies and some affirmed the accu-racy of production detail in this respect. But others took the view that there was a hint of Paul Smith in Tyler's stripes to indicate the noughties from which he has travelled back. One friend, a classic car restorer by profession, was able to confirm that not only was Gene Hunt's car *not* a Ford Granada as used in *The Sweeney*, but rather that it was actually a 'ringer' of a Mark 3 Ford Cortina, badged at the front as a GXL but badged elsewhere as the later 2000E (boot lid and roof pillar). The car's interior is also from the later 2000E. So much for the doxa of television audience theory that viewers watch TV inattentively.

Two general points might be drawn here. First, that viewers take pleasure in period detail in the *mise en scène*. As Richard Dyer half-ironically observed a decade ago, '*Fortunes of War* [the 1987 BBC version] would have been worth it for Harriet's cardigans and tea-cups alone' (1992: 15). And, perhaps particularly for a northern audience of *Life on Mars*, a special pleasure is taken in the reasonably accurate depiction of Manchester street life rather than the textured bourgeois materialism of so much period drama based on nineteenth-century novels. Secondly, the accuracy of domestic detail serves also to ballast the seventies perspective, rendering more forceful the broader thematic comparisons between life at that time and life today. Where *Heartbeat* invites viewers to indulge for a while in a Ruritanian idyll, *Life on Mars* opens up a space for complex seeing by evoking recollections; not sentimental nostalgia, but memories framed explicitly through modern perspectives which entail reflection on the cultural distance travelled between then and now. Moreover, a critical comparison between the two time frames is elicited because Sam Tyler constantly references aspects of policing and society in the noughties. These points of comparison are made not for Tyler's colleagues who, if they hear them, can make nothing of them, but rather for the benefit of viewers. And the comparisons are frequently pointed by a camera lingering on Sam, inviting viewers to take his point of view in pondering on the difference. For a range of reasons, then, *Life on Mars* was popular to the extent that it often drew an audience of 7–8 million on a Monday night, which is a considerable achievement against the stiff competition in the context of today's multi-channel, fragmented audience. It was popular, but it was also complex and challenging.

At best, the series drew viewers to think reflexively about their culture. *Life on Mars* went out of its way to evoke the seventies, the paradigmatic example being a reconstruction in the animated style of *Camberwick Green* of an unhappy Sam Tyler emerging from the magic box and the cause of his sorrow, Gene Hunt, 'kicking in a nonce' (episode 2.1). Such an evocation of the seventies does nothing to advance the plot (though it does reinforce the different approaches to policing of Tyler and Hunt). Its primary function is a self-conscious sharing with the audience of a sense of the experience of the period, and particularly television watching in the seventies.

Some episodes, notably 2.6, drew attention to much tougher cultural issues such as racial bigotry. In respect of broader cultural concerns, my survey sample acknowledged a strong interest in how the series marked social change and indeed its surprise at how much things had changed in a kind of gradual revolution. Attitudes to women, to sexual orientation, to ethnic groups, as shown from Sam Tyler's 'noughties' perspective, undoubtedly suggest British culture is more tolerant today. 'Outside the law' policing methods, notorious in the West Midlands and London 'Met' forces in the seventies, are less common today. In these respects, *Life on Mars* might be accused of encouraging an ideological quietism, a satisfaction with the present in comparison with the past, suggesting that British society has progressed in a liberal tradition. But in the very possibility of Tyler's choice to relinquish the contemporary world and return to the seventies, there is an interrogative suggestion that, for all its apparent liberalism, contemporary society might lack the vibrancy and social engagement of former times, inviting us perhaps to view a little more critically the fragmentation and privatisation of experience in twenty-first-century culture.

The grounding detail of the *mise en scène* of *Life on Mars* is the trigger for specific memories of seventies Britain and broader evocations of British cultural history. In whatever ways different viewers might have read and responded to *Life on Mars*, they tend to share in the British specificity of its context, and its location in British acting, televisual and cultural traditions. And that is why *Life on Mars* should ultimately be celebrated as a British 'quality' TV drama which nevertheless drew a substantial audience.

Multi-channelling notwithstanding, a distinctive television culture remains discernible in the UK, affording those 'local' resonances that audiences are known to want. Some dramas are more powerful simply by being more pertinent to the everyday lives and circumstances of inhabitants of British culture, as compared with, say, *The Sopranos*, which for all its undoubted excellence, cannot carry such 'local' resonances. British TV drama production has a history of being good at this, and the independent sector – and Kudos in particular – is to be applauded for making a significant contribution in recent times to sustaining the British quality TV tradition.[6]

British quality TV drama output gives pleasure to – and on occasion challenges – large numbers of British television viewers. However, its cultural specificity, almost by definition, limits its transnational reach and puts it in jeopardy in a global market where, as noted at the outset of this essay, producers are required to have an eye for broader market potential. Format sales are not always viable or successful. An American 'best-selling show' is not the same as British quality TV drama and we need to ensure, to evoke a lyric from another iconic David Bowie song, 'Changes', that we are not simply obliged to 'turn and face the strange changes' of transnational production.

NOTES

1   *Life on Mars* was conceived by the writers of *Blackpool* (BBC, 2004) as *Ford Granada*, seven years prior to its ultimate commission as *Life on Mars* by BBC Wales. It was developed over a two-year period by Jane Featherstone and Claire Parker for Channel 4 before it was turned down over concerns about its genre (cop show or sci-fi?). However, needing a cop show for BBC schedule, Jane Tranter ultimately green-lit the show within seven days of reading the script. Julie Gardner (BBC Wales) and Claire Parker (Kudos) brought the project to realisation.

2   The long-running *Antiques Roadshow* (BBC, 1979–) and *One Man and his Dog* (BBC, 1976–) typify enjoyable but unchallenging television thought

suitable for early evening viewing on a Sunday, a slot which in British public service television still retains a sense of religious service overtly visible in the, again long-running, *Songs of Praise* (BBC, 1961–). *Antiques Roadshow* involves ordinary people bringing their heirlooms to a heritage location where resident television experts contextualise and value them for the participants. *One Man and his Dog* covers a competition for television of shepherds' skills in rounding up sheep with the assistance of their working dogs.

3   My use of 'complex seeing' owes a debt to Raymond Williams (1981 [1968]: 321 ff) who in turn acknowledged Brecht's usage in his retrospective notes on *The Threepenny Opera*. Where Brecht emphasised the impact upon audiences, however, Williams insists that complex seeing 'had to be realised in a play' (ibid.), within its principles of composition. In part following Brecht, Williams wanted the work to show people's dreams and potential but also to offer a commentary on how the achievement of what was desired is constrained by social forces.

4   *Dixon of Dock Green* revolved around the avuncular figure of George Dixon, literally a 'bobby on the beat', a policeman who served his local community by patrolling the area on foot. By instinct, Dixon knew a villain when he encountered one but aimed to prevent crime by supporting people whose circumstances might otherwise lead them astray.

5   Though I have some reservations about the value of industrial quantitative audience research such as informed the production of *Heartbeat* (see Nelson 1997), I find qualitative research through informally distributed questionnaires and viewing groups helpful in indicating how viewers are engaging with television. Having become aware that a group of fifty-somethings with disparate backgrounds revealed a strong commitment to *Life on Mars*, I held an informal viewing at my house, followed by an informal discussion which I documented. I followed this up with a questionnaire consciously distributed to a range of ages, genders and dispositions. The findings inform this chapter.

6   Kudos is also responsible for the production of *Spooks* (BBC, 2002–11).

REFERENCES

Clark, A. 'Sweeney, The (1975–78)', *BFI Screenonline* [website], *http://www. screenonline.org.uk/tv/id/473709/index.html*, accessed 24 May 2010.

Dyer, R. (1992). *Only Entertainment*, London, Routledge.

Eco, U. (1981). *The Role of the Reader: Explorations in the Semiotics of Texts*, London, Hutchinson.

Graham, M. (2008). 'Backstage: questions: inspiration', *BBC Drama: Life on Mars*, *http://www.bbc.co.uk/lifeonmars/backstage/questions_inspiration.shtml*, accessed 24 May 2010.

Hills, M. (2000). *Fan Cultures*, London, Routledge.

Johnson, C. (2005). *Telefantasy*, London, British Film Institute.

Nelson, R. (1997). *TV Drama in Transition*, Basingstoke, Macmillan.

Williams, R. (1981 [1968]). *Drama from Ibsen to Brecht*, Harmondsworth, Penguin.

'AM I MAD, IN A COMA OR BACK IN TIME?'

GENERIC AND NARRATIVE COMPLEXITY IN *LIFE ON MARS*

2

Nichola Dobson

HIS CHAPTER EXAMINES *Life on Mars* and discusses both the generic characteristics and the narrative complexity of the show. The series establishes its cop show characteristics very early but at the same time introduces the series-long mystery of a man apparently out of his time. By engaging with the possibility of the supernatural or time travel, *Life on Mars* differs from conventional crime fiction. While the writers were keen to align themselves to crime genres rather than sci-fi, there are generic characteristics present in the show which are undeniably science fiction.[1] This chapter examines the characteristics of both and suggests that it is the interpretation of the protagonist Sam Tyler (John Simm) of generic clues from his own mediated experiences which have influenced his perception of his new universe. By considering the generic characteristics of television crime fiction and science fiction, the chapter will suggest that *Life on Mars* and *Ashes to Ashes* conform to the notion of the hybrid genre.[2] Though audiences are increasingly familiar with the concept, these shows are unusual in their approach by combining genre with nostalgia and creating subtle hybrids, which are often difficult for the audience to decode. While there have been other series which combine sci-fi with crime fiction (see below) it was the situation of a contemporary policeman in 1973 which set *Life on Mars* apart. By engaging with the long tradition and history of police drama in British television, *Life on Mars* references styles and character traits familiar to the audience from the point of view of noughties man Sam. This is portrayed through a very specific narrative space and *mise en scène*, the complexity of which adds to the mystery of the series and will be examined below. Sam is lost in two contrasting worlds, and this makes him an unreliable narrator who cannot resolve how to 'come home'. This constitutes the 'myth arc', or season-long mystery, with clues that are only resolved in the season finale. The chapter will examine this story arc, which was developed to lead the overall narrative across both seasons, separate from the weekly plots and provide clues for the observant viewer. It will be argued that this arc is central to the narrative and generic complexity of both *Life on Mars* and *Ashes to Ashes*, posing the question of whether this represents true generic innovation or ultimately an exercise in nostalgia.

GENERIC CHARACTERISTICS – TV CRIME FICTION

It has been suggested (Dobson 2009: 77) that the defining characteristics of television crime fiction, though not exhaustive, can be described as the commission of a crime; the crime-solving process (arrests, questioning, examining forensics and chasing suspects, prosecution); the narrative space of the police station (and associated areas); the characterisation of heroic cop, clever side-kick, officious superior; resolution or outcome of the justice system. These dominant features have defined television crime fiction, in various forms, over the last fifty years on both sides of the Atlantic in shows such as *Dragnet* (NBC, 1951–9), *Hill Street Blues* (NBC, 1981–7), *Miami Vice* (NBC, 1984–9), *Homicide: Life on the Street* (NBC, 1993–9), *NYPD: Blue* (ABC, 1993–2005), *Law & Order* (NBC, 1990–) and *CSI: Crime Scene Investigation* (CBS, 2000–). However, it has not been a stable genre, and variations have come through a particular emphasis on one or more of the central characteristics. For example, the prosecution became a major focus in the *Law and Order* franchise, the personal lives of the police were more in evidence in *NYPD: Blue*, and the crime lab became the focus of the *CSI* franchise. The level of realism has varied, with documentary-style filming (connoting a more direct connection to 'reality') in *Hill Street Blues* and *Homicide: Life on the Street*, whereas in *Miami Vice* and *CSI* the Hollywood visuals and soundtrack are central.

The contribution to the development of the genre made by these shows is writ large in *Life on Mars*, with aspects taken from many of them, demonstrating the creators' awareness of the history of TV crime fiction on both sides of the Atlantic. This is of particular importance to the success of the show as the audience is required to recognise not only the contemporary generic codes (Neale 2000), but also those of the 1970s. One of the most iconic British series of the 1970s was *The Sweeney* (ITV/Euston Films, 1975–8), which the writers (and directors – see Julie Gardner's comments elsewhere) have consciously referenced throughout the series. It was in *The Sweeney* that television audiences began to see a more action-oriented aspect to police work, which had previously been highly procedural, albeit realistic in the case of shows such as *Z Cars* (BBC, 1962–78). *The Sweeney*'s characters took more risks and adopted a more aggressive approach to policing. The stars of the show were in the mould of the tough guy/hero who had what Cooke suggests 'was a self-righteous belief in the validity of their own methods, even if those methods involved a degree of violence and bending the rules' (2001: 22). The series capitalised on the success of similar characters from films of the early 1970s such as *Get Carter* (1971) and *Dirty Harry* (1971). Some of the hallmarks of *The Sweeney*, which have been re-created in *Life on Mars*, are the general seventies 'look', the use of (authentic) cars, the representation of the UK as a gritty, crime-ridden society and the use of violence when apprehending and questioning suspects. The blend of fast-paced action with particular character types – the contrasting 'buddies' – became common generic features throughout the seventies, seen in shows such as *The Professionals* (ITV, 1977–83) and the US series *Starsky and Hutch* (ABC, 1975–9).

By recalling the characteristics of the seventies, the writers provoked a sense of nostalgia for the audience while at the same time reinforcing the difference between the two time frames and Sam's alienation from both. This is done initially through the *mise en scène* and the plotting of the narrative. In the opening scenes of *Life on Mars* the generic characteristics of the contemporary crime show are presented through the paraphernalia of the modern police station, a high-tech (though sterile) environment. In the course of the investigation references are made to forensics and modern procedures. The show initially shares the noughties aesthetic and techniques of crime solving, using surveillance and forensics, seen in *Law & Order* and *CSI*. After his accident Sam comes to in an environment which looks similar, in general terms, to that of *The Sweeney*. From this point, the audience and Sam are made very aware of the differences between these two worlds – and within the police genre as well – and are asked to assess them. While the series follows individual cases in each episode the narrative becomes increasingly complex, developing over the entire run of the show (this will be explored further later). It has been argued that the notion of the complex narrative in a cop show helps define it as 'quality television' (see Jenkins 1984) because of the demands it makes on an audience to be sophisticated enough to follow the multiple plot threads. This is clearly the case in *Life on Mars* with a requirement for the audience to have both patience for a long-term mystery and an understanding of the evolving conventions of the cop show.

GENERIC COMPLEXITY AND HYBRIDITY

While the key aspects of *Life on Mars* are clearly grounded in crime genre, there are also elements of science fiction, presenting the audience with a generic hybrid. In the last fifty years television sci-fi has focused primarily on space travel and alien life forms in shows such as *Star Trek* (NBC, 1966–9) (and its many spin-offs), *Doctor Who* (BBC, 1963–89; 2005–) and *Blake's 7* (BBC, 1978–81), but generally sci-fi deals with contemporary fears placed in the future. These can range from the fear of ageing and disease, to societal unrest and anxiety, as well as what Hockley suggests is a fear of 'the Other' as seen in such shows as *V* (NBC, 1984–5) and the various *Star Trek* series (2001: 27). A common theme is of being lost, or away from home, in an alien environment which the protagonist must negotiate: the key aspect of *Life on Mars* and *Ashes to Ashes*.

Science fiction TV, like crime fiction, has developed from an early focus on space and time travel, with frequent explicit representations of alien life and space, to the earth-based shows where aliens were among us, such as *V*, *Alien Nation* (Fox, 1989–90) and recently *Invasion* (ABC, 2005–6). Early shows reproduced the tropes of previous genres, with the frontier exploration of *Star Trek* borrowed from the western. The narrative space of these shows (including such examples as *Space 1999* (ITV, 1975–7) and *UFO* (ITV, 1970–1) typically featured alien worlds with barren hostile landscapes. The costumes in the shows set in the future were characteristic of the genre with gender-neutral jumpsuits featuring heavily.

By the eighties, science fiction television referenced the second Cold War more directly (as seen, for example, in *V*). Here, the narrative space was on earth, in familiar locations but with the threat of disruption to the status quo. Another common theme was the misuse of science, or scientific progress gone wrong. This was the focus of *Quantum Leap* (NBC, 1983–93), which featured a scientist whose time-travelling experiments backfired. The long tradition of time travellers in fiction being unable to, or advised not to, interfere with time was turned around in *Quantum Leap*, which saw the protagonist Dr Sam Beckett – another Sam – trying to alter the course of history or, in some cases, maintain it to avoid catastrophe, attempting to find his way back by 'fixing' reality. Beckett's negotiation of the unfamiliar was the main focus of the show and reinforced the notion of 'Other' in sci-fi; this time, like Sam Tyler, he was the other, trying to make sense of the world.

In 1993, *The X-Files* (Fox, 1993–2003) brought together the crime series with sci-fi for the first time. The show featured two FBI agents who investigated 'unexplained' cases, often serial killers or larger conspiracies, but all with a sci-fi, alien or supernatural cause. Over ten seasons the show introduced several season (or longer) myth arcs combined with 'monster of the week' episodes which could be quirky and different from the established mythology of the show. The series dealt with the notion of the other among us, but used the narrative structure of the crime fiction or mystery drama, with the outcome having a supernatural or extra-terrestrial explanation, often accompanied by suggestions of a government conspiracy. This resulted in a hybrid of the crime and sci-fi series, increasing the potential fan base.

Johnson (2001: 30) suggests that the reasons for the international popularity of *The X-Files* are complex and include its referencing of contemporary popular culture and its reflection of a crisis in society – a 'pre-millennial tension'. This could describe the success of any hybrid series, particularly one with science fiction characteristics. As with *Quantum Leap*, the viewers did not have to be sci-fi fans as such, but could engage with other elements in the mix. The producers went on to replicate the hybrid of mystery, crime, horror and sci-fi, creating *Millennium* (Fox, 1996–9) and, with some of the same production personnel, *Supernatural* (WB, 2005–). These shows reinforced the generic mix and arguably brought sci-fi closer to the mainstream. Likewise, the use of a season-long mystery or plot thread became more common.

The hybrid genre has long existed in television and, according to Altman (1999), Hollywood has been mixing genres since the days of the studio system. One of the key issues in genre categorisation is who is doing the categorising and for what purpose. Producers want to mix genres to appeal to as wide an audience as possible, whilst critics want to label the texts in order to maintain their critical discourse and audiences want to identify what they consume. Studios do not want to alienate mainstream viewers, who may not enjoy particular genres, and try to promote shows in the widest way possible. The relative success of both *The X-Files* and *Quantum Leap* in the mainstream (as well as having a very devoted fan base) demonstrated that mixed-genre sci-fi was able to reach a wider audience than perhaps more 'space'-based sci-fi, such as *Babylon 5* (Prime Time/TNT, 1994–8). It also suggests that television audiences have become familiar with hybrid programmes that are increasingly self-reflexive and intertextual. Altman suggests that such viewer sophistication is one of the key elements of a mixed-genre text, what he terms 'multiple framing' which requires particular 'spectator processing' (ibid.: 136), although in *Life on Mars* the multiple aspects are not constantly present. Science fiction elements are mostly in the form of subtle references to time travel and messages from the future/elsewhere, which run throughout the series-long mystery.

The genre of crime fiction, however, is clearly established in the opening scenes of the first episode of *Life on Mars* with the aforementioned narrative space, the questioning of a murder suspect and the examination of a potential crime scene. However ,the episode takes a generic twist when Sam is hit by a car and wakes up in 1973. Sam's confusion increases throughout the episode, as he begins hearing voices from 2006 and seeing personalised messages on his seventies television screen. The audience shares Sam's confusion, and at the start of the second episode a new dimension to the mystery is added in a pre-credits voiceover. Sam tells us who he is and what happened to him, asking if he 'is mad, in a coma or back in time', introducing the suggestion of time travel, and reinforcing the aspect of science fiction. But he also says, 'maybe if I can find out the reason I can get home', as though this could be resolved by fixing something. This recalls *Quantum Leap*, which said in its pre-credits voiceover that Sam was always leaping through time, hoping his next would be 'the leap home'. The quest was the narrative device driving the entire series, shared by *Life on Mars*. Even if the audience is unfamiliar with *Quantum Leap*, the notion of time travel and being 'out of time' is reinforced on a weekly basis, through the opening credits sequence.

NARRATIVE COMPLEXITY

The narrative of *Life on Mars* is formed by the structure of individual episodes as well as the overall series, by the narrative space, or setting, and by the unique perspective of the protagonist. Sam assumes the role of narrator; however, this position becomes unreliable as soon as he begins to question his place in 1973. The messages from 2006 are clues to the larger mystery that Sam (and the audience) must decipher in order for him to 'get home'. The narrative enigma of *Ashes to Ashes* differs somewhat from *Life on Mars*, with the protagonist DI Alex Drake seemingly aware of what has happened to her. She has woken up in 1981 after being shot, but has read Sam's file from 2006 and believes she has created this time which she inhabits, and is already familiar with the main 'characters', Gene Hunt and his colleagues, who have conveniently moved to London. She actively participates in what she believes is a psychological effect of her injury. This adds a new dimension to the mystery for the audience. Like Alex, we know what happened to Sam in the end and as such the mystery is lessened. However, we are still unsure what this 'time travel' means to her or how it happened, and this maintains and reinforces the generic mix of sci-fi and crime drama.

The narrative space is an important part of the generic characteristic of any show, and the specificity of the space of *Life on Mars* adds to the series mystery. The location and exterior of Sam's police station are the same in 1973 and 2006, creating a sense of familiarity for Sam, but upon entering the building after he wakes up in 1973 he finds the place has changed. What were previously ultra-modern, sterile interiors, filled with high-tech equipment, are now drab, brown and very low-tech offices. The details have been set up to be in stark contrast, noticeable in the clothing and indeed the demeanour of the police officers inhabiting the office. This contrast between the future and the past is used throughout the series; whenever Sam becomes comfortable in the world of 1973, there is a reminder of 2006 which confirms that he does not really belong in this time or place. The problematic nature of Sam's sense of place/time is particularly evident in the final episode when he returns to 2006, only to once more experience the high-tech sterility of a world in which he no longer feels at home. What was once familiar has now become alien and this leads to his actions at the conclusion of the series.

The exterior spaces in the series play an important role in evoking the world of the seventies cop show. The inclusion of high-speed, stylised car chases in period cars reinforces the ideas of both Sam and the audience of what the seventies would look like. We discover in later episodes that Sam would only have been four years old in 1973, so if this is not time travel the imagery could not have come entirely from his coma 'dream' or memory, but would rather be based on his knowledge of the TV cop shows of that era. This again suggests that Sam's position as narrator is a questionable one. Likewise in *Ashes to Ashes*, the 1980s world in which Alex has arrived presents us with every nostalgic image and stereotype of the decade, from the fashion and cars to the changing styles in police work. Like Sam, Alex shares a collective nostalgia with the audience, whose familiarity with the time may be informed by memory and television.

The contrasts of Sam's worlds are emphasised to great effect in episode 1.3 when he investigates a murder in a textile mill. We discover that Sam knows this building well. In 2006, he lives in one of the flats in the converted building; in fact, the murder scene is in his kitchen. The scene shows images of his flat intercut with the murder scene, which prove disorienting for Sam. The episode's main theme, the price of modernisation, also presents another conflict for Sam as he sees, at first hand, the power of unionism in 1973, which he knows will ultimately fail. Not only is he out of his time, but he is out of his place in the political and social struggle, as he is ultimately a beneficiary from the decline of this industry.

The theme of modernisation and progress is also present in the make-shift forensics which Annie uses to preserve a bloody footprint. Sam and the audience are aware of the progress made in crime scene forensics, typified in the contemporary TV crime fiction genre, but these techniques are unknown in 1973. The contrast between technologies once more stands in for Sam's divergent worlds. His knowledge of the future is another complicating factor in the narrative. Remarks are made about future events, yet to happen in 1973, but all too real to Sam; this suggests that he has come from the future and is not delusional. The references to politics and news maintain the accuracy of the period and also serve as comic relief (and provide dramatic irony for the audience), as, for example when a joke is made by Gene Hunt about the 'unthinkable' possibility of a female prime minister, which Sam knows will be Margaret Thatcher.

A key part in the negotiation of the narrative by both the audience and Sam is the characterisation of the supporting players. The characters who inhabit 1973 are familiar from the cop shows of the time and the particularly aggressive, dominant male typified by DCI Gene Hunt, who is strongly reminiscent of Jack Regan in *The Sweeney*. There is an element of sexism and homophobia which rings true of the era. However, Gene is never as racist as the character would perhaps have been had this been written in the seventies (the creators acknowledged this in the 2006 BBC documentary *Creating Life on Mars*[3]). If it is the case that Sam is in a coma and is controlling the narrative, then he has constructed the elements from his own knowledge of the period and from what he has seen on TV, and this also extends to the characters: Gene could be merely a combination of perceived stereotypes from the era. This complicates the narrative still further, but does not provide a resolution to the enigma. Sam attempts to engage with these characters, even occasionally emulating their behaviour in early episodes, but this only lasts until he is reminded of something from the future, and returns to his more sensitive, noughties character

Alex's position as narrator of *Ashes to Ashes* is perhaps more complex still as she is conscious of her problem and refers to those around her as 'constructs' playing out what she believes is a delusion, sharing the audience's knowledge of what came before. At the end of the first series we discover that she may have met Gene when she was a child, though this may also have been coloured by her knowledge of Sam's case. The role of narrator in both series thus adds to the narrative complexity which, when combined with the mixed-genre codes, contrasted narrative spaces and recurring echoes of the future, creates an overarching mystery as to what has happened to the protagonist.

MYTH ARCS

Life on Mars and *Ashes to Ashes* are introduced as mysteries with a series-long question of how the protagonists ended up out of their time. The mystery forms the mythology, or myth arc, which is present throughout the series. In many sci-fi and crime fiction TV series, the myth arc, once established, is only occasionally alluded to. In *The X-Files* for example, the government conspiracy over the cover-up of alien activities is not featured in every episode. Other shows, such as *Supernatural*, use the myth arc as a driving force for the narrative, but again only make occasional direct references.

The mystery in *Life on Mars* has to be examined in every episode, since Sam is never *not* wondering why he is now in the seventies. Likewise, Alex is always trying to figure out how to get home, but unlike the other series where a myth arc episode deals with the mythology in depth, here the whole mystery is only resolved at the end of the series. *Life on Mars* offers clues throughout for both the audience and Sam to decipher. Since they are often subtle, the programmes demand a close reading from the audience. They may be direct references to Sam's past (in the future), for example, his relationship with Maya, his parents, his flat or cases he worked on in 2006. There are also particular lines of dialogue and actions that are repeated from episode one in the series finale. In the first episode, when Sam is questioning the reality of 1973 and trying to understand what has happened to him, he feels Annie's heartbeat as though its existence will prove his. In the final episode, when he is trying to decide whether to stay in the past or return to the future, this happens again. On this occasion he is confirming his choice of where to exist. Another echo from the first episode into the last comes when Sam is going to jump from the roof of the police station. In the first episode, he is prevented from doing so by Annie, but he thinks that if he jumps he will wake up in his own time. In the final episode, he jumps out of 2006 and back into 1973, making a conscious choice to leave the contemporary world. They are subtle but important references that provide a sense of completion and closure, with the audience rewarded for their investment in the series' premise. As well as the series-long mystery (which for *Life on Mars* lasted two seasons), the first season had its own mystery, as did *Ashes to Ashes*.

In series one, Sam has recurring visions of a girl in a red dress running through the woods, and the whispered words 'Where are you?', suggesting that someone is looking for him, possibly from the future. In the season finale, the conundrum as to whether this is time travel or a coma is heightened when Sam believes that he is in the middle of the event which caused his father to leave the family when Sam was just a child. Sam decides that if he can prevent this event then he has resolved a key part of his life and will somehow be sent home. The episode reveals that this is a broken memory of when Sam was a child and was looking for his father. In the original time his dad killed Annie, the girl in the red dress, but Sam saved her this time round. This implies that the people are real as this event happened so are not figments of his imagination; not entirely at least. This episode revealed the truth about his dad's leaving, but little else.

The attempt to alter a past event is replicated in *Ashes to Ashes* when Alex tries to prevent her parents' death. She is unable to do so, but finds out what really happened to them. Like Sam, this only provides an insight into her father's true actions, and does not result in her return home. In both cases the resolution of the mystery only serves to deepen the narrative complexity, and the audience is still left wondering if this recovered memory is part of the coma, or if there could still be a possibility that the protagonist has travelled in time, as they are apparently real historic events. Alex is particularly distraught as she was convinced that this was the resolution which would send her home, but we find out at the end of the episode that she is still in 1981 and indeed shows no sign of going anywhere else.

More indications of the myth arc occur throughout season two of *Life on Mars*, including a clue to Sam's past in the seventies. He receives phone calls from a stranger telling him to be patient and that he will return home soon. To Sam this means that he is communicating with the future, but the number is said to come from Hyde, from where, according to Gene Hunt, Sam had been transferred. Once more, the narrative becomes problematic for both the audience and Sam. It is not until the final episode of the series that we discover 'Hyde' is the name of the hospital ward in which Sam is lying. Throughout the second series, Sam is increasingly convinced that he is in a coma in the future, reinforcing the notion of 1973 as a world constructed in his head. He hears sounds from hospitals and in one episode is ill from an apparent change in medication. A new police inspector, Frank Morgan, is introduced and seems to know everything about Sam, hinting that he can help him get home. By the finale the evidence is mounting that Morgan is really the surgeon who is going to remove the tumour which is keeping him in the coma and therefore in 1973.

Morgan has been cryptic with Sam since their first meeting, but in a pivotal scene he outlines a plan to remove Gene Hunt from the force. Sam questions this and tells Morgan he knows what really happened to him and that he is from the future. Morgan contradicts this, revealing that Sam's accident was in fact in 1973; the family and names he knows are part of an undercover operation to remove Hunt. This revelation sends Sam, and the audience, spinning. If Sam is really from the seventies then why does he know things about the future? Or is the audience assuming that he is in a coma because we saw the earlier version of his life, which may be a dream? Until this final episode, we share Sam's confusion as to what is real: we followed the narrative and generic codes and thought we had deciphered the mystery. This revelation is a double bluff from the writers as the ending reveals the truth; it seems that Sam *was* in a coma and none of this actually happened. He emerges from the tunnel in 1973 to wake in his hospital bed in the present. We see Sam struggling to recover his pre-coma life, but even the therapeutic act of recording his experiences (which will later be of use to Alex Drake in *Ashes to Ashes*) does not help him to adjust. Left feeling nothing, and no longer 'belonging' in this world either, he decides to complete the act he could not in the first episode and jumps from the police roof. This time he wakes up in 1973, where he left Gene, Annie and the others in danger, and ultimately saves them. He agrees to stay with Annie forever, and the series ends with Sam silencing the radio messages, suggesting that his future self is dying.

The creators have maintained that the ending is finite, and that Sam is dead, but viewers are still left to wonder the extent of the construction of Sam's alternative time. Were they constructs of his memories and knowledge of history and television, or is it an actual other place, an afterlife or limbo for Sam, as he is held between life and death in his coma? The suggestion the narrative is finite means that the experience of the mystery for sixteen episodes is heightened; we know we are going to finally get the answer that we have been waiting for, even though in some cases it was not what people expected. Several newspaper reviews and online forums suggested a degree of dissatisfaction with the outcome amongst the programme's audience.[4]

The conclusion of *Life on Mars* shaped the expectations that the audience brought to *Ashes to Ashes*; we share the information that Alex has, and her understanding of the world in which she has appeared. This would suggest that the mystery cannot have the same impact as in the previous series. However, we are still unaware of whether this is a dream construct or, in view of the inclusion of so many events from both protagonists' real past, time travel in some form. The success of *Life on Mars* has been attributed to the uniqueness of the plot and the nostalgia for the period, as well as the quality of acting and the production values. By drawing on the iconic nature of *The Sweeney*, the show engages with the audience in a knowing, postmodern way. This strand is not present in *Ashes to Ashes*, which lacks any similar reference. The only UK crime series in the 1980s which might bear any influence would be *Dempsey & Makepeace* (ITV, 1985–6), though this show was never as generically significant, or innovative, as *The Sweeney*.

Narrative complexity in *Life on Mars* comes from the myth arc mystery that requires the keen viewer to negotiate the series. Episodes appear to follow a standard pattern; however, clues to the myth arc appear alongside the 'monster of the week'. Small clues are littered throughout, adding to or creating the mystery of the protagonist's predicament. Each one of them appears designed to confuse the protagonist and viewer. Even the final reveal of both seasons continued to confuse by taking the clues 'we' had gathered and offering alternative explanations. The standard narrative of the genre is lost as we try to connect the codes.

GENERIC INNOVATION?

Ashes to Ashes does not seem to have achieved the same level of critical acclaim as *Life on Mars*, though it sustained similar ratings for its first series. It could be argued that because it already knows the outcome, the audience does not have the same degree of investment in what happens to Alex, or that the very unique approach to the series was what made *Life on Mars* a success and that this simply cannot be replicated. However, as often happens as a result of generic mixing, there are attempts by other producers to emulate the success of the original show. In 2008, NBC's *Journeyman* premiered in the USA, featuring a journalist transported through time in order to correct history, but unaware of how or why this happens. The show was cancelled after just one season. The US version of *Life on Mars* initially received some acclaim, though it did not follow the narrative resolution of the original. Other television drama series with ambiguous genres, such as *Lost* (ABC, 2004–10) and the recent *Flash Forward* (ABC, 2009–10), have developed the notion of the complex narrative and time travel, but they are not hybrids of an established genre such as crime fiction; rather they begin as mysteries with some sci-fi, adventure and romance in the mix and are determinedly 'high concept'. As such, they do not appeal to the same established audience as a show like *Life on Mars* can with its arguably nostalgic take on crime fiction.

This chapter has argued that the use of the hybrid genres of crime fiction and sci-fi, combined with nostalgia and a highly complex narrative, has resulted in a particularly innovative series in *Life on Mars*, and, to a lesser extent, *Ashes to Ashes*. There are many factors to consider in generic categorisation and progression and it could be argued that patterns of generic development cannot be observed until they have become truly established; however, innovation in one series does not guarantee that a new generic cycle will be created (Altman 1999). It remains to be seen what effect *Life on Mars* will have on the crime fiction genre, or if it will simply lead to more hybridisation, but in the meantime viewers have been able to continue the journey with Gene Hunt, via Alex Drake.

NOTES

1   At the symposium 'Life on Mars', held at the University of Glamorgan, Cardiff, November 2007, producer Julie Gardner was keen to stress that the show was not sci-fi.

2   Dunleavy (2008) suggests that the hybrid is overstated without understanding the nature of the fluidity of TV, and refers to John Fiske's definition of TV genre, 'a shifting provisional set of characteristics which is modified as each new example is produced' (Fiske 1987: 111). Though discussing sitcom, she suggests that hybrids can offer more innovation in TV.

3   'Creating Life on Mars' was part of the BBC 'Time Shift' series and aired on 2 April 2006. The programme was hosted by Andrew Collins and featured an interview with the creators.

4 *Manchester Evening News* Blog 'The life of Wylie' (Wylie 2007) summarises the final episode with responses from the creators about the outcome and some of the clues in the show. He discusses the fans' confusion and the occasional dissatisfaction with the ending.

REFERENCES

Altman, R. (1999). *Film/Genre*, London, British Film Institute.

Cooke, L. (2001). 'The police series', in G. Creeber (ed.), *The Television Genre Book*, London, British Film Institute.

Dobson, N. (2009). 'Generic difference and innovation in *CSI: Crime Scene Investigation*', in M. Byers and V. Johnson (eds), *The CSI Effect*, Lanham, MD, Lexington Books.

Dunleavy, T. (2008). 'Hybridity in TV sitcom: the case of comedy verité', *Flow* – Volume 9.04. [website], *http://flowtv.org/?p=2244*, accessed 25 August 2010.

Fiske, J. (1987). *Television Culture*, London and New York, Routledge.

Hockley, L. (2001). 'Science fiction', in G. Creeber (ed.), *The Television Genre Book*, London, British Film Institute.

Jenkins, S. (1984). '*Hill Street Blues*', in Jane Feuer, Paul Kerr and Tish Vahimagi (eds), *MTM 'Quality Television'*, London, British Film Institute.

Johnson, C. (2001). '*The X-Files*', in G. Creeber (ed.), *The Television Genre Book*, London, British Film Institute.

Mittell, J. (2004). *Genre and Television: From Cop Shows to Cartoons in American Culture,* New York, Routledge.

Neale, S. (2000). *Genre and Hollywood*, London, Routledge.

Wylie, I. (2007). '*Life on Mars*: the answers', *Life of Wylie* [website], 11 April 2007, *http://blogs.manchestereveningnews.co.uk/ianwylie/2007/04/life_on_mars_the_answers.html*, accessed 25 August 2010.

3 IMMERSION VERSUS ALIENATION

LISTENING TO *LIFE ON MARS*

Rob Smith

EVEN THE MAKERS OF *Life on Mars* seem to agree that the series' premise leaves neither characters nor audience knowing whether Sam Tyler (John Simm) is either hallucinating from his 2006 hospital bed or has been physically transported back in time to 1973. However, this is a productive uncertainty. Tyler can know he lived in Manchester 2006, but cannot be certain about anything that has happened since the accident. The viewer can sift the evidence within the series' diegesis, and bear witness as Tyler shifts between alienation from, and immersion in, the world in which he finds himself. This chapter focuses upon the creative exploitation of this tension as it is reinforced by the music and sound used in the series.

The original score for *Life on Mars* was composed by Edmund Butt. After rising through the British classical music world, Butt moved into 'composing to picture' whilst also working as a musical director for the London shows of artists such as Madonna and Puff Daddy. In media composition his music is recognisable for its dark, ominous but fairly static soundscapes as well as clear influences from contemporary dance music. In addition to *Life on Mars* series one and two, Butt has also scored *Ashes to Ashes*, and series one, two and three of *Murphy's Law* (Tiger Aspect, 2003–).

To write about music for television is to enter an undeveloped field. With the exception of Phillip Tagg's (2000; Tagg and Clarida 2003) musematic analyses, there is little substantive analysis of the contribution made by music to television narrative. Perhaps musicologists are put off by addressing a cross-disciplinary audience, fearing their analysis will either be compromised for a general audience or fall on deaf or uncomprehending ears. Meanwhile, television scholars often lack musicological training, having migrated to the discipline largely from the literary or media subject areas. In reading television's music as being as much about carefully constructed timbres and qualities of sound as it is note to note sequences, this essay is indebted to some of the work of Eric F. Clarke (1999: 347–71). Clarke asserts that some levels of musical discourse are regarded as universally shared, accessible to anyone:

> [M]ore complex and abstract levels are more idiosyncratic as a result of the specific training and experience of particular listeners . . . [W]hile the simpler perceptual attributes are a more tractable proposition for empirical and theoretical accounts. (348)

On the other hand, avoiding harder data such as notes and the theoretical relationships between them renders commentary more vulnerable to the 'So what?' chide often levelled at popular music study. By discussing it at all we are looking for planned musical thinking behind decisions that might just as well be arbitrary and which may in fact work best when unnoticed. As Cook points out in relation to music in commercials:

> It is not just the messages . . . that are subliminal. In a sense, the music is too. That is to say, viewers rarely hear the music as such; they are rarely aware of it as an entity in itself . . . Music transfers its own attributes to the story-line and to the product: it creates coherence, making connections that are not there in the words or pictures; it even engenders meanings of its own. But it does all this, so to speak, silently. (1998: 20)

Music and the creative use of sound design in *Life on Mars* may reveal more about the story than can be read in the diegesis alone. The music and sound of *Life on Mars* makes 'connections that are not there in the words or picture' and can also be said to 'engender meanings of [their] own' (ibid.).

Avoiding detailed discussion of precise pitches, this essay concentrates instead on general features of timbre, instrumentation, sound perspectives and editing. Their timing on the DVD within the episode in which they occur identifies cues. In examining the role of music in *Life on Mars*, the analysis refers to five key areas, with the aim of making evident the full range of narrative, temporal, generic and affective roles played by the music in the drama. These areas are: the creation of a distinctive sonic environment; the use of aural leitmotifs; the affective use of music in relation to Sam's mother; musical intertextuality, and, finally, the breaking in series two of conventions established in series one.

THE MUSIC AND SONIC ENVIRONMENTS OF *LIFE ON MARS*

Several delineated layers of musical activity and potential meaning may be found in *Life on Mars*'s soundtrack. A key feature to note is how early seventies pop and rock music is used frequently when Tyler, who in the first series is in every scene and from whose point of view we viewers see almost everything that happens, is most immersed in his 1973 world. Tyler's immersion usually happens through action such as a chase, a problem to solve or being surrounded by activity such as in a nightclub, party or Nelson's pub. In the latter cases, the diegesis could explain the presence of music more than Tyler's attitude to his 1973 surroundings. These instances differ from those articulating Tyler's drifting in and out of immersion in 1973 on several occasions and, elsewhere, being yanked out of it by the intrusion of sounds from 2006. The music used in the immersed sequences is usually already social music because it was played by groups – usually groups of men of around the same number as the team – and was commonly intended for sharing in social situations such as dancing. In other words, it is already heavily laden with values in regard to male bonding and self-image before it is used to reinforce these values and actions as portrayed on screen. As a general rule, when cues of seventies music are used they burst into the soundtrack with a very hard edit thus maximising their aural impact in a style reminiscent of the aggressive music edits in Sergio Leone's 'spaghetti western' films.

Notable in the commissioned score is the use of synthetically created original music cues; brooding dronescapes and percussion tracks to move us eerily through the world of 1973 (and through the world of 2006 in episode 1.1). Together, these help remind us that Tyler is from elsewhere. In fact the present contemporary soundworld is often an indicator of Tyler's alienation from the 1973 world, his unease with certain modes of behaviour of the characters within it (such as police brutality, bullying, crass sexism) and an awareness of his own 'otherness' and issues that reach across to his other world and time. The lack of human, in favour of mechanical and digital, performance here contributes to Tyler's alienation and isolation, which he frequently feels in relation to the world of 1973. This music also has a unifying influence on the series as a whole. It is modular in nature. Familiar musical sounds, textures and melodies recur across the whole series in different combinations: high metallic ticking percussion, a nasal throbbing drone, slow-moving string orchestral passages to name just three of many possible examples. The constant re-combination of these elements, which themselves quickly become familiar, contributes to the series' sense of sonic unity.

One of the most important roles played by sound and music in *Life on Mars* is in helping us move between the two temporal worlds that Sam inhabits. Portal sounds – that is, sounds that operate as a doorway between two worlds – are used when Tyler senses the world of 2007 bleeding into 1973. Such portal sounds often involve voices – whether they are those he recognises or those that he does not recognise but believes are talking to or about him – medicalised sounds such as defibrillators or heart monitors, and drone sounds of various kinds, sometimes musical and sometimes associated with technical or technological equipment. These elements are used in various combinations throughout the two series and, often, they bleed into other musical or sonic cues with other meanings.

45

Specific episodes are often characterised by distinct musical themes, some of which are original or sourced music from the seventies. The plot of episode 1.2, for example, is framed by Wings' 'Live and Let Die', already the frame and incidental music for a 1973 James Bond film with the same title. This is the first episode that sees Tyler inescapably caught up in the 1973 world. The music frames the episode in a filmic way, beginning and ending it, allowing the episode to function as a complete story as well as finding its place in the flexi-narrative continuum of the series (Nelson 2007: 120). The music's lyrics could also be taken as comment on Tyler's need to behave like his new colleagues in order to survive, or, more specifically, to let his 2006 persona and mindset die in order that a 1973 version might live. At the very least, it lends a quick-paced and exciting cutting rhythm to a chase scene at the beginning of the episode. By using this piece thus, the series' makers are buying into a big-budget orchestral sound, a soundworld very different from the small-group rock and pop and computer-performed soundscapes that dominate the vast majority of *Life on Mars*.

One of the most striking elements in the series' narrative soundscape is the use of voices from the 2006 world to destabilise the perceived reality of the 1973 world. For instance, in episode 1.8, Tyler is trying to influence events that will have ramifications through time. Here we experience a more mundane time shift as Tyler recovers a memory of himself running through a wood in summer. This is a memory re-emerging in Tyler's mind: there is no recourse to a portal as is the convention for temporal dislocations elsewhere in the series. The soundtrack is a *horspiel*-like montage of a rich, drone chord, distressed breathing and the reassuring voice of Tyler's 1973 mother with a very intimate sound perspective. All these sonic elements add up to a rich and evocative piece of sound design. The fact that it is an intimate memory, rather than an alien incursion via a portal, gives the impression that Tyler is close to a happy resolution of his series-long temporal dislocation.

LEITMOTIFS

The musical term leitmotif refers to a practice, ascribed in particular to the operas of Richard Wagner (1813–83), whereby 'a recurrent theme [is] associated throughout a musical . . . composition with a particular person, idea or situation' (*OED*: 1996). A more recent example can be found in the spaghetti western scores of Ennio Morricone who makes frequent use of leitmotif. This is especially marked in *Once Upon a Time in the West* (1969) where each of the four main characters has their own associated piece of music. The music of two of those characters ('Harmonica' and 'Frank') frequently appear together, though the reason for this link is only revealed at the film's climax: a gunfight between the two and a flashback to a time when 'Harmonica' was forced to stand with his brother in a noose on his shoulders until the boy 'Harmonica' gave way under his brother's weight, leaving his brother unsupported and consequently strangled to death. The score is then revealed to have been foreshadowing the film's key cathartic moment by reference to the harmonica which 'Frank' pushed into the mouth of the young boy in the flashback. This is a clear example of music's ability to tell us more about a scene than we can actually see.

Morricone's work is not an arbitrary example for Sergio Leone's spaghetti westerns are referred to frequently in *Life on Mars*. We see Gene Hunt (Philip Glenister) putting up Leone film posters and he's outraged in episode 1.8 on discovering that the titles of Leone's films have been subverted to provide the titles for porn films (for example, 'Once Upon a Time in her Vest'). In the DVD accompanying the first series, Butt professes a love for Morricone 'because of his melody writing . . . he is just one of the best in the world at writing beautiful melodies . . . but with unusual instruments' (Butt 2006). Earlier in the same featurette Butt explains that:

[I]t took a long time to get the structure right, you know, themes for characters, soundscapes and stuff that basically would work for television as opposed to a cinema because you do have to write a little bit differently for television.

Writing music for television series might well be different from writing for film, given the exigencies of flexi-narrative devices (Nelson 2007), radically differing budgets and the problems of catering for the vagaries of domestic television set speakers, but the gap is closing due to rapid developments in television set technology, high-end production values and the convergence between films and 'cinematic' television such as *The Sopranos* (HBO, 1998– 2006). In the light of such developments, and given Butt's evident fascination with film music techniques, it is difficult to agree with his comments beyond the obvious budgetary concerns: in *Life on Mars* all Butt's original music is technologically created and performed. All the 'real' instruments are in the sourced music. Nevertheless, the leitmotif technique, and the time tricks it can play within narratives, is an important feature of the music of *Life on Mars*.

A clear echo of this Morriconian technique, in which music is used to foreshadow and reveal narrative elements, is evident in episode 2.5. The action is ostensibly based upon a kidnapping in 1973, but it is motivated by a desire to redress crimes committed the previous year. This is an unusual episode inasmuch as the plot concerns itself with events that happened before Tyler's appearance in the team. These events are recounted to Tyler by other characters, particularly Hunt, with the consequence that Tyler is absent from many scenes. Events are remembered, seen or filmed from another character's point of view, and Tyler – who spends much of the episode hyperactively feverish or blacked-out – views many of the episode's events on television. From timing 19.10 through to 19.30 we hear a cue previously heard in episode 1.6 and, in that episode, associated firmly with fantasist kidnapper Reg Cole (Paul Copley). Only the most observant listener might pick up on this on first viewing. However, this sonic association underlies the narrative action when it transpires that the dead girl's father in episode 2.5, Don Witham (Jonty Stephens), who we see viewing the body of his murdered daughter, and who implores Hunt here to 'leave no stone unturned', turns out to be the kidnapper. This giveaway musical clue, a high whistling tone, has the notes A flat rising a 5th to E flat rising another minor 3rd to G flat and then falling a 4th to D flat. This melody is heard here and later at 45.17 to 45.35 as Annie discovers a letter from Witham leading her to him and the resolution of the kidnapping. Over the course both of the episode and the series, this leitmotif works not only to establish a mood of anxiety, but also indicates to the observant audience that Witham is the kidnapper.

The use of memorable themes within and across episodes and series does more than simply flag up plot developments in advance of their narrative resolution. In episode 1.5 we have a somewhat different example of a leitmotif operating at the level of emotional subtext; it seems aurally to emphasise Tyler's recognition of his feelings about his father through the experience of a young boy he encounters in a police case. Tyler and the team are investigating the murder of a Manchester United fan with the hope of completing their work in time to prevent the repeat of a violent showdown between City and United fans. The investigation and its context rekindle in Tyler happy memories of going to see Manchester United with his father as a very young boy. Music creeps in subtly as the team view the dead body. The music is pulsing and fairly quiet but, thirty seconds later, a series of high-pitched string chords enter, moving slowly over the droning pulse below. The slow isolated chords, some mixing in sounds other than strings, gradually cohere to form a recognisable chord sequence, which, with the introduction of a harp sound emerging gradually from the mix, begins to form a recognisable and memorable musical theme.

As elsewhere, Tyler's interactions with characters from the 1973 world trigger memories and realisations about his self. Here, his dealings with the murdered United fan's son, Ryan (Michael Lawrence), again scored by the falling string chords in what is increasingly becoming a recognisable sequence, lead him to a happy memory of being on the terraces at Old Trafford, presumably with his own father. We learn from his exchanges with Ryan that Tyler does not know where his father is. Here, the music implies a closeness where, narratively speaking, we know there is none, given that we have already learned that Tyler has not seen his father for a long time and has no idea where he is. Later, we see Tyler walking to an undercover stake-out in a pub, and, as he passes Ryan and his Manchester City-supporting 'best mate', we again hear the high string chords. By now we can surmise that they are triggered by, or are meant to make us think of, encounters with Ryan and memories for both Ryan and Tyler of football games watched with their (now-absent) fathers. Tyler breaks up a fight between Ryan and his City-supporting friend, after which Ryan tells Tyler that it will be alright if he, Tyler, breaks his promise to catch Ryan's dad's killer, to which Tyler replies 'That's what grown-ups do innit?' Here the leitmotif cue re-enters, this time very noticeably in a break in the dialogue. Both are talking about the unreliability of grown-ups, but both miss their fathers. The music links Ryan's and Tyler's experiences of lost fathers, although it is clearly Tyler's feelings with which we are meant to identify. This impression is reinforced later in the series when in episode 1.8 the same music is used several times in a story about his father who disappears in ignominy at the end of the episode and series.

At 51:45 in episode 1.5, when Tyler has caught the killer and is giving him an impassioned speech against football violence, the leitmotif reappears. There is no reference to Tyler's father and Ryan is not present, although Ryan's father and his murder is the reason we are here watching Tyler making the arrest. At the episode's conclusion, as Tyler is walking away from Ryan, having given him the killer's ticket to the match, he recognises his own young self walking past. Here a shock of recognition beyond what he thought was possible is signalled by a heavy, loud electronic drone with a wide spectrum which seems to absorb and block off all diegetic or incidental sound. Tyler is wrenched out of 1973's reality, but out of this sound emerges the recognisable first chord of the leitmotif. This time it is only the first chord that we are given before we segue quickly into Nina Simone's 'I Wish I Could Know How it Would Feel to be Free' (Taylor/Lamb, Westminster Music Ltd. 1972). However, this one chord functions as a recognisable trigger of the leitmotif, a sonic resolution to the episode and a signal of what is to come later in the series.

MOTHER MUSIC

Whilst leitmotifs operate at narrative levels, they also establish the mood and tone of characters' relationships and nowhere is this more powerful or emotive than in the case of Tyler's relationship with his mother. In episode 1.4, the sequence that introduces her begins, musically speaking, at 11:47 and continues through to 17:07. There are three important sections that have distinct musical themes. First, Tyler is left at the team's usual pub after a drinking session, telling Nelson the barman that he has had money planted in his pocket at The Warren, a nightclub owned by local gangster Stephen Warren (Tom Mannion). Tyler hates corruption and suspects that his colleagues are in Warren's pocket. The music is slow, mid-range dense bowed string-like chords, underpinning Tyler's disgust with what he has discovered around himself. Next we are in Tyler's flat and there is a children's programme on the television featuring a talking puppet of a horse. In a portal moment, the horse begins to speak with the voice of his 2006 mother trying to communicate with him through the comatose condition. The music skilfully lightens and a rich string sound with a lighter, treble-rich timbre comes in and a simple melody is played on a slightly distorted and de-tuned piano accompanied by the continuing rich strings and harps. We cut to Tyler walking through the streets of his boyhood (we already know from earlier in the episode that Tyler is searching for the house where he used to live). The music connotes innocence and a pleasant nostalgia as Tyler recognises Alfie, a rag and bone man from his youth, followed by Ivanhoe, the family's pet cat who is lounging in the doorway to a terraced house. The music then darkens as Tyler realises he has found the house he has been looking for. As Tyler waits nervously on his own long-lost doorstep we hear a couple of hesitant descending minor phrases mixed very quietly, almost behind the hovering, droning strings, and then his mother appears accompanied by a distinctive and instantly memorable theme on reverberant piano over static strings that lighten in timbre as the theme strengthens. Tyler moves into the house and surveys the domestic interior in which he spent part of his childhood. His sense of unreality is hinted at as the recognisable theme on reverberant piano is re-played without the harmony but with a trembling pitch distortion.

Time never stands still in *Life on Mars*, but the pace is sufficiently varied to allow moments of stillness and these piano leitmotifs have a timeless suspended quality allowing us to register Tyler's shock as a talking horse channels his 2006 mother, and later awe at his rediscovered surroundings and his longing for this lost time with his 1973 mother. The music that links these moments has movement, a sense of progression which carries us along on Tyler's physical journey to this childhood house. The sequence as a whole, uniting these moments, is elegant.

Warren sets a honey trap to discredit Sam, using a 'dancer' from the club called Joni (Kelly Wenham). Joni inveigles her way into Tyler's flat and just before she drugs him in order to take compromising photographs, we hear optimistic piano with timbrally rich, light strings. This music is similar to the cue we heard behind the talking horse that mouthed the voice of his mother, but the melodic material is different and the piano is not de-tuned. Tyler then dreams of his mother (Joanne Froggat) and we hear what has quickly become established as *her* theme, although the dream is interrupted by interference and hallucinations from both Joni's sexual antics at Warren's behest, and from an LSD-fuelled trip containing images of Britney Spears which can only be from his 2006 subconscious.

Later, as Joni repents, burns the negatives of the blackmail photos and tells Tyler how Warren forced her into the kind of work she has had to do for him, she is accompanied by a piano playing simple major tonal music, a self-contained cue with its own resolute ending as if to say Joni has gone. Whilst this episode has introduced us to a piano-led leitmotif, that of Sam's mother, which will recur later in the series, the use of piano so prominently for the other cues around Joni and the talking horse-puppet portal can be no coincidence. The consistent use of piano helps create within-the-episode unity in a story which, because much of it is set in and around a nightclub, could have otherwise been dominated by snippets of diegetic music. Moreover the use of the piano for both Joni's story and Tyler's mother's leitmotif could indicate a link between Joni and Tyler's family: all were beholden to Warren and sub-ject to his regime (Warren is Joni's boss and Mrs Tyler's landlord). At times Tyler seems acutely aware of his mother's vulnerability, at other times, such as when he offers her money, insufficiently aware of her strength and pride.

INTERTEXTUALITY

In her analysis of quality television, Sarah Cardwell argues that a defining characteristic of American Quality Television is its tendency to:

> [E]xhibit high production values, naturalistic performance styles, recog-nised and esteemed actors, a sense of visual style created through care-ful, even innovative camerawork and editing, and a sense of aural style created through the judicious use of appropriate, even original music. (2007: 26)

This is one of relatively few analyses to recognise the contribution music, and, by implication, composers and sound designers, plays in quality television storytelling. This essay has thus far emphasised the narrative, affective and mood-creating function of music and sound. Yet music may also be part and parcel of what critics such as Jonathan Bignell (2007) have identified as qual-ity television's reflexive, self-conscious mode.

Intertextuality is one example of such reflexivity, and it is audible in *Life on Mars*'s use of seventies popular music, perhaps most dramatically when a song's lyrics comment upon the diegetic action. One such example occurs in episode 1.4. This sequence covers the discovery of Joni's body and an argument and fight between Tyler and his least sympathetic colleague, Ray Carling (Dean Andrews). Throughout this sequence the music is loud. The song 'I Can't Change It' and its lyrics are clearly audible in between the dialogue, which sounds as if it has been worked around the song. Tyler is trying to change the web of corruption spun by Warren and which encompasses the police. However, in Joni's case he has failed.

My friends can't fight some things I do,
Must be the way I do those things
I can't change
But I'm trying
To do right

'I Can't Change It' by Frankie Miller:
(P) 1972 Chrysalis Records Ltd.

The next intrusive cue in episode 1.4 is Sweet's 'Blockbuster' which begins with its distinctive siren opening as Warren's sidekick is informing Hunt and Tyler that Warren is responsible for Joni's murder. The lack of conventional music under the siren and its place in the edit, combined with the ubiquity of technological portal sounds in the *Life on Mars* soundtrack, make this piece of sound ambiguous and confusing at first hearing. The creators were no doubt aware of this aural punning.

Once 'Blockbuster' is established, we see Tyler and Hunt striding with some considerable swagger, and in slow motion, through 'The Warren' to a lyric about a destructive force. Tyler seems to be thoroughly immersed in the task at hand, carefully worked towards, painfully won. Interestingly, Hunt professes a dislike for the accompanying music, and that 'Me and the wife like, er, Roger Whittaker . . . well no, more her than me.' Hunt here is not as immersed in the moment as Tyler is: it is Tyler's victory and Hunt's refusal to enjoy the music probably reflects his ambivalence about Warren's defeat.

This prepares the way for a closing instance of intertextuality. Tyler has attempted to visit his mother and young self only to discover that the family has fled. Interestingly, the score replays the de-tuned piano music from the first portal scene with the talking horse. The fact that this music has been substituted for the expected leitmotif could indicate or highlight the mother's absence, or could refer to the earlier portal moment: a failure to get through, a breakdown in communication. Most significant, however, is the fact that for clues about how Tyler feels about this missed opportunity we are left with only the soundtrack. In a closing sequence, the television skips to footage of Roger Whittaker singing:

> No you won't believe in if anymore
> If is for children
> . . .
> Building daydreams . . .
>
> > 'I Don't Believe in If Anymore'
> > R. Whittaker: (P) 1970 BMG Publishing Ltd.

Breaking into this, Tyler's 2006 mother is again speaking through the talking horse-puppet 'I'll be here for you . . .' and the voice has a more intimate sound perspective as it morphs between 2006 and 1973 versions of his mother. The accompanying music is the leitmotif for his 1973 mother, but once again, in this key moment, there is a blurring between diegetic truth and hallucination. The impression that Tyler hears his 2006 mother through the portal but 'reimagines' it as his 1973 mother is reinforced by the leitmotif's presence.

BREAKING CONVENTION IN SERIES TWO

In series two, the central plot driver changes from Tyler trying to put his personal 1973 world in order to trying to engineer Hunt's downfall. Concomitantly, there is a detectable change of emphasis towards the use of commissioned music from Butt in more immersed contexts. Whilst there are occasions when scenes are not seen from Tyler's point of view, such as episode 2.5, there is also a series-long narrative drive towards Tyler's distancing himself from Hunt, his team and 1973. Subtle changes in the protocols of immersion and alienation reflect this.

Early in series two, certain conventions of the first series are either eroded or flouted. Butt himself states that he had no intention in scoring the series of trying to recreate the music of the seventies, saying instead that he would leave that to the original artists. However, in episode 2.2 we see a police operation where CID people an entire post office with police employees to catch a group of armed robbers. At 20.00, as the planted officers within the post office await the expected bank raid, we hear some synthesised brass chords, which, after percussive ticking and throbbing pulses are added, begin to sound like classic American police drama soundtracks as the swelling brass section circles around the uneasy rhythmic parts below it. The tension is increased when a terse, electric piano melody is added. It is easy to hear this music as a pastiche of, or even a reference/homage to, classic American cop-show scores of the early seventies.

Previously in the same episode, beginning at 6.28, there is an original music cue when Hunt gets involved in the investigation with his usual lack of subtlety and unwillingness to observe standard procedure. In the conventions of the first series we would expect to have the usual music of immersion – pop music from 1973 – at this juncture, but the pace of the investigation is instead increased by original music. Is this telling us that Hunt is on shaky ground, though he does not yet know it?

CONCLUSION

When studying music for television it is useful to look diachronically at the occurrences and recurrences of particular melodies, textures and harmonic features both within and across episodes and series. The music and sound in *Life on Mars* works to reinforce the show's productive dilemma: is Tyler hallucinating from 2006–7 or has he travelled through time? Should he just accept that he is where he is and be in the moment and enjoy it? Or should he try to heal his fractured self and get back home? As well as articulating these two possible realities, the music and sound conspire in creating portals between the two via a combination of highly effective sound design and shocking, wrenching musical textures behind them. Furthermore, taking techniques from Morricone and Leone, the series' creators are able to hint at meta-narratives, give us clues as to what is coming, and articulate themes and experiences that ripple through the entire two series sequence.

However, within the sequence of the two series, there is a subtle shift in conventions. Dramatically, Tyler believes in series one that the key to his returning home lies in healing the rift in his family caused by the desertion of his father. In series two, this motivation is replaced by Frank Morgan's (Ralph

Brown) appearance, as he seems to offer a way out if only Tyler will cooperate in bringing about Hunt's downfall. This shift in the engine of the overarching plot is accompanied by subtle changes in musical style and methods, an increase in the use of original music to engage with the 1973 world. This, perhaps, is geared towards keeping the viewing and listening audience on its toes.

REFERENCES

Bignell, J. (2007). 'Seeing and knowing: reflexivity and quality', in J. McCabe and K. Akass (eds), *Quality TV: Contemporary American Television and Beyond*, London, I. B. Tauris, pp. 158–70.

Butt, E. (2006). 'The music of *Life on Mars*', Disk 2, Bonus Features, *Life on Mars: The Complete Series One*, Contender Home Entertainment.

Cardwell, S. (2007). 'Is quality television any good? Generic distinctions, evaluations and the troubling matter of critical judgement', in J. McCabe and K. Akass (eds), *Quality TV: Contemporary American Television and Beyond*, London, I.B. Tauris, pp. 19–34.

Clarke, E. F. (1999). *Music Analysis 18/iii*, Oxford, Blackwell, 347–74.

Cook, N. (1998). *Analysing Musical Multimedia*, Oxford, Oxford University Press.

Cooke, M. (2008). *A History of Film Music*, Cambridge, Cambridge University Press.

'Edmund Butt', *Cool Music Ltd* [website], *http://www.coolmusicltd.com/Composers/Edmund-Butt/Edmund-Butt.html*, accessed 2 February 2009.

Life on Mars, BBC Drama [website], *http://www.bbc.co.uk/lifeonmars/*, accessed 2 February 2009.

Neal, C. (2006). 'Gangstas, divas, and breaking Tony's balls: musical reference in *The Sopranos*', in D. Lavery (ed.), *Reading the Sopranos: Hit TV from HBO*, London, I. B. Tauris, pp. 121–6.

Nelson, R. (2007). *State of Play: Contemporary 'High-End' TV Drama*, Manchester, University of Manchester Press.

McCabe, J. and Akass, K. (eds) (2007). *Quality TV: Contemporary American Television and Beyond*, London, I. B. Tauris.

Tagg, P. (2000). *KOJAK Fifty Seconds of Television Music: Towards the Analysis of Effect in Popular Music*, New York, The Mass Media Scholars' Press.

Tagg, P. and Clarida, B. (2003). *Ten Little Title Tunes: Towards a Musicology of the Mass Media*, New York and Montreal, The Mass Media Scholars' Press.

'The Sopranos', *IMDb* [website], *http://www.imdb.com/title/tt0141842/*, accessed 31 March 2009.

PART II

CONTESTING THE PAST

TELEVISION AND HISTORY

4 | MEMORY BANKS FAILING!

LIFE ON MARS AND THE POLITICS OF RE-IMAGINING THE POLICE AND THE SEVENTIES

Andy Willis

THE INITIAL THINKING for this chapter was sparked by reading Manchester-based DJ and journalist Dave Haslam's book *Young Hearts Run Free: The Real Story of the 1970s*. In his introduction Haslam states that:

> The seventies are frequent fodder for nostalgia TV, and the image of the decade is dominated by a selection of the most anodyne symbols . . . We've allowed the Abbafication of the seventies to create a powerful but partial version of the history of the decade . . . History without the rawness and unpredictability. (2005: 1)

On the surface the television series *Life on Mars* may not seem to be part of this process of 'Abbafication' as its version of the decade would seem far removed from such sugar-coated images. Indeed, many of the series' episodes deal with the very things that Haslam argues today's nostalgia shows omit: terrorism, sexism, political activism and, most repeatedly, attitudes towards policing and the role of the police in society. This chapter will explore whether *Life on Mars* offers anything other than a rather comfortable trip back to a nostalgic version of the seventies, a version that, even if it does not omit the difficult moments, still manages to present the decade in a much more palatable and ultimately conservative version than one might at first expect. What becomes striking as one looks in detail across the two series of *Life on Mars* is the fact that this conservatism is rooted not only in the nostalgic version of the past, but also in its representation of the attitudes and ideals of the present. This leads to the conclusion that one of the most interesting aspects of the programme is the way in which it uses the past to engage in a critique of the policing of today. However, in order to understand the politics of the series and its attitude to today's police we need to begin by looking closely at its re-imagining of the fictional seventies and its representation of the police force of that time.

MISREMEMBERING THE PAST?

In an interview with the *Manchester Evening News* at the time of its first broadcast, John Stalker, the former deputy chief constable of Greater Manchester Police, made a rather obvious dismissal of *Life on Mars*'s representation of the police of the seventies as being well wide of the mark in terms of his experiences:

> It's a combination of every cliché from every cop show . . . but it's got nothing to do with real policing in the 1970s. It could not be more inaccurate in terms of procedure; the way they talk or the way they dress. In all the time I was in the CID in the 1970s I never saw a copper in a leather bomber jacket and I never heard an officer call anyone 'guv'. (King 2006: np)

Whilst it might be easy for those, such as Stalker, who see themselves as 'in the know' regarding the 'reality' of policing in the period to dismiss the programme as inaccurate, for those viewers who had watched seventies television, the series would not seem to be, even remotely, attempting to recreate an accurate picture of policing in that decade. Rather, it seemed the programme makers were far more interested in recreating fictional representations of the police from that era, such as *The Sweeney* (ITV/Euston Films, 1975–8)[1] that still circulate on UK re-run channels such as ITV 4, rather than creating a historically accurate image of the actual organisation. However, even the BBC press office seemed to have missed this point when it offered up the programme's historical fidelity as something positive, thereby providing the likes of Stalker with a stick with which to beat the series:

> *Life on Mars* will remind viewers of life in the decade that taste forgot, but it is not a trip down memory lane to get nostalgic or reminisce about the good old days; it reflects life as it really was: an era of social and civil change. There was considerable industrial unrest, unemployment was on the increase, especially in the North West as the textile and mass manufacturing industries were reaching crisis point and the unions were becoming more vocal and militant. (*Life on Mars* Press Pack, 2005)

Whilst *Life on Mars* engages with a number of important social and political issues that one associates with the seventies, the programme manages to mis-remember some of the key things with which the police force of that period is associated. Of course, the inclusion of events in a television programme does not necessarily mean that they are going to be portrayed accurately. However, rather than focus on the procedures and dress codes as Stalker does, it is more rewarding to look at the way in which the police are shown in relation to some of the movements for social change from that period, particularly their involvement in wider operations that worked against forces committed to progressive social change. For example, in a period marked by widespread industrial strike action often led by left-wing militants, the police force of the seventies played a key role in working to counter such class-based actions. This ranged from the heavy-handed policing of the mass pickets at trade union strikes, such as that at the Grunwick Film Processing Laboratories in 1976 (Dromey and Taylor 1978), to dealing with organisations such as the anarchist urban guerrillas, the Angry Brigade, a few years earlier. In the case of the latter, there still remains a strong feeling that the convictions in 1972 of four supposed members of the group were achieved through the planting of evidence by police officers (Carr 2008). More widely, and at all levels, the police of the period were connected to the establishment via organisations such as the Freemasons, and the seventies was a period when the level of police–Masonic links was starting to cause broader concern in society. Alongside these, throughout the seventies there were persistent accusations of serious corruption in the police force, and high-profile instances involving the Vice Squad in London and the West Midlands Serious Crime Squad were widely reported at the time and caused a rising mistrust of the police in many quarters. Stalker may have wanted to focus on incorrect jackets, but the real omission in *Life on Mars*'s fictional version of the seventies is the police force's role in maintaining the established social order.

Ultimately, whilst many of these political and social issues and their contexts are touched upon in *Life on Mars*, the series still presents such events and characters from the perspective of the police, and the force of the seventies is shown as a gang of rather oafish but ultimately likable men/children. The actions of the police may be, at times, a little bit risky but they are always done with the intention that their results will always, broadly speaking, promote the public good. This reveals that *Life on Mars* continues a fictional representation of the force that came to the fore in the seventies. As Lez Cook has observed, these characters shared:

A self-righteous belief in the validity of their own methods, even if those methods involved a degree of violence and a bending of the rules. In a decade in which the social consensus of the postwar years was breaking down, the old, gentlemanly codes . . . no longer applied. Now the ends justified the (often illegal) means. In an increasingly lawless society extreme tactics were sometimes needed by these fictional policemen in the performance of their 'duty'. In the 'law and order' decade of the 1970s, television police series became an arena where the ideological and coercive work of the police was foregrounded as never before. (Cook 2008: 32–3)

Episode 1.1 sets up how the audience might read the 'old school' approach of the 1973 force in *Life on Mars*, and nowhere more so than its introduction of one of the show's main protagonists, DCI Gene Hunt (Philip Glenister). A disorientated Sam Tyler (John Simm) arrives in the squad office and his shouting disturbs Hunt who, appearing in his doorway smoking a cigarette, says, 'A word in your shell like pal.' He then grabs Tyler, pulls him into his office, slams him against a filing cabinet and says, 'They reckon you got concussion. Well I couldn't give a tart's furry cup if half your brains are falling out, don't ever waltz into my kingdom acting king of the jungle.' Tyler asks him who he is and he answers, 'Gene Hunt, your DCI and it's 1973' and it is through this that the brusque, no-nonsense attitude of the 1973 police force is established from the outset. Unsurprisingly, by the end of the episode there has been a reworking of the idea that rules can be bent for the good of all by the copper whose ultimate aim is just. A note is discovered that indicates that Kramer, the dangerous criminal the team are trying to bring to justice, has some sort of mental problem and if this comes to light when he is taken for trial it is likely he would be sent to a hospital rather than a prison. Gene Hunt suggests that the note might find its way into the bin, thereby ensuring that a criminal is punished in a suitable fashion and not released early to continue committing even worse crimes. Sam Tyler, with his 2006 methods of policing, considers Hunt's suggestion for a moment and then, with the whole weight of the programme's morality, both in 1973 and 2006, behind his decision, crumples up the paper and drops it in the waste bin. Whilst we are shown that Sam seems to be aware of what it takes to succeed in his contemporary version of the police force, here, through his time-travelling experiences in the past, he has found that there is a more timeless version of policing that centres on a different version of 'doing the right thing', one that supersedes the liberal perspectives of the present.

From the outset, then, the dominant perspective of *Life on Mars*, whether in the past, the present or indeed the future, is one that ultimately sees contemporary liberal attitudes towards the maintenance of law and order as what has led to criminals escaping punishment when a 'correct', that is a more conservative, attitude to policing would ensure that they paid for their actions and remained off the streets and behind bars unable to perpetrate future crimes. *Life on Mars* therefore seems to suggest that good policing is in fact something that is timeless and not fixed by its – or indeed any – context. In the final analysis, be it 1973 or 2006, a good policeman will always make the 'right' decision as Sam Tyler, despite his liberal inclinations, has done. Such representations of the police have increasingly been in circulation since the seventies. As Charlotte Brunsdon has argued, such a discourse of law and order is a staple of the television police series and one that, 'occupies, and contributes to, a Manichaean universe in which guilt, innocence and blame can be clearly attributed. Wrong is wrong, and should be recognised as such and punished' (Brunsdon, 2000: 198). Indeed, there are many versions of fictional policemen and women who might on occasion have to use methods that would normally trouble society's liberals for the ultimate good scattered across the history of the television police series from Theo Kojak[2] in the USA to Jim Taggart[3] in the UK.

POLICING THE NATION IN THE TWENTY-FIRST CENTURY

Whilst some, such as John Stalker, have chosen to critique *Life on Mars*'s representation of the past, we should remember that any television drama that is set in the past will always also offer us a perspective on its present. In the case of *Life on Mars* this is more obvious because of the fact that one of the central characters, Sam Tyler, is actually from our 'present' world and brings a range of contemporary attitudes to his job to the era in which the drama is set. This is most obvious in his and Gene Hunt's contrasting attitude to the working methods of the police force. Far from critiquing the past and championing the present, *Life on Mars* finds contemporary policing problematic and overly bureaucratic. This is reflected in Sam's contemporary existence being dominated by meetings, thereby suggesting it is ineffective in its primary goal of stopping criminals. Ray King, writing in the *Manchester Evening News*, went so far as to describe the image of the contemporary force present in the series as 'limp-wristed, politically correct, stressed out, bureaucratic and invisible' (King 2006: np).

Life on Mars can therefore be read as a deeply conservative, even reactionary programme when it comes to its attitude and perspective on contemporary policing. As is the case with a number of police dramas there is at the core of *Life on Mars* a structural opposition between the instinctive, rule-bending copper who gets results and a 'system' whose structure is always presented as being overly bureaucratic and obsessed with its cumbersome procedures being followed to the letter by its officers. Perhaps surprisingly, at first Gene Hunt represents the former and our erstwhile hero, Sam Tyler, with his twenty-first-century perspectives, is often portrayed as being closer to the latter. This is repeatedly indicated by his wanting to adhere to procedure and his continual admonishments throughout both series of Hunt's less-than-liberal perspective on the world and its inhabitants. This opposition, and in particular Hunt's connection to other historical representations of the police, goes some way to explaining the character's popularity with viewers. For many, he will be a familiar character type, easily understandable, and in turn read as positive within the context of the police drama, unlike the more liberal-minded and bureaucratic Tyler whose generic precursors were usually at odds with the likes of Hunt. This opposition is nothing new, and those who have written about television drama have addressed its repeated manifestation within the genre of the police series. Geoff Hurd discusses such structural oppositions between the approach and attitude of members of the fictional police force in television series in his consideration of *The Sweeney*.

Hurd's main concern is with 'the actual programmes and more specifically with the ways in which an image of policing is constructed and mediated through the fictional forms of the television police series' (Hurd 1981: 53). He puts forward a series of oppositions which he suggests have created the points of tension that British Film Institute drive the drama on screen:

> The points of tension within the police series can be revealed by considering the major oppositions identifiable within the programmes, the ways in which they are resolved within the drama and their relation to the structural contradictions which they manipulate and redefine. (1981: 65)

Though written almost thirty years ago, the tensions and oppositions Hurd identifies remain relevant when thinking about *Life on Mars* and its evocation of the past; they help shed some light on how we are invited to view the two central characters that inhabit the fictional worlds of the 1970s and 2000s. Hurd's complete list looks like this:

Police v. Criminal
Law v. Rule
Professional v. Organisation
Authority v. Bureaucracy
Intuition v. Technology
Masses v. Intellectuals
Comradeship v. Rank (1981: 66)

Hurd's analysis is an interesting one to apply to *Life on Mars* as much that has been written about the series has commented upon the ways in which it actively evokes police shows of the past and connects Gene Hunt's attitude to policing to that of his fictional predecessors, including *The Sweeney*'s Jack Regan (John Thaw). Hurd's article is also useful as it helps to re-foreground the idea that *Life on Mars* is a representation of the police both past and present and as such, as Matt Hills explores in his contribution to this collection, is very much a self-conscious, television-literate programme. With this awareness of how television police series work, Sam Tyler's contemporary liberal attitude can be read as more of a structural necessity of the genre than an earnest and realistic critique of today's police force and their working methods. As in Hurd's seventies examples of the genre, the central opposition within the police drama elements of *Life on Mars* is between the police force and the various criminals whose activities they endeavour to stop and seek to arrest. So, whether the fictional police officers are from 1973 or 2006, they are still represented as working to protect the law-abiding public from crime and criminals, even if their methods differ greatly.

Hurd's list continues with his opposition of 'Law' with 'Rule'. Here he argues that, '[t]his is most obvious in *The Sweeney* and in productions in the same trajectory, in which the short-circuiting of legal niceties is the accepted method for establishing guilt' (1981: 66). In *Life on Mars* Hunt and his approach to his work clearly connects with the policing of *The Sweeney* whilst Sam's seems to be closer to the procedural world of *Z Cars* (BBC, 1962–78)[4] or even *Dixon of Dock Green* (BBC, 1955–76).[5] In the seventies police series that are Hurd's focus, the 'good' coppers – that is, those we were invited to believe – were working in the interest of society, however much they bent the rules. They accord with the left-hand side of his list. In *Life on Mars* it is Gene Hunt whose attitude, characteristics and actions are summed up by the left-hand side whereas Sam Tyler's style of 'contemporary' policing is more in line with those on the right. Indeed, Hunt often refers to 'instinct', 'gut-feelings', and he continually taps his temple, suggesting that it is in fact Tyler who needs to use *his* head more and think about what he is doing rather than just following established procedures in an unquestioning fashion. In episode 1.3 Hunt makes his views on policing clear when he says that it always works on instinct. Tyler, on the other hand, makes continual references to 'procedure', always wanting the team's investigations to be done 'by the book' and in the correct – what might be termed 'politically correct' – manner. One of the striking things the programme does is too easily to suggest that the reason for an increasingly bureaucratic police procedure is outside political desires to get the force to appear politically correct. In this fashion, Tyler's version of the correct way of doing things always seems to involve some sort of ordered system or approach and the gathering of evidence through technology or new scientific methods such as forensics and autopsies. His actions are often dictated by the results of these methodologies, rather than any innate feel for crime solving or police work. For much of *Life on Mars*, Sam Tyler is not an instinctive copper; he is a twenty-first-century modern man overtaken by new technologies, so much so that the techniques and equipment that are meant merely to assist policing have now seemingly become more important than the people who actually police. The most important lesson both Tyler and, by extension, contemporary viewers must learn from the seventies of *Life on Mars* is to allow the people who can to do their jobs and to have less red tape and bureaucracy preventing them from doing so.

In contrast to Tyler, Hunt is presented as pragmatic, willing to shift and change his approach in order to get results and put the bad people behind bars. Because of this it is Hunt who most resembles the traditional police drama heroes of previous decades. This fact perhaps goes some way to explaining why he became the character most liked by many audience members. Furthermore, the approach to the part utilised by Philip Glenister, evoking other quiet tough guy actors such as Clint Eastwood and Chuck Norris, makes it easy for audiences to quickly understand and read the character. Reflecting this, Glenister himself has stated that, 'I'm an instinctive actor . . . I just see the part and play it. I'm more interested in what isn't said – the silences' (*Daily Mail*, no date). By episode 1.2 Tyler is already beginning to acknowledge that, as much as he does not want to admit it, Hunt's approach may have something to offer. This is shown during the episode's final moments. After dealing with armed robber Kim Trent (Andrew Tiernan), thanks to Hunt's intervention with his fist, the team play a game of cards. As they do so Hunt asks Tyler, 'Are you sure you're in?' to which the latter replies, 'Deal me'. Here, by accepting Hunt's invitation to join 'the game', Tyler seemingly accepts the fact that to deal with criminals of the calibre of Trent one might just have to do some things the Gene Hunt way.

Episode 1.4 of *Life on Mars* is an important one in this respect as it shows that, even though he may be tinged with corruption and ignores rules and regulations, Hunt is not a totally irredeemable character. Here, even though there have been suggestions that his integrity might have been compromised through his association with members of the criminal underworld, he helps Tyler to arrest local criminal kingpin Steven Warren (Tom Mannion). Following his brusque introduction in episode 1.1, Gene Hunt became increasingly sympathetic, with the series characterisation offering the audience the opportunity to read him as the 'good' cop. By episode 1.3 this has been further established through the introduction of the Regional Crime Squad and its arrogant, unsympathetic leader, DCI Litton (Lee Ross). Litton's unequivocally negative presence in the series is crucial – it allows the audience to read Hunt in a less critical manner and enables them to be more willing to embrace his redemptive moments, such as those in episode 1.4.

In contrast to Hunt's pragmatism and ability to get the job done, in 2006 the ordinary copper, as represented by Sam Tyler, is the personification of the final victory of the attitude represented in Hurd's list of oppositions by terms such as 'Organisation', 'Bureaucracy', 'Technology' and 'Intellectuals'. With the advances in technology and the clear ways they can in fact help today's policing, *Life on Mars* cannot reject Tyler's crime-solving approach out of hand. Rather, it seems overall to suggest that it might be some combination of Tyler's and Hunt's approaches that offers the best approach to policing, with Hunt's instinctive approach humanising Tyler's dependency on procedure and forensic science. However, the way in which this balance is suggested remains vital to understanding the series' attitude to contemporary policing. It is Hunt who seems better at actually detecting and catching thieves whilst Tyler has something of a laboured, almost learned, approach to his work. Sam's approach ensures that the arrests are sound and not achieved through unfair means, but it lacks the obvious flair offered by Hunt's individualism. Episode 2.5 is interesting in this regard. Here, we see that Hunt has been overly aggressive in the past – significantly before the arrival of Tyler – when he violently interrogated a supposed criminal called Bathurst (Adam Beresford) (whom we ultimately find was wrongly convicted of killing a young girl). At the end of this episode, Tyler and Hunt come together to realise that the real killer was in fact another character, Mr Lamb (Reece Dinsdale). As the episode concludes, they both simultaneously call out and walk over to him united as one force as they arrest the real criminal. The ending here seems to sum up the overarching ideas about policing offered by the programme; that is, whilst new technologies harnessed to crime solving can prove helpful they should, or indeed can, never fully replace the individual 'instinct' of a good copper.

The drawing together of Tyler and Hunt may suggest an idealistic, almost utopian, policing method that combines the best of both characters. However, a closer look across the episodes of *Life on Mars* suggests that it is in fact indicating that contemporary policing needs to take a leaf out of the seventies book. As Hunt says in episode 1.2, reflecting Tyler's view and his own unease with it, 'Are they all like you in Hyde? It must be a bloody dangerous place.' His concern, in line with many of those that appear in contemporary newspapers such as the *Daily Mail*, is that an overdependency on procedure prevents instinctive policing and thus makes his and, by extension, our twenty-first century, streets as dangerous as those in Tyler's mythical Hyde. Interestingly, during an edition of current affairs programme *Tonight with Trevor McDonald* (ITV, 1999–), shown on 11 November 2007, police officers complained that they had too much paperwork and therefore not enough time to carry out proper policing. These debates circulating about the role of the police further reinforce the idea that a programme such as *Life on Mars*, in its representation of policing and the conflicts about how it should be undertaken, are indeed speaking to the present as much as they are about the past.

Unsurprisingly, given its historical importance, the idea of corruption within the seventies police force is central to many episodes of *Life on Mars*. However, it is also for the most part confined to the seventies and as such is not presented as something that is part of Sam Tyler's contemporary police force. This absence from Tyler's present-day force might again be seen as a rather conservative reading of today's police. In 1998, the Association of Chief Police Officers Taskforce on Corruption was established, and as recently as 1999 Gloria Laycock, in the foreword to a Home Office document on this area, accepted that:

> Throughout the 1960s and 1970s discussion of the Police Service and policing in the United Kingdom was punctuated with examples of malpractice and misconduct. Twenty years on, several high profile scandals involving officers at all ranks of the police service in a number of forces, have again placed the police service, and discussion of police corruption in particular, under the official and public spotlight. (Laycock, 1999: iii)

Corruption and malpractice within the police force remains a serious concern in British society as evidenced in July 2011 by the resignations of Sir Paul Stephenson, Metropolitan police commissioner and John Yates, assistant commissioner in the wake of the *News of the World* hacking affair. Seeing liberal Sam Tyler as representative of the contemporary force may be as much an act of fictional re-imagining as *Life on Mars*'s creation of Gene Hunt and the seventies.

ASHES TO ASHES: THE RETURN OF GENE HUNT

Gene Hunt's re-introduction to the audience in episode 1.1 of *Ashes to Ashes* reveals how important the popularity of the character and his attitude had become to those involved in the production and wider media promotion of the series. Eleven minutes into the first episode of *Ashes to Ashes*, following her awakening in 1981, Drake (Keeley Hawes) is being threatened by a man. On the soundtrack we can hear a car engine and there is a cut to reveal in the distance a red Audi Quattro accelerating towards them, followed by a series of shots that culminate in it skidding to a halt in front of the pair. This is then followed by a shot of the bottom of the car door; this opens and a foot clad in a snakeskin boot steps out, and continues with another shot of the two boots hitting the ground in slow motion accompanied by screeching guitar riffs. This sequence is clearly designed to celebrate the arrival of Gene Hunt into the world of *Ashes to Ashes* and finishes in a shot of Hunt in the mid-distance framed through Drake's legs, recalling the poster for the 1981 exploitation film *Ms. 45: Angel of Vengeance*. As episode director Jonny Campbell states on the DVD commentary track, for him this was 'the moment we've all been waiting for' (Campbell 2008). As he goes on to confront the man holding Drake, Hunt's dialogue reinforces this sense of celebration as he states, with an attitude and delivery familiar to the audience from *Life on Mars*, that, 'Today my friend your diary entry will read: took prossie hostage and was shot by three armed bastards', before, echoing his original appearance in *Life on Mars*, kneeing him in the groin. Hunt's appearance here, wielding a large 'Magnum-style' gun, suggests that, if anything, his attitude has become even more uncompromising than before; more Dirty Harry than Jack Regan. However, whilst this shift might reveal an even more reactionary approach to policing, in an instant the audience are comforted by the fact that in the intervening eight years Hunt has not been softened by the police hierarchy. As Jonny Campbell states, here, 'familiarity is important . . . when the knee goes in you think, at last!' (2008). Ultimately, *Life on Mars* and *Ashes to Ashes* seem to suggest that we in the twenty-first century could do with more of the old-fashioned 'attitude' displayed by Gene Hunt; as suggested towards the start of this chapter, however, this leaves something of a sour taste in the mouth when one recalls aspects of the actual approaches to policing utilised in seventies Britain.

NOTES

1   *The Sweeney* is an iconic 1970s series that has remained familiar to newer generations through continued repeats and the use of sounds and images from the series across popular culture. It has its own unofficial celebratory website at *http://www.thesweeney.info/*.

2   Theo Kojak, played by Telly Savalas, was the central character in *Kojak* (CBS, 1973–8).

3   Jim Taggart, played by Mark McManus until his death in 1995, was the central character in *Taggart* (STV Productions, 1983–).
4   Initially praised for bringing a new realism to the police drama, *Z Cars* ran on BBC 1.
5   Often seen as something of an outdated, comfortable and somewhat soft representation of the police force, *Dixon of Dock Green* ran on BBC 1.

REFERENCES

BBC Press Pack (2005). 'A sign of the times: How the seventies were brought back to life', *BBC* [website], *http://www.bbc.co.uk/pressoffice/pressreleases/stories/2005/12_december/08/mars_life.shtml*, accessed 23 October 2007.

Brunsdon, C. (2000). 'The structure of anxiety: recent British television crime fiction', in E. Buscombe (ed.), *British Television: A Reader*, Oxford, Oxford University Press, pp. 195–217.

Campbell, J. (2008). 'Commentary on episode one', Disk 1, Bonus Features, *Ashes to Ashes: The Complete Series One*, Contender Home Entertainment.

Carr, G. (2008). *The Angry Brigade: The Spectacular Rise and Fall of Britain's First Urban Guerrilla Group*, Oakland, PM Press, DVD.

Cook, L. (2008). 'The crime series', in Glen Creeber (ed.), *The Television Genre Book* (second edition), London, BFI/Palgrave, pp. 29–34.

Daily Mail reporter. 'Philip Glenister: drugs, shoplifting and why he loves cuddling babies', *Mail Online* [online news resource], *www.dailymail.co.uk/femail/article-1168290/Philip-Glenister-Drugs-shoplifting-loves-cuddling-babies.html#ixzz0TpkK7qIy*, accessed 9 October 2009.

Dromey, J. and Taylor G. (1978). *Grunwick: The Workers' Story*, London, Lawrence & Wishart.

Hammond, S. (2006). 'Top cop's race charge', *The Asian News*, 29 June.

Haslam, D. (2005). *Young Hearts Run Free: The Real Story of the 1970s*, London, HarperCollins.

Hurd, G. (1981). 'The television presentation of the police', in T. Bennett et al. (eds), *Popular Television and Film*, London, British Film Institute, pp. 53–70.

King, R. (2006). '*Life on Mars* writers on another planet – top cop', *Manchester Evening News*, 27 February.

Laycock, G. (1999). 'Foreword', in T. Newburn, *Understanding and Preventing Police Corruption: Lessons from the Literature*, London, Home Office.

5 | SAM TYLER AND THE 'NEW NORTH'

John Curzon

Twenty minutes into episode 1.2 of *Life on Mars*, Sam Tyler (John Simm) seeks solace in a local pub after his textbook methods of policing have resulted in a young woman being in a coma. Frustrated by the perceived inadequacies of 1973, he complains to the barman (Tony Marshall) of the Railway Arms,

> Why does it have to be now, Nelson? Why this particular year? . . . eighty-eight was a good vintage. Year I graduated from the force. Colour television, central heating. It was like bloody *Star Trek* compared to this. Can I change it?! I'll have 1988 please, quick as you like. See I don't mind staying if that's how it's supposed to be but, please can I have a year that's AD as opposed to BC!

This essay will attempt to provide an answer to Sam's question, 'Why does it have to be now?', by exploring and explaining the historical setting of *Life on Mars*, and elaborating upon his distinction between 'BC' and 'AD'. In particular, it will use the space of the cotton mill as a way of understanding Sam Tyler's status as a post-industrial 'comer-in' and how it relates to competing ideas of northern masculinity.

In terms of genre one of the most significant influences on *Life on Mars* is the 1975 police drama *The Sweeney* (ITV/Euston Films, 1975–8). However, *Life on Mars* is located at a slightly earlier point in history, which appears to create a discrepancy in the programme's retrospective logic. However, what follows will argue that by locating its narrative action in 1973, *Life on Mars* engages with an important historical moment, and in doing so, provides clues to the political, economic and, more importantly, cultural changes that have taken place in Britain over the last thirty years. Central to this idea is the significance of the year 1973 within the context of post-industrial theory. In the work of prominent sociologists such as David Harvey (1989), Manuel Castells

(1998, 2000), Scott Lash and John Urry (1988, 1994), 1973 is commonly identi-fied as marking the beginning of the post-industrial society for advanced west-ern economies. For Britain during this period, the difficulties of rising inflation and unemployment were compounded by industrial disputes and a deteriora-tion in Britain's balance of payments. In the aftermath of the Arab–Israeli war, the quadrupling of the price of oil by the OPEC cartel of oil-producing coun-tries precipitated an energy crisis, the imposition of a state of emergency on five separate occasions and the imposition on industry of a three-day working week. Strikes by miners and workers in power stations put enormous pressure on Edward Heath's Conservative government and they were forced to fight an election in which they asked the electorate 'Who governs Britain?' (Jenkins 2006: 29). These domestic crises were related directly to the international situation and changes that were occurring within the US economy. The year 1973 marked the beginning of the first major post-war recession in America, with foreign competition threatening its hegemony in international trade, and the dollar being undermined as the world's stable reserve currency following the breakdown of the Bretton Woods agreement in 1971 (Harvey 1989: 141). The 'oil shock' of 1972–4 represented the end of the post-war boom and the exhaustion of the Fordist–Keynesian consensus, a tacit social contract achieved between labour, capital and the state in which full employment, welfare and low inflation were achieved through a mixed economy and state intervention. From the end of the seventies, the viability of this system was questioned and subsequently rejected by the neo-liberal economic policies of political figures such as Margaret Thatcher and Ronald Reagan, and from 1973, restructuring in the global economy led to the internationalisation of business and markets, the contraction of manufacturing in advanced western economies, and the shift to a new strategy of capitalist accumulation reliant on core and peripheral non-productive, white-collar service-sector work. The year 1973, therefore, marks a decisive point in the emergence of the 'post-industrial society', and the decline of a factory-based working class in the western world.

In the following discussion, Sam's idea of 'bc' is positioned in terms of an 'Old North' represented by manufacturing and extractive industries, while 'ad' is taken to represent a 'New North', ostensibly centred on a post-industrial, white-collar class. The most significant example of this dichotomy occurs in episode 1.3 when the police are called to investigate a murder at Crester's textile mill. In a striking montage sequence, two ideas of the North are seen to share the same mill space, albeit at different times. The focus of the episode is the death of a loom operator, Jimmy Saunders, who, by defying the advice of a recently merged and increasingly powerful union, has attempted to stave off redundancy by working triple shifts. He does so in order to com-pete with newly installed mechanical looms, which are capable of doing the work of three men. Suspicion for the crime quickly falls on Ted Bannister (John Henshaw), a union man and ageing patriarch who is wedded to the old labour movement. Ted has a stubborn determination to fight for what is ostensibly a doomed project, and a significant relationship with his son that is played out against the backdrop of a dying industry. The episode consistently exploits the audience's extra-textual knowledge regarding the fate of Ted's project, generating a degree of pathos that is most obviously conveyed through reaction shots of Sam, who, like the audience, is already aware of the painful outcomes of the industrial confrontations of the eighties. This extra-textual knowledge is conveyed most explicitly through Ted's view of people like Saunders who, in his opinion, defy the solidarity of the group and the powerful trade union movement. This is expressed most clearly by Ted's son, Derek (Andrew Knot): 'Dad always said there's two types of enemy. The one's above you: management and government. The one to fear's the other kind. The enemy within your own ranks.' Later in the same episode, Gene provides an even more explicit reference to Thatcher's characterisation of the NUM miners during the 1984–5 strike as 'the enemy within'. In this sense, *Life on Mars* suggests that the transition from BC to AD can be located at some point during the economic restructuring of the eighties; in 1984, or perhaps even, as Sam suggests in his conversation with Nelson, in 1988, a year after the third and decisive election victory of the Conservative government. It is tempting therefore to view the advanced world of Anno Domini as a reference to the post-industrial society that emerges following the decline of manufacturing and the rise of service industries in the British economy. In short, Sam longs for a world that is 'After Thatcher'. Coming from the 'New North', in which manufacturing and extractive industries have contracted, where the power of trade unions has declined significantly and in which the 'labour' movement no longer subscribes to traditional orthodoxies such as Clause IV,[1] Ted's union rhetoric seems as archaic as anything else Sam encounters in 1973.

In *Loft Living: Culture and Capital in Urban Change* (1982), the sociologist Sharon Zukin examines the structural and social factors behind the development of loft living in seventies New York. At the same time, she is keen to stress the relevance of her findings for other 'post-industrial' cities across the world. For Zukin, an emphasis on the 'lifestyle' of apartment living masks a bitter class struggle for civic terrain and local markets, entailing the re-conquest of the downtown areas for 'high-class and high-rent users' (ibid.: 145). She identifies a close connection between strategies of capitalist accumulation and cultural consumption by arguing that the demand for lofts is based on a type of social and cultural change that valorises investment capital and the service class at the expense of the traditional manufacturing base (15). In her view the 1973 US recession, which marks the end of the Fordist–Keynesian regime of accumulation, contributes to the increased supply of lofts for the purposes of gentrification. Zukin argues that lofts, which developed commercially exploitable cultural associations with artists in the late sixties, are indicative of an Artistic Mode of Production, which forecloses a return to the older manufacturing mode of production, and reduces the 'immediacy of industrial society and its problems to a distant historical perspective' (ibid.).

Cresters Mill, the site of Jimmy Saunders's murder in episode 1.3, is the location for a subjective sequence linking the mill space in 1973, a space of manufacturing production, with the 2006 apartment space, a post-industrial space of consumption. Arriving at the mill, Sam steps out of Gene's Cortina and is immediately distracted by the presence of the mill, which is viewed from a low angle. 'I live here,' he tells Annie (Liz White), 'I mean, I *will* live here.' Inside the mill, as the police officers approach the crime scene, Sam indicates the way in which the mill will be reconfigured to become a twenty-first-century living space. 'This is all going to be flats in thirty years', he says, and he remarks on how he finds the situation 'unbelievable' before being checked by the sight of the dead body. The camera tracks across the factory floor, capturing row after row of mechanical looms, the white cloth and fine strips of cotton attached to the machines indicating the working condition of the mill as a space of production. Sam regards the dead body of Jimmy Saunders with a squeamish expression and we see the dead man lying in a pool of his own blood. This provides the motivation for a rapidly edited sub-jective sequence which intercuts images of Sam's apartment kitchen in 2006, complete with stainless steel appliances, painted brickwork, and an imagined pool of Saunders's blood, with the dead body lying in 1973.

Sam's incredulity about the idea of his apartment acting as an industrial space provides an interesting inversion of the logical response to a factory floor functioning as a place to live. For seventies factory workers such as Ted Bannister, part of a self-styled 'cotton army' who, like the Luddites before them, conduct an ongoing and ultimately futile struggle against the forces of economic change, there is a lingering hope that the mill will continue produc-tion long enough to support another generation in the form of Derek, Tina (Rebecca Atkinson) and their unborn child. The Bannisters' personal invest-ment in the future of the mill arises from necessity: it is a space to *work* in order to support a family. For Sam, however, the mill is a space to live for one-self, a part of the lifestyle of the young professional who has no family com-mitments. Located in close proximity to the city centre, its offices and leisure services, the flat fits into a lifestyle pattern fashioned by a different economic base to manufacturing. In fact, the idea of a factory as the site of one's home life is as 'unbelievable' to seventies Mancunians such as Annie as the thought of Sam's home acting as an industrial space is for him. The mill is built to serve a specific function and throughout the episode a connection is made between the idea of the mill as a living, breathing entity and the life force of the indi-vidual workers and the community it supports. Again, as Ted tells Sam outside the mill, 'Living things need to keep working on the inside, once the inside stops . . . [and Sam finishes the sentence] It's just a shell.'

The subjective juxtaposition of images otherwise separated in time and space is extremely significant in terms of the BC/AD dichotomy. The image of a modern apartment block splattered with the blood of a textile worker could be said to function metonymically: the blood of the manual worker stains the flat of the white-collar professional; the death of the old working class taints the spaces of the post-industrial middle class. And it is perhaps for this reason that Sam recoils in the way he does, finding it difficult to face the socio-economic traumas of BC which have helped to create the luxurious domestic spaces of AD.

The changes in the function of the mill space are therefore revealing in terms of Sam's association with a post-industrial middle class of core workers who have emerged alongside the development of white-collar service industries, in particular through his status as a 'comer-in'. In this context, the term 'comer-in' derives from a verse commentary written by the Yorkshire-born poet Simon Armitage to accompany a documentary made in 1996 for the BBC 2 *Modern Times* series. Following four individuals and their experiences of a Saturday night in Leeds at a time when the city was experiencing employment growth in white-collar service industries, it provides a snapshot of the northern English city at a particular historical moment, one which is intimately linked to changes within national and global economic structures. The selection of different character types in the documentary includes Jackie from Croydon, a middle-class, white-collar worker who has been sent from the south to the north as part of a business relocation. As Armitage writes:

[JACKIE, driving.]
Each to their own, anything goes.
Jackie's a comer-in, can't get into the swing of it,
Came Up North from The Smoke
But can't get a feel for it.
She's staying at home,
She's making a meal of it.
(Armitage 1999: 180)

The comer-in brings with them a sense of affluence, educated-ness and cultural sophistication perceived to be lacking within northern settlements coded as working class. Potentially, there are similarities between the comer-in and the 'scholarship boy' described by Richard Hoggart in his landmark work of cultural studies *The Uses of Literacy* (1957). Hoggart used his term to refer to a working-class student removed from his (or her) social class background as a result of educational advancement (Hoggart 1969 [1957]: 224–31). Hoggart's valorisation of a traditional northern working-class culture and his acerbic critique of mass culture accompanied a particular historical moment of sociological interest in the working class, which included the northern metatexts of *Coronation Street* (ITV, 1960–) and the films of the British New Wave (1958–63). Both the comer-in and the scholarship boy can be seen as ambiguous figures whose physical presence within the northern community, yet cultural distance via an education acquired elsewhere, position them betwixt and between the imagined communities of north and south to encourage an exterior view of northern subject matter. The comer-in draws attention to contrasting cultural associations between north and south. However, the north is not always viewed pejoratively in the sense of lacking social and economic advantages since the unpretentious modes of behaviour characteristically associated with the working class are often portrayed as more desirable due to an alleged 'authenticity'.

Life on Mars offers an interesting variation on the figure of the 'comer-in' because Sam's relocation is not from 'the south' to 'the north', but from 'AD' to 'BC', thereby highlighting the transition from an industrial to a post-industrial Manchester. Sam can be identified as a comer-in, not only in terms of his class position, but also in terms of his masculinity, offering a sophisticated 'metrosexual' variant of masculine work and lifestyle which contrasts with the unreconstructed masculinity of his fellow officers Gene, Ray and Chris. From the beginning, Sam's application of professional and scientific police procedures, or what the other officers are quick to denigrate as 'gay boy science', generates suspicion and tension within a department that traditionally relies on instinctive or authentic responses. The manner in which Sam first enters the seventies police station identifies him immediately as an outsider figure by working within the conventions of the American western. Sam flings open the saloon-like doors of the department and in doing so, is positioned in the role of 'the stranger', the comer-in figure of the American west played by Clint Eastwood in the seventies spaghetti westerns of Sergio Leone.

In 2006, as a detective chief inspector in charge of his own plain-clothes department, Sam's high income and property value position him within spaces occupied by the city's post-industrial middle class. Sam's kitchen in 2006, which contains a bottle of balsamic vinegar and an expensive coffee machine, is significant not only in terms of the quality of domestic and decorative appliances and their value as symbols of status and lifestyle, but also for what they reveal about the importance to Sam of food, and the way it functions as an indicator of social class. In *The Road to Wigan Pier* (1937), George Orwell's classic study of living and working conditions in the industrial districts of the north following the depression of the thirties, he devotes chapter six to the dietary arrangements and deficiencies of working-class people in the north (2001 [1937]: 84–96). Evidently, a good diet maintains physical health, yet it can also serve to maintain class distinctions through the exhibition of a superior cultural knowledge. Sharon Zukin makes a connection between food and gentrification by comparing the latter, which she defines as the appropriation and transformation of dilapidated urban environments by a homogenous middle-class culture, to the contemporaneous spread of *nouvelle cuisine* (Zukin 1991: 214). For Zukin, gentrification and food share a critical infrastructure and a new organisation of consumption predicated on new forms of capital investment and production that have developed since 1973. The idea of food is equally important to the comer-in, as an indicator of social status, modes of consumption and specialised knowledge, and specific choices of food and drink consistently distinguish Sam from the less enlightened figures of the 'Old North'. For example, in episode 1.4, Sam takes the nightclub dancer Joni (Kelly Wenham) back to his flat and prepares a Mexican dish using the exotic ingredient of a jalapeno chilli, taken from a recipe he acquired on holiday in Central America. Joni, by contrast, simply doesn't understand why Sam can't crack open a 'can of baked beans'. Sam's choice of food therefore reflects his cosmopolitan knowledge and experience, and is contrasted with a prosaic and recognisably 'local' item of food. Similarly, in episode 1.5, while working undercover in a pub kitchen, Gene receives Sam's talk of olive oil and coriander with incomprehension. The comer-in is required to 'educate' the unsophisticated Gene by imparting his superior knowledge. 'It's a herb', he says half-heartedly, knowing that his attempt is likely to be futile.

John Hill has argued that the films of the British New Wave, synonymous with the north of England despite some of their Midlands settings, respond to the decline of a working-class male culture of production, and the rise of a materialist culture of consumption coded as female (Hill 1986: 154–7). Similarly, in an article considering gender in the British New Wave, Terry Lovell (1990) shows how the sexually active male protagonist of the New Wave films is associated with exterior locations outside the domestic space, while interior spaces are coded as female (ibid.: 365–7). Indeed, Lovell describes the fitted kitchen of the new house in *Saturday Night and Sunday Morning* (1960) as indicative of the new consumerism associated with the female. In *Life on Mars*, Sam's associations with the kitchen space of his flat position him within what in the seventies is more likely to have been regarded as a feminine domestic space, and align him with a particular mode of consumption rather than production. Sam's choice of food reflects the cosmopolitanism of his experience as a member of the post-industrial middle class. By contrast, the male officers of the 'Old North' provide a regressive idea of masculinity that venerates instinct rather than intellect and furthers a sense of political incorrectness presented throughout the series as comical. The new forms of consumption suggested by the lifestyle of the comer-in are also linked to new forms of masculinity, which demonstrate a more fluid characterisation of gender roles within the spaces of AD, and could be seen as consistent with a relative 'feminisation' of northern representation in contemporary television drama, exemplified by the centrality of female characters in *Cutting It* (BBC, 2002–5), *Cold Feet* (Granada/ITV, 1997–2003), *No Angels* (C4, 2004–6) and *Playing the Field* (BBC, 1998–2002), and the prominence of female writers such as Kay Mellor and Debbie Horsfield.

Sam Tyler and Gene Hunt represent two different ideas of the north, BC and AD, which are associated with contrasting representations of masculinity and male gender roles. However, despite the apparent progressiveness of Sam's modern world view and the feminine influences associated with his metrosexual lifestyle, the series seems to invite greater sympathy with, and nostalgia for, the unrefined masculinity of birds and boozers represented by Gene. The sense of archaic and progressive masculinities linked to old and new ideas of the north of England, and the amusing complexities and contradictions generated by their juxtaposition, are also pertinent to a much earlier interpretation of the north. Set in seventies Tyneside, and transmitted during the period depicted in *Life on Mars*, the situation comedy *Whatever Happened to the Likely Lads?* (BBC, 1973–4) contrasted the post-war working-class north-east of its sixties forerunner *The Likely Lads* (BBC, 1964–6), with a 'New North' of increasing affluence and the reconstruction of the built environment. After spending some time in the British Army in Germany, Terry Collier, an Andy Capp[2] figure who embodies an older northern masculinity, returns to discover that the north-east has been transformed by the general social changes experienced since the sixties. Bob, his best friend, is now engaged to Thelma, a female figure consistent with the portrayal of women in the films of the British New Wave and the putative source of Bob's new-found interest in conspicuous consumption and upward mobility. As temporally disorientated as Sam Tyler, Terry frequently scorns Bob's new-found lifestyle and aspirations, dismissing his new house as 'characterless' and 'depressing', and looking back nostalgically to his old terraced house overlooking the 'brewery, glue works and lead factory'. The opening title sequence of the series highlights this tension between an older, industrial north associated with Terry, who symbolically 'misses the bus' on a street of Victorian terraced housing, and the modern 'New North' associated with Bob and Thelma. The north-east of 1973 appears to represent a decisive break from the urban-industrial north of the pre-war era, and the modernity of the new north is articulated spatially in terms of the changing built environment. Despite his retrogressive behaviour, however, the audience is often subtly encouraged to root for Terry and his artlessness and stubborn resistance to change prove to be endearing qualities in a manner which is shared by Gene Hunt in *Life on Mars*. In both cases, the acknowledgement of a 'New North', linked subtly to the feminine, contains within it a lingering affection and nostalgia for the 'Old North', which can be linked to a crucial observation made by John Urry in his critique of post-industrial theory:

> The PI (post-industrial) thesis . . . ignores how once industry has declined, so it can and will be celebrated and preserved . . . Nostalgia then for industrial times past is a widespread and permanent feature of PI Britain. It is believed that there has been a huge loss, that a plethora of skills, solidities and meanings, which were bound up with particular places, have been eroded for ever. The PI thesis is therefore far too modernist. (1995: 124)

This essay has suggested that the contrast between BC and AD made by Sam Tyler in the Railway Arms, which appears initially to be a comic reaction to his situation, is also caught up in a narrative of progress, and on examination tells other important stories about the wider structural and social changes that have taken place in the north of England since 1973 and which have led to the emergence of 'AD'. Despite its seventies setting, *Life on Mars* is therefore an important text in terms of thinking about the post-industrial present and the complexity of our emotional responses to economic restructuring and social change.

NOTES

1   Clause IV refers to that part of the constitution of the Labour Party, dating from 1918, that committed it to the 'common ownership of the means of production'. The clause was revised, and its core principles effectively abandoned, when the party constitution was rewritten in 1995, prompted by the then party leader, Tony Blair.
2   A popular figure in a cartoon strip that has appeared in the *Daily Mirror* since 1957, Andy Capp represents an archetype of the northern, working-class male, replete with flat cap.

REFERENCES

Armitage, S. (1999), *All Points North*, London, Faber and Faber.
Castells, M. (1998). *End of Millenium: Vol. III: The Information Age – Economy, Society and Culture*, Oxford, Blackwell.
Castells, M. (2000). *The Rise of the Network Society: Vol. 1: The Information Age: Economy, Society and Culture* (second edition), Oxford, Blackwell.
Harvey, D. (1989). *The Condition of Postmodernity: An Enquiry into the Origins of Cultural Change*, Oxford, Blackwell.
Hill, J. (1986). *Sex, Class and Realism: British Cinema 1956–1963*, London, British Film Institute.
Hoggart, R. (1969 [1957]). *The Uses of Literacy*, London, Pelican.
Jenkins, S. (2006). *Thatcher and Sons: A Revolution in Three Acts*, London, Penguin.
Lash, S. and Urry, J. (1988). *The End of Organised Capitalism*, Cambridge, Polity Press.
Lash, S. and Urry, J. (1994). *Economies of Signs and Space*, London, Sage.
Lovell, T. (1990). 'Landscape and stories in 1960s British realism', *Screen*, 31, 4, 357–76.
Orwell, G. (2001 [1937]). *The Road to Wigan Pier*, London, Penguin.
Tiratsoo, N. (ed.) (1997). *From Blitz to Blair: A New History of Britain since 1939*, London, Weidenfeld & Nicolson.
Urry, J. (1995). *Consuming Places*, London, Routledge.
Zukin, S. (1982). *Loft Living: Culture and Capital in Urban Change*, New Brunswick, NJ, Rutgers University Press.
Zukin, S. (1991). *Landscapes of Power: From Detroit to Disney World*, Berkeley, University of California Press.

6 'MOONAGE DAYDREAMS'

NOSTALGIA AND CULTURAL MEMORY CONTEXTS OF *LIFE ON MARS* AND *ASHES TO ASHES*

John R. Cook and Mary Irwin

NOSTALGIA AIN'T WHAT IT USED TO BE. From the mid-seventies through to the early nineties, the sixties figured frequently in British media discourses as the 'golden' decade of nostalgia: a time of untrammelled freedom and greater innocence, to be looked back upon wistfully from the vantage point of a more complex, cynical and troubled present. Examples appeared in the early years of British TV: in his epic seventeen-part TV documentary history of popular music, *All You Need is Love* (ITV, 1977), director Tony Palmer deployed extensive interview footage of doyen rock critic, Lester Bangs, filmed in 1975 lamenting the decline of sixties idealism into the more empty spectacle of seventies glam rock, not least the louche theatricalism of David Bowie. In 1982, one of the first major documentary series of the fledgling Channel 4 was *The Sixties* (RSO, 1982), a six-part series which looked 'at the optimism of the 1960s in the light of the 1970s and the early 80s' (Various 2008); in this way helping to construct for an eighties audience a sense of aching regret for a present less optimistic, particularly amongst those too young to have experienced the sixties first-hand.

The series producer of *The Sixties* was a young, ex-Westminster University media studies graduate, Michael Jackson, who, when he had risen to become controller of BBC 2 in 1993, cleared the August Bank Holiday schedules of that year to broadcast *One Day in the Sixties*. This featured transmission of complete sixties programmes from the TV archives, together with a whole host of archive footage from the decade, plus interviews and other links (Various 2008). Again, the emphasis was very much on the sixties as a special time of optimism and change. However, the concept also gestured towards a desire for escape from a greyer present through a total re-immersion in the past: an attempt to experience all the media sights and sounds of that 'golden' decade once more, if only for a single day.

By the end of the century, the special place of the sixties as the decade of golden nostalgia had begun to be replaced by the seventies. There had been a nostalgic seventies cultural revival since the early nineties across fashion, popular music and film,[1] but by the millennium that nostalgia had been personalised for audiences by a rising generation of media practitioners depicting the seventies as the memory of a happy time of childhood compared to a less happy adult present. The seventies were celebrated as the 'golden' decade for the very simple reason that for the current thirty- and early-forty-something audience it was the decade of their childhood. In the early noughties, examples in the British media of this phenomenon included the rise and rise of 'nostalgia clip' shows: cheap programming from the archive in the digital multi-channel age which the BBC began in earnest with BBC 2's successful Saturday night series in the summer of 2000, *I Love the 1970s*; soon to be followed up in the autumn and winter of 2001, respectively, by the 'instant' nostalgia of *I Love the 1980s* and *I Love the 1990s*. Note that there was no *I Love the 1960s*: the sixties having receded further back in cultural memory, the terrain now of the less fashionable fifty- and sixty-something audiences, whose interests were increasingly catered for in the 2000s through nostalgia programming on smaller, niche digital channels such as BBC Four.[2]

One of the regular contributors throughout *I Love the 1970s* and its successor series was the journalist and film critic Andrew Collins. In 2003, Collins published the popular memoir, *Where Did It All Go Right? Growing Up Normal in the 70s*, a paean to the joys of being a suburban child in the seventies. This development made it clear that the seventies children had come of age and were emerging as opinion-formers in the British media. It seems no coincidence that after the first series of *Life on Mars*, it was Andrew Collins who was chosen to front a short BBC documentary on the making of the series, *Creating Life on Mars* (BBC, 2006), in which he quizzed the show's main writers on their inspirations and influences. In *Life on Mars*, Sam Tyler (John Simm) is the fictive representative of Collins's ascendant thirty- and early-forty-something generation. Born in 1969, Sam's coma-induced memories and fantasies of TV in his seventies childhood – test card, BBC 1 logo and *Camberwick Green* (BBC, 1966) – are that audience's formative TV memories.

Life on Mars, however, is no simple 'nostalgia' show. Its escapist seventies idyll is constantly problematised. This is most vividly symbolised by the memorable *Camberwick Green* sequence from episode 2.5, in which Sam hallucinates a scene from the classic children's show, a clever pastiche by the drama's makers in which an animated puppet version of Gene Hunt (Philip Glenister) suddenly intrudes and is seen 'kicking in a nonce'; a 'lawman beating up the wrong guy' if there ever was one. As a still-hallucinating Sam later shouts at the flesh-and-blood version of Gene Hunt in the same episode, 'You can attack me all you like, Gene. But stay out of *Camberwick Green*!' The intrusion of Hunt into the memory of the children's show is portrayed here as the ultimate sacrilege of a seventies childhood: the golden childhood memory 'polluted' by later adult experience, particularly the adult's retrospective knowledge and understanding of the real difficulties and crises of the period; its general 'primitiveness' and 'backwardness' when looked back upon from the vantage point of the present, not least in the quality of its policing.

Whilst Sam Tyler certainly experiences the heady and exhilarating freedoms of policing within his seventies environment, where rules, regulation and red tape rarely stand in the way of chasing down a villain before dinner time, where a couple of double scotches in the pub before the afternoon shift are de rigueur, and where Gene Hunt's instincts, gut-feelings and encyclopaedic knowledge of his beat lead to vigorous and speedy conviction, nonetheless there is equally much about policing in Manchester in 1973 that leaves the adult Sam frequently reeling with shock and an overwhelming sense of disbelief at what he is witnessing. He may enjoy the rush of being 'one of the lads' racing to the crime scene in the Mark III Cortina. However, episode after episode illustrates the grimness of the period for those unfortunate enough to be on the margins or outside the mainstream of Britain in the seventies. It is in these situations that we see the flip side of the much-admired cavalier policing style practised by Gene and his colleagues and its impact on those unfortunate enough to feel its force.

In episode 2.3, Gene's brutal and ignorant treatment of the Irish community in the city and the level of prejudice he shows towards them articulates with Sam's and our own present-day knowledge of the indiscriminate hatred that was the experience of many Irish people living in Britain during the period. Gene blithely greets the assembled Irish workforce he is about to ask about a spate of bombings with a facetious 'Top of the morning to you lads. Know anything about some missing dynamite?', delivered in an outrageous cod-Irish accent. Despite scant evidence, he is convinced that the bombings must be the work of the IRA. He cold-bloodedly brutalises a petty local criminal of Irish origin in the hope of forcing him into a confession. As the suspect says with ironic resignation: 'All our kind are good for is shovelling shit and making bombs.' This is something for which there should be no nostalgia, and Sam's distress at what he witnesses problematises simple readings of the series as some kind of glorious seventies nostalgia-fest.

Likewise, episode 2.6 explores the bigotry shown towards the newly arrived Ugandan Asian community when Gene and his team are on the trail of heroin dealers. Attitudes towards race in seventies Britain, as manifested in many now unwatchable TV sitcoms of the period such as *Love Thy Neighbour* (ITV, 1972–7) or *Mind Your Language* (ITV, 1977–9), are, of course, nothing to be nostalgic about. Gene's sidekick Ray (Dean Andrews) states he has 'got nothing personal against "Gunga Dins"' but also comments: 'All these bloody Ugandan Asians – why do they have to come here?' Gene asks Layla (Alex Reid), the white girlfriend of Deepak Gandhi (Paul Sharma), one of the suspects: 'What's it like stepping out with one of our Pakistani brethren; a bit kinky in the sack, is it all Kama Sutra and Arabian Nights?' Once again, Sam as our 'avatar' brings a twenty-first-century perspective to the kind of behaviour which is now simply incomprehensible to contemporary eyes.

On a smaller scale, but equally telling, is the treatment and experience of a deaf witness in episode 1.7. Whilst Sam does his best to build the witness's trust and confidence, for Gene and company his disability is a source of both comedy and irritation. Phyllis Dobbs (Noreen Kershaw), the formidable desk officer, wants Gene or Sam to rip the hearing aid out of the witness's ear since she claims it is 'messing with our station radios'. Gene tries to humiliate the witness by mimicking the effects of a broken hearing aid whilst conducting an interview. Sam, by contrast, makes visible efforts to talk slowly and clearly to the suspect, giving him the opportunity to read Sam's lips. He also points out to Phyllis that 'He is a key witness. Could you treat him like a person?' With such incidents, the dramatic message is clear that a huge amount of progress has been made since the seventies in creating a fairer, less discriminatory Britain, in which attempts are at least made now to treat *all* people with a greater degree of consideration and understanding, regardless of who or what they are.

Sam is equally appalled by the slapdash and casual approaches to police procedure that recur throughout both series. Much has been made in popular commentary about the positive aspect of a less hidebound approach to policing than that which has evolved in the past thirty years, and there can be little doubt that certain sections of the UK audience derived tremendous satisfaction from watching Gene dispense a little well-called-for rough justice to a criminal who would receive far more circumspect treatment today.[3] Nevertheless, it is Sam whose cool, considered and more reflective style of policing often brings the cases to a satisfactory conclusion. Sam collates evidence carefully and puts thorough search procedures into operation, basing his judgements on a consideration of the facts rather than operating on a thump first, think later basis.

Nowhere are the limitations of 1970s-style policing more evident than the way in which WPC Annie Cartwright (Liz White) is treated throughout both series of *Life on Mars*: in fact, it is only through the efforts of twenty-first-century man Sam that, as both series progress, Annie achieves a marginally more respected position amongst her colleagues and the opportunity to take on a more challenging role within the team. It may be that many male (and female) viewers have relished the return of the alpha 'retrosexual' male in the form of rough, tough, street-fighting Gene Hunt; however, less attention is given to the way in which such men treat women in the workplace, and the experience of women in the workplace more generally. *Life on Mars* offers a sobering depiction of the role and treatment of women in the police force, a particularly dark aspect of the indirect social commentary offered by this text.

Annie's situation and treatment are particularly revealing in this regard. She is considered by her colleagues to be a 'plonk' – a person of little or no knowledge – and assumed to be a lesser being. Indeed as one female witness remarks of policewomen generally in episode 1.1, 'It's no life for them!' When Annie and/or her views are considered by her office colleagues, it is either in the context of sexist banter, or with disbelief that she might have something worthwhile to contribute to the department. The fact that Annie has a degree in psychology is treated as risible by her fellow officers. This is highlighted in episode 1.1 when Sam asks Annie to explain the behaviour of a suspect to the team. Annie is greeted with hilarity and derision as she explains what in fact turns out to be the precise psychological motivations for the suspect's actions. Tellingly, Annie herself can be seen covertly checking her responses to the treatment that she receives, either because she knows that there is little point in taking them on, or because she has little sense of how else to react.

A typical Hunt quip on observing Sam pick up a soft porn magazine he finds lying around is: 'No need for that smut in here, not now we've got Cartwright's arse to look at. Come on, love, go and make me a cup of tea.' When Sam points out that 'She's as good a detective as anyone here', Gene ripostes: 'Well, see if you can detect me a packet of Garibaldis, love' (episode 2.6). Annie stops Sam from further intervention by saying she is happy to make Gene's tea. Sam's interventions can have little impact when Annie's daily workplace experiences confirm women's inferior professional and personal status. It is interesting that the only other example of a woman police officer that we encounter in the series is Phyllis, a hardened and cynical older woman, whose stock in trade is the withering put-down. The female professional characters are much like those of the classic seventies sitcom, where the available representations of women are either young, naive and sexually available, or a 'past-it battleaxe', unattractive and worthy of little further consideration. In *Life on Mars* the women characters are not generally proactive, positive or successful, tending instead to be portrayed in stereotypical terms as frightened and reluctant witnesses, victims or long-suffering girlfriends.

Sam, conversely, sees women in the workplace as colleagues doing the same job as him and his fellow male officers. More generally, he treats women – be they suspects, witnesses or cleaners in the police station – with unthinking respect. Interestingly, there have been a number of internet fan forum threads about the series which reflect on Sam's 'success' with women.[4] This seems less to do with Sam's sexual prowess and much more with the fact that he accords women the same consideration he would other men. He is constantly horrified by the attitudes to women he encounters throughout both series and in contrast to Gene, he treats them as individuals rather than as 'dolly birds', 'tarts' or 'doddery old dears'.

Alex Drake (Keeley Hawes) in *Ashes to Ashes* is certainly not a woman who plays a subsidiary role in life. When we first encounter her in twenty-first-century London, at work as a detective chief inspector and expert in psychological profiling, she commands both respect and recognition from her colleagues. She is neither a dizzy 'dolly bird' nor a deskbound police station dragon but a thirty-something professional woman sharply dressed in functional dark blue jacket and trousers. It is worthy of note that when Alex's accident pitches her back to 1981, she regains consciousness dressed in an extremely provocative manner as an undercover officer masquerading as a prostitute – stocking tops and cleavage prominently on display. Thus it is as an object of undisguised lust and mild contempt, rather than a highly trained police psychologist, that Alex enters the world of Gene Hunt and his team.

In fact, taken as a whole, Alex, translated back to the early 1980s, fares considerably less well than Sam, who eventually finds that for him there are pleasures to be had and even some advantages to life in seventies Manchester. While the Metropolitan Police of the eighties is an institution in the process of change and, indeed, a place in which a transferred Gene Hunt is forced to rethink his ways to catch up with how the police service is developing in the eighties, nevertheless it is still a place in which a female officer faces significant challenges. Alex is viewed with suspicion both as a female boss and as a police psychologist, one in a flaky new discipline to boot. (Similarly Shaz (Montserrat Lombard), the office WPC, while bolder and more likely to express an opinion than Annie in *Life on Mars*, is still regarded as less able and less worth listening to than male officers.)

Whilst *Life on Mars* offers Sam a working relationship in which he and Gene learn from each other and this is characterised by grudging, growing mutual tolerance and some degree of limited respect, that between Gene and Alex in *Ashes to Ashes* develops quite differently. *Ashes to Ashes* plays with different points of reference and a completely different cop show format to *Life on Mars*; that is, the 1980s 'Will-they-won't-they' unresolved sexual tension of crime-fighting comedy dramas such as *Dempsey and Makepeace* (ITV, 1985–6) and *Moonlighting* (ABC, 1985–9), rather than the cop buddies of *The Sweeney* (ITV/Euston Films, 1975–8). Consequently, we see less of a running comparison between different policing cultures and much more of a burgeoning romance developing between Gene and Alex. Whilst Sam and Gene's relationship combines for the audience the professional pleasures of watching the pair negotiate the least painful way they can find of working together whilst observing what makes the two individual men tick, Alex and Gene's relationship, at least in series one, pivots on the far more simplistic premise of whether or not the two will finally come together in a romantic partnership. Little is made of Alex's ability to solve cases and the fact that her skills, for example, prevent multiple deaths in episode 1.2 due to her ability to work with personality profiles. She remains a clever but slightly daffy 'posh bird', nicknamed by Gene, with fondness but also contempt, 'Bollyknickers'. In this sense, the relationship offers perhaps a rather singular, closed potential conclusion, whereas Sam and Gene's ever-evolving understanding of the other contains within it a much more open-ended set of pleasures.

Indeed, for a sector of the female viewing audience in particular, much pleasure is to be had in Alex's very unreconstructed romance with macho, domineering Gene Hunt. As evidenced by a very busy thread on 'Hunt's

Housewives', one fan forum on the entertainment website *Digital Spy*, this is a key aspect of the series. Much of the forum's discourse centres on key 'romantic' scenes that take place between Alex and Gene, on the attractions of Gene Hunt as a fantasy partner and the forum members' desire to be in the same position as Alex, involved with the kind of heroic alpha male hero whom they see embodied in Gene.[5] They make much of a number of occasions in the first series which one poster calls 'heart flutter' moments when Alex faints and is rescued by Gene, and in particular the scene in episode 1.6 where, to the muted strains of Ultravox's 'Vienna', Gene smashes through a plate-glass window in order to carry an unconscious Alex from near death in a deep-freeze, in the manner of the archetypal romantic hero.[6]

Is the 'liberation', then, that Alex experiences in the eighties simply that of the ultimate traditional feminine romantic heroine, who can surrender to her desire to be with a man who takes the lead? It is interesting that a number of the 'Hunt's Housewives' posters initiate threads which discuss classic fictional romantic heroes such as Mr Rochester from *Jane Eyre* and Mr Darcy, the ultimate nineties romantic hero as realised by Colin Firth in the BBC's 1995 *Pride and Prejudice*.[7] Rather, as fans of *Pride and Prejudice* combined Darcy the character and Firth the actor in a complex and problematic hybrid, so many fans of *Ashes to Ashes* read Hunt and actor Philip Glenister as extensions of each other. From such discussion it does seem clear that the nostalgic pleasures offered in *Ashes to Ashes* are very different from those in *Life on Mars*.

Whilst the engagement with cultural memory and nostalgia is therefore more provisional in *Ashes to Ashes* (Alex's psychic excavation of her early eighties childhood in series one culminates, after all, in the shocking final revelation that her own father was responsible for both his and her mother's deaths), *Life on Mars* works through a different set of internal tensions, namely a constant oscillation between the seventies as a 'golden' time of freedom (compared to now) and the seventies as a time of restrictive unsophistication (also compared to now). In a sense, the different audiences this popular drama must attract and reach on the mainstream BBC 1 channel help provide a measure of explanation for this constant oscillation. The series has clear appeal to thirty- and early-forty-something adults who, like Andrew Collins, remember growing up in the seventies: as a popular drama for the mainstream BBC 1 channel, however, *Life on Mars* also has to embrace (and not alienate) other demographics, including, for example, the youth audience, ethnic minorities, older audiences who may remember the decade with much less pleasure, and so on. And while the series' 'Ford Granada'[8] aspects offer a comparatively rare opportunity for a contemporary BBC TV drama to appeal to a 'traditional' male viewer, it cannot allow itself to alienate the female viewer since today 'women control the remote' (Tranter 2004), constituting the majority of the British TV drama audience.[9] In turn, this helps to account for *Life on Mars*'s constant balancing act in its representation of the 1970s: the vivid 'freak-out' aspects of the music, fashions, pop culture, counterbalanced with all of the depictions of the sexism, racism and violence considered above (especially in relation to the more established series two).

This oscillating 'heart' versus 'head' view of the seventies – as shown in the symbolic *Camberwick Green* sequence, the nostalgic emotional identification with the period simultaneously counterbalanced with a more jaundiced intellectual understanding of its limitations – helps to provide a context for reading *Life on Mars*'s overall ending. Having worked desperately to get home throughout the duration of the two series, Sam finally wakes up from his coma, only to find himself ill at ease and emotionally bereft back in the twenty-first century, reflecting ruefully, as he sits in on yet another pointlessly bureaucratic police meeting relating to procedure, on the burdens and constraints of his present compared to the undoubted freedoms he experienced in the seventies. Climbing on to the roof of his office building, he finally decides to make his leap for freedom by taking a long run and propelling himself off the building into the ether, seeing this as the only way he can return to his fantasy of the seventies which now seems more real to him than the so-called 'reality' of twenty-first-century life. In this way, his heart finally decides to reject the present and make his big leap for freedom back into the past. But is it quite that simple? Because if the leap back into the past is certainly the emotional end of series payoff ('the heart'), at the same time, from a present-day dramatic vantage point ('the head'), all Sam has done is simply jump off a building and commit suicide, just one more casualty of all the stresses of contemporary policing.[10] In this way, the series, as an interesting example of popular drama as open text, manages to sustain its oscillating ambiguities right to the very end. Sam trades his mortal millennial life for seventies perpetual fantasy, joining Gene Hunt and his gang for a permanent cops and robbers hurrah in the 1973 setting sun, whilst the test card girl runs up to camera and switches us off from the action, like someone switching off a seventies TV set at closedown. However, the underlying emotional truth of the drama seems clear. In its deliberately oscillating view of the period throughout its two series, only at the very end can the drama allow the 'heart' to win over the 'head' in its view of the seventies. Only then can the series fully embrace and play to the nostalgic childhood yearnings of its 'upscale' thirty- and early forty-something BBC 1 audience, the 'stressed-out', 'over-burdened' audience of twenty-first-century citizens who, like Sam, were children in the seventies and who, *pace* Sam Tyler, Andrew Collins et al., seem particularly afflicted with this general, 'crick in the neck' nostalgic disease of constantly yearning to look backwards, part of them longing for total re-immersion in a mythical, half-remembered past of lost moonage daydreams.[11]

NOTES

1   Examples from pop culture include the Beastie Boys' 1994 video for their song 'Sabotage', which spoofed seventies US TV cop shows, as well as the retro chic

of Quentin Tarantino's films *Reservoir Dogs* (1993) and *Pulp Fiction* (1994). In the UK in the nineties, there was the rise of new lad culture, through magazines such as *Loaded*, with their valorisation of unreconstructed seventies masculinity ('beer, birds and football') including seventies masculine icons in British film (such as Michael Caine in *Get Carter*, 1971) and TV (such as the character DI Jack Regan in *The Sweeney* (ITV/Euston Films, 1975–8), played by John Thaw. Regan became, as the series progressed, a direct model for Gene Hunt in *Life on Mars*).

2   BBC Four regularly screens a range of archive programming and seems to make a conscious effort to target an older audience demographic (certainly compared to its sister digital channel, BBC Three). In 2004, the channel devoted a whole season of archive programming to the sixties: *Summer in the Sixties*.

3   See, for example, Lisa McGarry's comments in *The Sun*, 8 February 2008: 'Phil Glenister has revealed that he receives bags of fan mail from British cops who would like to dole out justice the Gene Hunt way. Phil told *The Sun*: "The success of *Life on Mars* has led to Gene Hunt becoming a hero to many policemen. He's a throwback to the days when there wasn't so much paperwork and fewer restrictions"' ('*Ashes to Ashes*: cops love Gene Hunt').

4   For example, on the fan website *The Railway Arms*, in a thread dedicated to the character of Sam Tyler and the topic of his 'animal magnetism', one fan 'Jillybean' says: 'Call me a crazed fangirl if you will, but don't you think that Sam carries around far too much animal magnetism for his own good ?' (*The Railway Arms*, 20 June 2006). Later in the thread, user 'Clover' adds: 'I don't really know if it's animal magnetism so much as it is that Sam's just a nicer guy than the rest of the seventies crew. He's learned modern police methods and has modern ideas about treating suspects and women, etc' (1 July 2006).

5   For example, user 'First Slip' posts: 'Gene carrying Alex through doors of station in ep 1 – me please!!!. And need I say it . . . Window rescue and subsequent as close as it came snog – ohhh – so near and yet so far' (*Hunt's Housewives*, 23 August 2007). Or user 'Mrs Gene Hunt': 'My best moment is when he strides through that shattered window, sweeps Alex into his arms, rips open her blouse, then cups her chin with his leather-gloved hand and stares deeply into her eyes. Okay, several moments!' (2 April 2008).

6   User 'QuattroKez': 'I went for those "heart-flutter moments"' (*Hunt's Housewives*, 26 October 2008).

7   From 'QuattroKez': 'It's made me go all gooey over Darcy again. Sigh, drifts off, remembering that gorgeous Colin Firth-obsessed autumn of 1995' (*Hunt's Housewives*, 4 September 2008).

8   'Ford Granada' was the original proposed title for *Life on Mars*, as revealed in the documentary: *Creating Life on Mars* (BBC, 2006).

9   Jane Tranter was the BBC Television Controller of Drama Commissioning between 2000 and 2006 and thus the person ultimately responsible for commissioning *Life on Mars*. Her comment also helps explain the subsequent, more female-orientated, nature of *Ashes to Ashes*.

10　This reading is reinforced by the fact that psychological profiler Alex Drake reviews Sam's file, stamped 'SUICIDE', in the opening of *Ashes to Ashes*.

11　This is a reference to the David Bowie song, 'Moonage Daydream', which appeared on his classic seventies album, *The Rise and Fall of Ziggy Stardust and the Spiders from Mars*, released by RCA Records in June 1972.

REFERENCES

'*Ashes to Ashes*: cops love Gene Hunt', *Unreality Primetime* [website], *http:// primetime.unrealitytv.co.uk/ashes-to-ashes-cops-love-gene-hunt*, accessed 10 June 2010.

Collins, A. (2003). *Where Did It All Go Right ? Growing Up Normal in the 70s*, London, Ebury Press.

Palmer, T. (1977). *All You Need is Love: The Story of Popular Music* UK DVD, TPDVDBOX1.

Tranter J. (2004). Interview, *The South Bank Show – TV Drama Stories Part Two* (ITV, 8 February).

Various (2006). 'Sam's animal magnetism', *The Railway Arms: Life on Mars/Ashes to Ashes Forums* [web forum], *http://domeofstars.com/forum/*, accessed 10 June 2010.

Various (2007–8). *Hunt's Housewives, Digital Spy Entertainment Zone Forums* [web forum], *http://www.digitalspy.co.uk/forums/showthread.php?t=765591*, accessed 10 June 2010.

Various (2008). *BFI Film and TV Database* [website], *http://www.bfi.org.uk/ filmtvinfo/ftvdb/*, accessed 10 June 2010.

PART III | RECALLING THE PAST
TELEVISION AS MEMORY

7 'UP THE WOODEN HILLS TO BEDFORDSHIRE'

TIME TRAVEL, CHILDHOOD AND THE UNCANNY HOME IN *LIFE ON MARS* AND *ASHES TO ASHES*

Peter Hughes Jachimiak

THIS CHAPTER IS, FIRST AND FOREMOST, concerned with childhood in both *Life on Mars* and *Ashes to Ashes*. Whilst DI Sam Tyler (John Simm) interacts throughout both series of *Life on Mars* with the TV of his childhood (most notably, the test card girl), childhood is even more of an issue within the first series of *Ashes to Ashes* than it is in *Life on Mars*. Wearing figure-hugging leather and denim, and with an enhanced cleavage, DI Alex Drake (Keeley Hawes) is highly sexualised throughout the entire series. Indeed, the audience's first glimpse of her 1981 self is when, draped in a feather boa and sprawled across satin bedsheets, she is taking part in a disorientating, drug-fuelled party aboard a boat on the River Thames. So, against such scenes of hedonistic adult decadence, the grainy 'flashback' visions that she has of her-self throughout the series (as a balloon-wielding schoolgirl) are the personifi-cation of childhood innocence. As such, this chapter contemplates time travel or, more particularly, temporal slips, as the means by which both Tyler and Drake tantalisingly engage with the possibility of coming face to face with their childhood selves – which is, of course, one of the age-old, theoretical para-doxes of going back in time. Furthermore, having gone back in time, Tyler and Drake return to their (now 'uncanny') childhood homes, and attempt to build adult relationships with their respective parents – yet another paradox of time travelling to one's childhood.

LIFE ON MARS AND *ASHES TO ASHES* AS TIME-TRAVELLING SCIENCE FICTION TELEVISION

Whilst, ostensibly, both *Life on Mars* and *Ashes to Ashes* are takes on cop shows of the seventies and eighties respectively, this chapter insists that, due to their appropriation of the concept of time travel, both series sit firmly within

British science fiction television. Matthew Graham (co-creator and executive producer) and Ashley Pharoah (co-creator) reminisce on their conception of the series during a hedonistic, all-expenses-paid trip to Blackpool in 1998.[1] Initially given the working title 'Ford Granada', it was from the beginning, according to Graham, typical 'time-travel' science fiction television:

> And then we came up with the basic time travel story. Back then there was no ambiguity about the main character Sam, about whether or not he was in a coma, or whether or not he was mad, or whether . . . It was just pure time travel: cop, modern-day cop, crashes his car, wakes up, he's fallen back through time, 1973. (Graham 2006)

With this time-travel concept developed, Graham and Pharoah proudly presented their script to an expectant – and, then, an immediately sceptical – Kudos. As Graham makes explicit, they openly admitted to Kudos that '[w]ell, we've got this show called *Ford Granada* about a time-travelling policeman . . . they all sat there with these increasingly fixed grins' (ibid.). Then, with Kudos eventually convinced, the creators pitched their still farcical 'time-travelling policeman' idea to Julie Gardner of BBC Wales. Expecting an equally incredulous initial response (as they had had with Kudos), Graham expresses his concerns of the time:

> Julie had just started making *Doctor Who*, which hadn't actually come out yet. So she was already out on a limb doing *Doctor Who* and probably feeling, I should think, quite exposed and taking quite a big gamble. And, suddenly, here was a time-travelling – another – time-travelling show. Erm, and I remember thinking, oh, she's not going to go for it, she's going to say 'No boys, two time-travel shows on one person's slate is one too many'. (Ibid.)

Yet, to the surprise of both Graham and Pharoah, Gardner willingly commissioned the show. So, seven years on from their Blackpool trip, and in the wake of the phenomenal success of a yet-again-regenerated *Doctor Who*, *Life on Mars* was, in 2005, eventually in production.

Brian Ash, in his classic text *The Visual Encyclopaedia of Science Fiction* (1977), asserts that time is frequently acknowledged as the 'fourth dimension' along which three-dimensional humans endlessly travel in a forward motion. For the author Fritz Leiber, time travel, as well as being impossible, is an unwanted, troublesome tinkering with human existence, 'because it would change the past, disordering history and unfixing the framework of reality' (cited in Ash 1977: 144). Yet Leiber also enthusiastically highlights the creative benefits of engaging with – at least at a conceptual level – time travel, for 'memory travels into the past and imagination into the future . . . Yes, it's quite impossible, time travel . . . and infinitely fertile, artistically' (cited in ibid.).

Leiber notes that time travel is often invoked via the use of a 'machine'. H. G. Wells, in *The Time Machine* (1895), for example, imagined his 'machine' as something resembling a bicycle – 'the humblest of vehicles employed for the most daring of purposes' (Leiber, cited in Ash 1977: 144). Furthermore, Leiber asserts that time machines, as narrative devices, are extremely useful in adding dynamism to a plot, as 'they can be lost or stolen, and they can give the reader something concrete on which to focus his attention' (cited in ibid.). Thus, for Eric Rabkin (1983), not only was Wells's development of the fictitious contraption, the time machine, 'one of the few tools now in the general writer's kit that originated with science fiction', but also '[e]ver since that invention, the possibilities for paradox offered by time travel have driven science fiction writers and readers into happy frenzies' (402). Thus, BBC Wales's re-imagining of *Doctor Who* continued with the employing of his signature time-travelling machine, the Tardis (as with Wells's machine, this was a 'humble' police box). Yet, as Brian Ash reminds us, following Wells's creation of his time machine, 'that is not to say that the use of a machine was immediately taken up by other writers' as, '[m]ore often than not, adventurers still travelled into the past by some means of temporal slip' (Ash 1977: 145). Thus, rather than being propelled backwards through time in a controlled manner by any form of powered machine, both Tyler and Drake find themselves having fallen haphazardly back through time as a result of them undergoing some traumatic event that, in turn, results in just such a slippage in time. In *Life on Mars*, a traumatic event results in Tyler not only arriving in 1973 (a car accident in episode 1.1) but returning to 1973 (his rooftop suicide in episode 2.8). Meanwhile, Drake's shooting in the inaugural episode of *Ashes to Ashes* is the traumatic event that lands her in 1981. Most significantly, these temporal slips take both Tyler and Drake back to the time of their respective childhoods, the seventies and eighties – and, more specifically, back to their childhood homes.

THE UNCANNY HOME AND TELEVISION AS SCIENCE FICTION

Gaston Bachelard's classic text *The Poetics of Space* (1958) implores us to examine closely, and appreciate fully, the minutiae of life – especially the intensity of the 'miniature', the 'universe' to be found within the 'house' (indeed, first discovered in our childhood home). Eulogising the worlds within worlds to be found in 'corners' and in 'drawers, chests and wardrobes', Bachelard conceptualises such an endeavour within the chapter entitled 'intimate immensity' (1958: 183–210). Freud, in *The Uncanny* (1919), made use of the terms *heimlich* ('homely') and *unheimlich* ('unhomely'). In relation to our understanding of the returns of both Tyler and Drake to their respective childhood homes, their literal translation is most appropriate here: for, as adults returning to their childhood home, the home is, at once, both homely (that is, comforting) yet unhomely (somehow, quite unsettling). More typically, as Nicholas Royle (2003) adds, the uncanny is, 'a peculiar commingling of the familiar with the unfamiliar' (1). Thus, for both Tyler and Drake as time travellers, the home can *only* be an uncanny place: it is familiar to them, as it is a place that they recognise (they did, after all, once live there), but it is also a place that is totally unfamiliar to them (as they have only ever lived there as children, never as adults). Marina Warner (2006) returns to Freud, and insists that 'Freud is interested in the Heimlich, or homely . . . and develops the idea that the feeling arises when a figure or an image stirs a memory of something familiar that has been mislaid, or lost' (53–4). Therefore, Tyler and Drake – 'mislaid' in time – are 'lost' within their uncanny childhood homes: an uncanniness made all the more uneasy as they are conscious of the dual loss of not only their childhood, but also their adulthood. Brian Dillon, in his loss-tinged autobiographical examination of his childhood home, *In the Dark Room* (2005), considers such 'intimate immensity' from the perspective of the uncanny – and how unsettling memories increase with the passing of time:

> In the furrows and expanses of the house, we uncover for the first time the surfaces on which memory and imagination can be set in motion . . . from one plane to another in imitation of thoughts and dreams which will one day occupy much larger and unsettling spaces. (40)

For Tyler and Drake, then, the notion of their childhood homes as uncanny, unsettling spaces has been intensified by their time-travelling return to the place of their childhood imagination along with their experiences and memories of adulthood.

Jeffrey Sconce (2000) insists that, in relation to the notion of television as a 'haunted media', for the American post-1945, baby-boom generation – that was the first generation to grow up with television sets as common-place objects in its living rooms – a duality of both fascination and fear accompanied their consumption of TV. Whilst television is recognised today as being part and parcel of normal family life, 'the television sets that entered American homes in the 1950s no doubt bordered on the wonders of science fiction' (2000: 130). With the broadcasting, at this time, of science fiction series such as *The Outer Limits* (ABC, 1963–5) and *The Twilight Zone* (CBS, 1959–64), '[t]elevision exuded a powerful presence in the household, serving in the active imagination as a fantastic portal to other worlds' (ibid.: 131). This is played upon in *Life on Mars*, for example at the very end of episode 1.4, where Tyler is seen lying fast asleep on his bed with the television still on in the background. The TV shows *Mr Sockley*, a sock-based children's puppet, who is talking to Tyler in his mother's voice. As if keeping a vigil at Tyler's hospital bed of 2006, whilst he is in a coma, the episode ends with *Mr Sockley*/his mother comforting him with the words 'I love you'. At moments like this, the television in *Life on Mars* does indeed become an extraordinary point of entry to another world. Moreover, *Life on Mars* is a televisual site of time travel itself, as the TV often provides fleetingly (in a frustrating uni-directional manner, through the entire two series) Tyler's only means of contact with his former 2006/2007 self.

THE HOME, TIME TRAVEL, CHILDHOOD AND THE UNCANNY HOME IN *LIFE ON MARS*

The tensions that are created when the adult Tyler has the opportunity to confront the Tyler of his childhood are the direct consequences of Sam Tyler's time-travelling exploits. Claire Parker (producer) insists: 'I think that at the heart of every story in *Life on Mars* there's a conflict' (Parker 2006). Such a 'conflict' is evident not only in the clash of policing styles personified in the differences between Tyler's (and Drake's) politically correct methods and Hunt's more unreconstructed approach, but also with the possibility of the main characters' meeting, as adults, their childhood selves – and, more controversially, the bringing together of adult 'children' with their 'younger' parents. *Life on Mars* episode 1.4 opens with a dream sequence whereby Tyler, wandering the red-bricked, back-to-back terrace-lined streets of his childhood hears his mother's (Joanne Froggatt) echoing voice calling out to him – 'Sammy!' The ethereal nature of the scene – where 'home' is not quite 'home' – is heightened by the spookily phased meowing of a ginger cat (the cat, it later emerges, is Ivanhoe, the Tylers' family pet). Waking in a disturbed state, Tyler then sets about searching for his 4-year-old self and his family home. Eventually finding the latter, and coming face to face with his mother, Tyler – posing as a DI Bolan[2] – claims that he is carrying out 'door-to-door enquiries' with regards to 'a spate of burglaries in the area' in an effort to disguise the true reason for his presence.

With his mother being an attractive young woman, and Tyler – her son, of course – now being a similarly aged man, the audience is aware of an immediate mutual attraction. John McKay (director 1.4), during the episode's audio commentary, substantiates such a sexually charged liaison: 'One of the things I like about these scenes is that it feels like they sort of fancy each other, which adds a very interesting undercurrent.' John Simm agrees, adding – rather more bluntly – that, upon following his rather glamorous mother into the hallway of their home, his character momentarily adopts a rather more lecherous persona: 'Yeah, there's a glance at her bum, ain't there, in a minute.' This is an example, of course, of the inherent 'conflict' that Parker alluded to, for, instead of Tyler yet again coming to blows with Hunt, we are confronted with a 1973 version of the Oedipus complex – a *Life on Mars* 'sexual conflict', the result of a time-travelling policeman meeting his own mother as a younger woman. As Ashley Pharoah quips in the audio commentary, this scene is pure 'Freud for beginners'.

Tyler, walking into the living room alone, fondly picks up his Action Man deep sea diver that is lying on the table, only to put it down again hesitantly when his mother enters the room. Then, speaking of her 'son' being ill in bed with 'the mumps', Tyler's eyes look up contemplatively to the ceiling. With them both taking tea (and Ivanhoe knowingly rubbing up against a seated Tyler), his mother asks if she should 'wake Sam up', stating that 'He'll be really disappointed that he missed you.' Tyler, answering in a cautiously resigned tone, insists 'No, don't wake him up.' To this his mother proudly admits that, with regards her young Sam, 'He wants to be a policeman one day, so he says.' Tyler's prophetic reply is, of course, 'He will be.'

All of the elements in this scene – the coexistence of Tyler as both child and adult, an adult life yet to be lived (that has been lived), and an adult's knowledge of how their life was lived (first, as a child and, then, as an adult) – is not only an embrace of the myriad of possibilities on offer within H. G. Wells's *The Time Machine*, but also an acknowledgement of objections to, and misinterpretations of, the novel/concept. For, as Gary Westfahl (2000) notes, critics insisted 'that a person could not go back and meet himself, [and] that a backward traveller should logically grow younger' (131).[3] So, for Tyler, Freud's notion of the uncanny is not only manifest amid an Oedipal liaison with his mother as her younger self, but embedded within his time-travelling return to the home of his childhood and the possibility – yet self-denial – of meeting himself as a boy.

THE HOME, TIME TRAVEL, CHILDHOOD AND THE UNCANNY HOME IN *ASHES TO ASHES*

In episode 1.4 of *Ashes to Ashes*, Drake has her first opportunity to visit her family home. In contrast to Tyler's cramped northern terraced abode, hers is the epitome of a spacious, semi-detached London townhouse, surrounded by immaculate white railings and shaded in leaves. Walking upon the stone steps towards the lead-glass door, Drake smiles inwardly as she fondly remembers herself (in what would become the series' trademark 'flashback' version of Drake, as a schoolgirl (Lucy Cole) in burgundy uniform) frolicking amongst the foliage, with dolls and daddy in tow. Invited inside by her mother (Amanda Bullmore), Drake is comforted even more to be amid the recognisable confines of the white gloss woodwork of the hall. Passing cool, Lincoln-green potted plants, her fingers linger in a melancholic manner along the rise of the wooden stair rail. Drake eventually makes her way into the sitting room, where her mother is entertaining a male friend, Evan White (Stephen Campbell Moore). Thus, with this episode of *Ashes to Ashes*, amid this early eighties middle-class afternoon tea party (complimented by a cheeseboard of grapes, Jacobs crackers and Danish blue cheese) we have – instead of the Oedipus-charged relationship between Tyler and his mother of *Life on Mars*

– an embarrassing Electra equivalent (all uneasy smiles and silences) between Drake and Evan White. The pair had already dined together (albeit within a professional context) earlier in the episode, and, in the opening episode set in 2008, he is seen as a protective godfather figure to Drake's daughter Molly (Grace Vance). This uneasy situation is then encapsulated in her mother's comment that Drake, indeed, finds herself in 'difficult territory'.

Unlike Tyler's close (yet uncomfortable) proximity to his childhood self in *Life on Mars* (the adult Tyler downstairs, whilst his childhood self is ill upstairs), Drake has no opportunity to meet her childhood self in person. Upon Drake asking her mother the whereabouts of her daughter (Drake as a child, of course), she is told, rather bluntly, rather coldly, that she is away – 'France, school trip'. As Tyler fondly held his Action Man in *Life on Mars*, Drake, feeling between the cushions of the sofa upon which she is sitting, discovers, and nonchalantly caresses, her childhood Troll (a diminutive doll, with a head of shocking-pink hair).[4] Again in contrast to Tyler's only chance to visit his bedroom upon his family's vacation of their rented home (discussed in greater detail later in this chapter), Drake – under the pretence of visiting the toilet – is here able to wander leisurely around her own childhood bedroom. Walking along the hall and, once again, caressing the wooden stair rail, she pushes open the door. Gingerly picking up both a 1981 *Jackie* annual and gaudy, fluorescent-coloured roller-skates, and momentarily playing Shakin' Stevens' 'Green Door' on her pink stereo cassette player, Drake reaches up into the chimney breast to retrieve her diary – only to be startled by her mother, who, having now entered the room after her, asks angrily 'What are you doing?' In her rather hasty defence (and, also, in sudden realisation that her 'home' is, now, no longer hers), Drake blurts out a rushed explanation that 'It's my room! [Correcting herself] It's exactly like my room when I was a child. [Correcting herself once again] Girl!' Then, rather unexpectedly, her mother's eyes mist over and, gazing across the bedroom (as if acknowledging Drake's time-travelling return to the bedroom of her childhood), muses that it is a '[s]pecial place, special time. It's her world.' This appreciation of Drake's childhood bedroom as 'her world' (extending even into adulthood), corresponds with Christopher Day's consideration of children and their environment, whereby '[b]edrooms are personal realms', where children are 'free to establish long-term mood' (2007: 124).

LIFE ON MARS AND ASHES TO ASHES AS TELEVISUAL TIME PARADOXES

Ash (1977: 145–54) stresses that time travel within science fiction takes place across many '*n*th dimensions', including 'backwards in time', from the 'present to future', from the 'future to present' – even 'time standing still'. Thus, in the cases of both *Life on Mars* and *Ashes to Ashes*, Tyler and Drake find themselves inadvertently in the role of time travellers operating amid the whole gamut of 'time and *n*th dimensions'. For example, across the entirety of both series of *Life on Mars*, Tyler travels: 'backwards in time' (from 2006 to 1973); from the 'present to future' (in the final episode of series two, he not only finds himself back in 2007, but lives out a disconnected [and brief] future along a linear narrative); from the 'future to present' (in the final scene of that episode he returns to a 1973 present, that he is clearly now more comfortable with, from a 2007 future that had increasingly become alien to him).[5] Crucially, all of these aspects of time travel and temporal slippages in both *Life on Mars* and *Ashes to Ashes* take place amid (and, furthermore, they help *create*) 'time paradoxes'. For, as Ash enthuses, '[c]ertainly the most intriguing factor in the portrayal of time travel is the collection of paradoxes to which it may give rise' (1977: 151).

Thus, in *Life on Mars* and *Ashes to Ashes* one crucial aspect of time travel is Tyler's and Drake's possible meeting of their own childhood selves. Later in episode 1.4, Tyler returns to his family home as his mother sweeps the pavement outside. There, mid-conversation, Tyler gazes up towards an open bedroom window (*his* bedroom window) and asks 'How is he?': the possibility of meeting, but little more. The episode then ends with Tyler making a final return to his family home. Bearing a present and a bouquet of flowers, he walks up to the front door and, noticing it is off the latch, pushes it open, and walks in. The house is deserted. Tyler walks upstairs slowly, and walks across the landing. Like Drake's lightness of touch on the stair rail, it is this act of walking upstairs – literally, 'up the wooden hills to Bedfordshire' – that gives emphasis to both stairs and stair landings as further 'fantastic portals to other worlds' to be found within the childhood home that are essential in order to make the child (and, as with both Drake and Tyler, the adult) feel secure in order to progress from one space to another:

> Threshold and transition spaces help children adjust mood and behaviour . . . Sometimes children can't feel at ease without such public–private transition places. Entries, garden gates and stair landings are intermediate zones between the security of house interior, private territory or upper step and the freedom of being outside, on the way somewhere. (Day 2007: 50)

No longer apprehensive, as he now clearly has a memory that, as a family, they had by this stage of their lives vacated their rented home, Tyler progresses from one space to another, and steps from the landing into his childhood bedroom. Spotting a fallen, broken photo frame on the floor, he picks it up, examining the now loose snapshot it once contained. The photograph shows Tyler as a child wearing an oversized police helmet. Yet, as the helmet sits so low on his head, it obscures his eyes. Tyler, despite his time-travel journey back home, is denied the opportunity to take a proper look at himself. Indeed, unable to enact the uncanny fully, Tyler is unable to look *into* himself.

Tyler is unable to gaze into the eyes of his childhood self in *Life on Mars*, but Drake is able to do just that early on in *Ashes to Ashes*. In episode 1.2, when Drake and her mother are having a drink together in a wine bar (their first real meeting), Drake's mother states that 'I have a daughter called Alex', to which Drake breathlessly extols 'I know! I know!', asking 'Can I see her? Do you have a photograph, or . . . ?' Upon being shown a blotchy photo booth snapshot of herself (again, clad in burgundy school uniform), Drake comments forlornly that 'She looks quite sad.' This 'sadness' is picked up upon by Jonny Campbell (director, episodes 1.1, 1.2, 1.7, 1.8):

> It wasn't a perfect relationship with the mum, I think that's what's important. The career mum was excluding the daughter, she was at boarding school. So, rather than it being a sentimental, cute, and here's my mum who died in a car bomb, actually, 'Did my mum love me?' is one of the real themes of this story. (Campbell 2006)

Whilst all of this touches upon one of the many paradoxes of time travel ('adult' children meeting their 'younger' parents), this scene also brings us back to the notion that time travel, as a central tenet of science fiction, occurs amid a continuum of 'nth dimensions': time travel not only involving the obvious desire to go back in time, but offering the opportunity to move from the 'present to the future', and from the 'future to the present'. For Drake is not only able to go back in time and converse, as an adult, with her own mother, she also – throughout the series (albeit in her own mind) – interacts with, and simultaneously contemplates her relationship with, her future daughter Molly. As producer Beth Willis states:

> She's a hardworking career woman, and she has a wonderful relationship with Molly, but she's not there – she's not there. And, even in 2008, she's not there all the time, she has to go off and do her police work. (Willis 2006)

Furthermore, considering the possibilities that time travel offers with regards to human relationships, Willis also asserts that 'it's a chance to maybe make amends', insisting 'If you asked somebody, if you were to go back in time, "What would you do?", building relationships with family or friends or people you knew would be the first thing you'd say.' With Willis's words in mind, this scene ends with Drake's mother stating that 'What would really help me, Alex, is for us to become friends.' Drake, incredulous, excitedly asks 'Really!?!' – only to eventually realise that her mother's offer of friendship is a false one, as it is only so that she can gain 'insider' information into the workings of the police force.

CONCLUSION

It is unsurprising that both *Life on Mars* and *Ashes to Ashes*, as science fiction television, revolved around the genre's tried-and-tested principle of time travel. As Brian Ash, even in the mid-seventies, insisted '[i]t is clear that the intellectual teasers involving other dimensions will retain their popularity, and the element of fun shows little sign of diminishing' (1977: 154). Yet *Life on Mars* and *Ashes to Ashes* are far more than predictable sci-fi, time-travelling TV. For both series can be fully appreciated as a peculiarly British quirky take on science fiction in its original guise, what Daniel O'Brien (2000) has termed 'scientific romance'.

> Scientific romance implies a conflict between scientific observer and romantic dreamer, but the central realization of the British genre is that in the end both are necessary, and all the really interesting work has to take place in the cramped space the two can share . . . [t]hroughout British sf, we find the figure of the scientific romantic – at once rigorous and eccentric, involved and detached, serious and ironic, important and trivial, whimsical and adult. (12)

Crucially, both *Life on Mars* and *Ashes to Ashes* tackle all these aspects of British science fiction, but in taking both Tyler and Drake back to their respective childhoods they engage absolutely with the last: the 'whimsical and adult'.

Furthermore, both *Life on Mars* and *Ashes to Ashes* also adhere to the characteristically British science fiction's characteristic emphasis on the dystopian. In the very first episode of *Ashes to Ashes*, Drake writes words on a whiteboard to describe her predicament, the first being 'Dystopian'. Yet, as Cook and Wright remind us, such dystopian imaginings do not mean all is lost:

> Even though their visions of the future may be wholly pessimistic and dark, all sf TV texts carry within them the seeds of a latent utopianism, because appealing to the dreamer in all of us, they refuse to accept the way things currently are, telling their audience, often to the latter's delight and mystification, that the way things are today is not the way they are always necessarily going to be. Tomorrow is most definitely another day and the future, they dare to tell us, can always be different. (2006: 19)

Thus, the time-travelling adventures of the main characters in both *Life on Mars* and *Ashes to Ashes* are located firmly within the tradition of British science fiction television. Both series emphasise that yesterday – that is Tyler's and Drake's childhood – 'is most definitely another day'. Yet, their respective present and the future, their adulthood, and the promise of adulthood, 'can always be different'.

In both *Life on Mars* and *Ashes to Ashes*, then, the childhood home, rather than being that bastion of familial comfort, is to Sam Tyler and Alex Drake uncanny in its unfamiliarity for one simple reason: those recognisable places (their family homes, the bedrooms of their childhood of 1973 and 1981 respectively) they had only ever experienced before as *children*, not as *adults*. Time travel allows their entering of what was once familiar, and turns them into strangers within their own home, alien adults as it were. What should be familiar and comforting (*heimlich*) to them is unfamiliar and uncomforting (*unheimlich*). Therefore, like Brian Dillon's return to the house of his childhood, it dawns on both Tyler and Drake that 'the house persists, of course, as something lost, as the image of an intimacy to which we can never return . . . [that] in the end we are banished from this idyllic enclosure and discover ourselves adrift' (2005: 41). As such, one of the many paradoxes of time travel in both *Life on Mars* and *Ashes to Ashes* is that it *denies* rather than facilitates the connection, the offer of 'making amends', of 'building relationships with family or friends or people you knew'. Time travel emphasises to both Tyler and Drake that they, quite simply, do not belong, as adults, in their childhood homes.

Life on Mars and *Ashes to Ashes*, then, are more than mere nostalgic TV. Certainly, they allow us all to travel back in time to our own childhoods, whereby we all remember our Action Men and *Jackie* annuals. Watching each and every episode encourages us to, once more, climb the stairs of our childhood homes, to re-enter the bedrooms of our youth once more (to go 'up the wooden hills to Bedfordshire'). But *Life on Mars* and *Ashes to Ashes* offer us a nostalgia that also grounds us firmly in our adult present, reminding us that we can never, ever go back. As Doreen Massey asserts, with regards to the folly of nostalgia and its associated desire to go back home:

> For the truth is that you can never simply 'go back', to home or to anywhere else. When you get 'there' the place will have moved on just as you yourself will have changed . . . A nostalgia which denies that, is certainly in need of re-working. (2005: 124)

NOTES

1   Adams and Thompson's *Life on Mars: The Official Companion*, with the chapter '"Ford Granada": writing *Life on Mars*' (pp. 20–33), provides a detailed insight into this 'all-lads-together' genesis of the series in Blackpool, 1998.

2   Tyler's hurried adoption of the pseudonym 'Bolan' is as a result of the policeman having admiringly approached, earlier in the episode, the glam rock musician Marc Bolan at the Warren discothèque.

3   Here, Gary Westfahl (2000), in his chapter entitled 'Partial derivatives: popular misinterpretations of H. G. Wells's *The Time Machine*' (pp. 129–41), is

making reference to the criticism to be found amid the readers' letters of *Amazing Stories*, July, 1927, following the reprint of the novel, in said magazine in May of that year.

4   This troll is handed, later in the episode, by Drake to her daughter Molly – although only an act of mother/daughter bonding in Drake's mind, it is an example of pure 'present to future'/'future to present' time travel.

5   Such time travel, of course, is not only restricted to Tyler and Drake. In *Life on Mars*, episodes 2.7 and 2.8, DCI Frank Morgan of Hyde Division, is – whilst being a present-day police officer (that is, a 1973 present-day police officer) – also a neurosurgeon operating on Tyler's brain tumour in the future (again, a 2007 future).

REFERENCES

Adams, G. and Thompson, L. (2006). *Life on Mars: The Official Companion*, London, Pocket Books.

Ash, B. (ed.) (1977). *The Visual Encyclopedia of Science Fiction*, London, Pan Books.

Bachelard, G. (1958). *The Poetics of Space*, Boston, MA, Beacon Press.

Campbell, J. (2006). Commentary, bonus features, *Life on Mars: The Complete Series One*, Contender Home Entertainment.

Cook, J. and Wright, P. (2006). "'Futures past": an introduction to and brief survey of British science fiction television', in *British Science Fiction Television: A Hitchhiker's Guide*, John R. Cook and Peter Wright (eds), London, I. B. Tauris, pp. 1–20.

Day, C. (2007). *Environment and Children: Passive Lessons from the Everyday Environment*, Oxford, Architectural Press.

Dillon, B. (2005). *In the Dark Room: A Journey in Memory*, Dublin, Penguin Ireland.

Freud, S. (1919). *The Uncanny*, London, Penguin Books.

Graham, M. (2006). 'Take a look at the lawman – the making of *Life on Mars*, part 1', Disk 1, Bonus Features, *Life on Mars: The Complete Series One*, Contender Home Entertainment.

Massey, D. (2005). *For Space*, London, Sage Publications Ltd.

O'Brien, D. (2000). *SF: UK – How British Science Fiction Changed the World*, Richmond, Reynolds and Hearn Ltd.

Parker, C. (2006). 'Take a look at the lawman – the making of *Life on Mars*, part 1', Disk 1, Bonus Features, *Life on Mars – The Complete Series One*, Contender Home Entertainment.

Rabkin, E. S. (ed.) (1983). *Science Fiction: A Historical Anthology*, Oxford, Oxford University Press.

Royle, N. (2003). *The Uncanny: An Introduction*, Manchester, Manchester University Press.

Sconce, J. (2000). *Haunted Media: Electronic Presence from Telegraphy to Television*, Durham, NC, Duke University Press.

Warner, M. (2006). *Phantasmagoria: Spirit Visions, Metaphors, and Media into the Twenty-first Century*, Oxford, Oxford University Press.

Westfahl, G. (2000). *Science Fiction, Children's Literature, and Popular Culture: Coming of Age in Fantasyland*, Westport, CT, Greenwood Press.

Willis, B. (2006). Commentary, bonus features, *Life on Mars: The Complete Series One*, Contender Home Entertainment.

THE MEDIUM IS THE MONSTER ...
8 OR THE WORLD?

DISCOURSES OF UNCANNY 'OLD MEDIA' AND IMMERSIVE 'NEW MEDIA' IN *LIFE ON MARS*

Matt Hills

L*IFE ON MARS* (BBC, 2006–7) may well have become infamous for many things – the character of Gene Hunt; the car; the seventies soundtrack – but among its many celebrated aspects, the first *Official Companion* picks out a further iconic image: the 'test card girl' (played by Rafaella Hutchinson and Harriet Rogers). Authors Guy Adams and Lee Thompson note that it is 'amazing that a small girl playing noughts and crosses can inject such an air of genuine menace into a television drama' (2006: 34). This chapter focuses less on nostalgic denotations surrounding 'old media' representations in *Life on Mars*, and rather more on how the programme uses representations of television to connote noughties' anxieties and fantasies. In this regard, I concur fully with Robin Nelson when he argues that '*Life on Mars* is more than nostalgic "heritage" drama. In providing undoubted generic pleasures, it has the potential also to be thought-provoking and to invite complex seeing' (2007: 179). Nelson's focus here is predominantly on issues of policing – he interprets *Life on Mars* as a dialectical interrogation of 1973 and 2006 norms of police activity (ibid.: 178–9). However, what tends to be glossed over in readings of *Life on Mars* as centrally nostalgic, or as critically contrasting 1973/2006 policing, are its complex depictions of media technology. The fact that Sam Tyler, seemingly trapped in 1973, receives messages from 2006 on radio and television makes these media highly significant not merely as conduits for narrative information, but also as potentially interstitial, monstrous disruptions of Sam's world.

What follows, then, will consider television's interstitiality in *Life on Mars* in two ways. First, this chapter will argue that the series represents the medium in relation to conventions of 'gothic television' (Wheatley 2006), denoting it textually as an 'uncanny', invasive media technology (Freud 1990). Secondly, it will go on to suggest that television simultaneously connotes a version of noughties 'new media', possessing powers of interactivity and immersion which speak to contemporary cultural discourses of media convergence (on denotation and connotation, see Barthes 1977). Loaded with fascination as much as fear, television is a privileged object in the diegetic world of *Life on Mars*.

OLD MEDIA: TELEVISION'S UNCANNY, RETRO SCREEN

Within the programme's diegesis, television is represented as an object of its time, which is used frequently to convey period detail such as the now-obsolete test card, or creaky 1970s public information films (both featured in episode 1.1). Sam Tyler repeatedly watches television while alone in his room, and the television screen thus becomes a potential source of comfort and solace. A familiar, domestic technology, television is even portrayed as outdated junk in episode 2.1, where one broken set is reclaimed by a rag and bone man. Linked to the textual details and stereotypical broadcasts of the seventies – test cards and extravagantly bearded Open University lecturers – television is, however, defamiliarised and converted into a source of narrative threat. In his cultural history of media representations as spooky and fantastical, Jeffrey Sconce argues that

> the television ghosts we encounter today may be less than frightening or even fantastic . . . [A]n important transition in the cultural conceptualization of electronic presence [was] brought about by the advent of television [linked to] uncannily sentient electronic entities or . . . crucibles for forging wholly sovereign electronic universes. (2000: 126)

Sconce suggests that relatively early in its cultural life in the 1950s and 1960s television was more readily depicted as monstrous and threatening, supposedly possessed of magical powers, before such representations thinned out and shifted as the technology became normalised and fully domesticated. Indeed, by the eighties, with the release of such films as David Cronenberg's *Videodrome* (1983), television had arguably already been displaced as a cultural source of anxiety by newer video technology. As such, Sconce argues that television is rarely thought of as frightening in the contemporary age, with media fears instead relocating once again around newer technologies, for example, the Internet, which begin to carry connotations of 'domestic invasion' and uncontrolled, corrupting information flow. Based on a range of different historical examples, Sconce's work is persuasive, implying that the 'television-as-monster' would be unlikely to offer a culturally plausible, fantastical threat for noughties' audiences.

And yet this is one of the achievements of *Life on Mars*, which very much figures television as an uncanny technology, but does so by virtue of throwing us back to a diegetic time that is distanced from the present day and from telly's cultural normalisation. *Life on Mars*'s diegetic television images seem to become co-present and sentient, breaking the frame and addressing Sam directly (from episode 1.1 onwards). Similarly, the scary test card girl crosses diegetic boundaries between 'text' and 'reality', stepping out of the television screen and into Sam's room (this occurs first in episode 1.2). These category violations and boundary crossings (Carroll 1990; Hills 2005: 65) approximate to aspects of the Freudian 'uncanny' such as the 'animation of inanimate objects' (Freud 1990: 373). Sigmund Freud argues that uncanniness, an audience's feeling of dread and horror, can be produced by a range of images and themes in fiction such as 'wish-fulfilments, secret powers, omnipotence of thoughts', provided that 'there is a conflict of judgement as to whether things which have been "surmounted" and are regarded as incredible may not, after all, be possible' (ibid.). For this reason, a text's realism is essential to securing an uncanny effect. So too is its genre, which must not wholly normalise or accept the existence of fantastical/supernatural events, and indeed Freud rules out the fairy tale on these grounds (see Wheatley 2006: 7). This quality of uncanny uncertainty, with seemingly fantastical events intruding into a realist diegesis, is crucial to representations of television in *Life on Mars*.

The opening episode of series one illustrates this uncanniness, featuring a scene in which Sam sleeps in front of an Open University broadcast. He wakes to find that the mathematics lecturer (Richard Sinnott) is apparently discussing his medical case in 2006 and addressing him directly: 'At times however, he moves, murmurs . . . this gives us some hope, despite the brain stem bruising.' Indeed, the lecturer on the television even appears to call out to Sam. This mysterious figure, portrayed with a glassy-eyed manic stare by Sinnott, is first shown in extreme close-up, emphasising his status as a grainy, televised image. Such a close-up also lends the character an air of implicit threat, despite his monotonous, calm vocal delivery. As the camera pans round to Tyler's sleeping form, the televised Open University dialogue switches from Pythagorean maths to medical discussion of Sam's situation just moments prior to his waking up. The precise timing of this narrative disruption contributes to audience uncertainty; as a result it is not immediately evident whether Sam is imagining, dreaming or hallucinating the television message targeted directly at him. In fact, the introduction of the television switch-over shortly before Sam is confirmed to be conscious suggests that the OU lecturer could be objectively speaking in such a way. However, his televised lecture begins as a 'normal' transmission; the audience may at first assume that it is merely a part of the show's seventies background colour, and the scene also concludes with Sam's television returning to a state of seventies normality and period detail via the test card's first appearance. Realism is set up and restored, featuring only a temporary breach of the fantastical which thus remains a textual object of 'intellectual uncertainty' or, in Freud's terminology, a 'conflict of judgement' (Freud 1990: 373). At this stage, it remains unclear whether we have been shown a subjective or objective narrative event

107

where the diegetic 'television image' and 'Sam's reality' can interact. The scene ends with John Simm performing Tyler's loneliness, despair and disorientation by literally (and hysterically) hugging the television set, setting up an ambivalence which will continue throughout the series' fantastical, uncanny representations of seventies television – the medium may be both a threatening monster and a salvational messenger.

When the OU lecturer returns in episode 1.7, his appearance is represented more clearly as an intrusive, disruptive television signal, as on this occasion his lecture cuts in and out of Sam's usual television transmissions via static fuzz. Again, the lecturer appears to speak directly to Tyler, his face filling the 'screen within the screen' as Sam sits immediately in front of it. Proximity and connection are connoted by an unusual two-shot framing of Sam and the lecturer's looming close-up face, but it is a connection, an interaction, which fails as Sam hits the television set and shouts, 'What the hell does that mean?' Though seeming to hold out an 'answer' to Sam's situation, the lecturer does not offer any such solution. Indeed, the dialogue promising an answer is itself ambiguous, falling liminally between talk clearly belonging to a maths module and that belonging to discourses of medical treatment. The precise timing of this, along with the ambiguous coding of an 'answer' (is it to a maths problem or to Sam's predicament?), once more works to sustain the uncertainty and disruption of realism that Freud attributes to uncanny narratives.

Having been established as a marker of safety and restored normality in the show's first episode, it is only in episode 1.2 that the test card is itself transformed into an uncanny 'TV ghost' (Sconce 2000: 126): the inanimate image seemingly becoming an animate, sentient being. Here, in an escalation of threat, the test card girl does not merely 'break the frame' by addressing Sam. Rather, she appears to step out of the television set and directly into Tyler's room. The sequence again features Sam waking up alone, roused from slumber by his television's close-down signal. As the test card girl is revealed standing behind him, lighting within the *mise en scène* changes dramatically, moving out of realist codes and towards what Noel Carroll has termed the 'ambiguous coding' (1990: 156) of numinous/apparitional lighting. Carroll argues that such self-conscious, artificial over-lighting can code subjective, psychological disruption, but that it can also be read as indicating the appearance of supernatural forces. This device is repeated, and intensified, towards the end of the series, in the red lighting of episode 2.8's 'none of this is real' scene.

Accompanying the lighting changes of episode 1.2, Sam's television screen is shown to carry an empty test card. The *mise en scène* is restored to its normal state only when we see Sam Tyler awake for a second time, suggesting strongly that the preceding events were a dream sequence. But again, the status of this fantastical, televisual intrusion is not entirely clear: is the test card girl a manifestation of Tyler's psyche, or does she have an independent, animate existence of some kind?

Like the 1970s OU lecturer (episodes 1.1 and 1.7), the test card girl returns across the run of *Life on Mars*, her appearances largely concentrated in series one (episodes 1.2–1.5 and 1.8; 2.3 and 2.8). However, given her frequent appearances, it is unsurprising that the character should have become emblematic of *Life on Mars*'s uncanny televisual imagery. Other candidates and moments are offered across the series, including children's puppet Mr Sockley (1.4) which speaks with the voice of Sam's mother (Joanne Froggatt), as well as episode 2.5 in which Sam effectively watches *Life on Mars* on a television set within the diegesis. This conceit – the most self-reflexive use of television in the series – is narratively rationalised via the notion that 1973 Sam is feverish because noughties' Sam has been given incorrect medication while in his coma.

Despite series two's displacement of the test card girl, and its escalation into self-reflexivity, the character's symbolic importance to the series is attested to by her appearance in its closing sequence. Here, a camera tilt (rendering the horizontal briefly vertical) mirrors the framing of Tyler's prone body after his accident in episode 1.1, and as the camera rights itself we see a group of children running down the road. Though this seems to restore more standardised, non-stylised patterns of realist representation, the final child is dressed in red and carrying a toy clown. As we realise that this is a version of the test card girl (this time played by Harriet Rogers), the character cocks her head quizzically, seeming to look out at us, the empirical audience. She then gestures as if reaching for a switch (off-screen, but in violation of depicted on-screen space) and the image disappears down to a white dot, signifying a television being switched off, retro-style. Even here, the test card girl condenses nostalgic images of 1970s TV – a 'quaint' time when television programmes were not broadcast twenty-four hours a day, and when television sets slowly switched on and off – with the threat of signal shutdown, or narrative cessation. Series co-creator Matthew Graham has positioned this ending as a playful gesture:

> It was written in the full knowledge that the show, and that episode, would be analysed to pieces . . . And that last moment is really me saying, ' . . . It's just a piece of television, it's just a story and it's come to an end.' It is an in-joke . . . in the spirit of the show. (Graham 2007)

But this reading – the writer's attempt at fixing 'official' interpretation – overwrites less frivolous possibilities whereby the final switch-off might be read as Sam's death in the present day, and as the switching off of life support (or simply the cessation of life signs). Such an articulation of the television signal and Sam Tyler's life is, after all, given earlier in episode 2.8 where a graphical, pulsing trace of Tyler's heart rate is shown on the television screen within the screen as Morgan begins to operate.

By focusing frequently on its uncanny moments of dread and supernatural disruption on Sam Tyler's television set, *Life on Mars* functions as a textbook instance of what Helen Wheatley has termed 'gothic television'. Wheatley suggests that television texts drawing on the codes and conventions of the horror genre, and the Freudian uncanny, frequently make reference to television's 'domestic reception context . . . we are constantly reminded that this is terror/horror television which takes place, and is *viewed*, within a domestic milieu' (2006: 7, italics in original; see also Johnson 2005: 147 on telefantasy's foregrounding of the TV image).

The fact that the test card girl, OU lecturer and suchlike appear to Sam when he is home alone can be interpreted as a narrative strategy which sustains audience uncertainty, or conflict of judgement, since no other character is present who can validate Sam's strange experience. Coincidentally, Noel Carroll has even linked the maintenance of audiences' uncanny uncertainty to cultural norms of evidence, invoking the police force in the process:

> the supernatural hypothesis cannot be accepted until we can eyeball the monster to our own satisfaction, and to the satisfaction of something like the police department or a court of law . . . horror [texts] . . . can engender . . . uncertainty . . . by playing off the standards of our culture for knowledge from observation, especially as those standards are embodied in such activities as legal testimony. (1990: 154)

Of course, *Life on Mars* restricts its eyewitness to a single policeman, Tyler himself, off-duty and sat at home in front of the television. At the same time, however, the presence of uncanny televisual events in Sam's domestic setting certainly works in the manner identified by Helen Wheatley:

> Gothic television can be characterised by the meeting of two houses: the textual domestic spaces of Gothic television (haunted houses, decaying mansions, permeable family homes under threat from within and without) and the extra-textual domestic spaces of the medium (the homes in which Gothic television is viewed). (2006: 200)

Mirroring the programme's reception, the use of seventies retro television icons is thus more than merely nostalgic, also speaking to current viewing contexts (that is, viewers watching in their extra-textual noughties' domestic spaces) as well as to audience memories of test cards, public information films and white dots. Having observed this much, the next section will argue that television's strong presence within *Life on Mars* further transcends its positioning as historicised 'old media' whose outdated quaintness carries both a patina of nostalgia and a threatening uncanniness. As well as being represented as an object of uncanny dread, I will suggest that television in *Life on Mars* simultaneously takes on a fascination for audiences – figuring contemporary discourses and fantasies of immersive, interactive 'new media'.

NEW MEDIA: TELEVISION'S IMMERSIVE, INTERACTIVE TOUCH-SCREEN

Television drama in the twenty-first century has undergone a series of reconceptualisations, including a new-found, technology-driven emphasis on multi-platforming and brand extension (encapsulated by the BBC's policy of '360 degree commissioning'; see Belam 2007). As Derek Johnson has put it:

> the *hyperserial* connectivity of multiplatformed television allows viewers to metaphorically enter and consume from positions within its vast, internally coherent, *hyperdiegetic* spaces. By creating more proximate relationships between the spaces of production, consumption and narrative, multiplatforming has reshaped the relationships between industry, audience and text. (2007: 73)

This participatory audience is characteristic of convergence culture and its transmedia storytelling, where extensive, massively detailed narrative worlds, sometimes termed hyperdiegetic spaces, are stretched across different platforms (television, the web, DVD, mobile phones, books). As a result, 'overlapping sites of the everyday and the hyperdiegetic' can be created via tie-in merchandise (ibdi.: 72), as the narrative world becomes ever more important to franchise creation.

As an experienced screenwriter told me:

> When I first started, you would pitch a story . . . Later, once sequels started to take off, you pitched a character because a good character could support multiple stories. And now, you pitch a world because a world can support multiple characters and multiple stories across multiple media . . . World-making follows its own market logic. (Jenkins 2006: 114)

Although 'convergence anxiety' (McPherson 2008: 321) might suggest that this process sounds a death knell for 'TV as we know it', Tara McPherson argues that what has been dubbed 'quality TV' benefits from this industry shift (322). By resonating with the need for distinctive, compelling, high-concept products whose narrative world (and brand) can be quickly recognised within a multi-channel environment, and readily extended across media platforms, such 'quality popular television' (see Nelson 2007: 176–9 on *Life on Mars*) has become more appealing to broadcasters.

Life on Mars is arguably marked extra-textually and textually by these industry developments, despite the fact that at first glance it seems backward-looking, retro or nostalgic, as well as minimally merchandised or multi-platformed. For example, discourses of immersion and brand extension are written into the *Official Companion*, with co-author Guy Adams adopting a self-reflexive approach to pondering 'how to get into it, how to . . .

immerse myself. It needs that . . . to feel like an extension of the programme. Nobody wants this to be another boring "overview" style book' (Adams and Thompson 2006: 10). What the reader wants is, instead, supposedly a seamless extension of the *Life on Mars* brand (indeed, the *Companion* includes a series of fictional pieces recounting how its own authors find themselves caught up in the diegetic world of 1973). Likewise, this tie-in book demonstrates a keen awareness of how the show's uncertainty and narrative puzzles may drive online fan speculation: 'Is Sam in a coma? Has he gone back in time? The audience may never know the answer, but the question will send shivers down their spines (and will no doubt become a source of fevered debate on the net)' (ibid.: 162).

As already noted, co-creator Matthew Graham was obviously also highly aware of fan analysis and interpretation when he penned the test card girl's final scene (Graham 2007). As for the textual impact of 'new media' discourses of audience immersion and interactivity, these are connoted in a variety of ways through Sam Tyler's narrative predicament and his relationship to 'old media' such as television. Narratively, Sam is placed in exactly the position of the ideal, fantasised twenty-first-century audience member: that is, he is immersed in a highly distinctive, high-concept narrative world (1973 disrupted by uncanny media and messages from 2006). It is a virtual, hyperdiegetic space so vivid, so seemingly 'alive', that Sam Tyler ultimately chooses to live inside it rather than inhabit the drab noughties' reality that he is briefly returned to in episode 2.8. Like the participatory audiences metaphorically *'invited in'* (Johnson 2007: 63) to transmedia, multi-platformed narratives, Sam chooses proximity and participation in his very own hyperdiegesis.

The series repeatedly emphasises Sam's immersion in the world of 1973 by utilising a 360 degree camera pan around his figure, reminiscent of a videogame animation. Deployed when Tyler first finds himself seemingly thrown back in time, this 360 degree sweep follows an extreme close-up on his bewildered reaction which is tightly focused on his eyes (also being multiplied and reiterated in the series' title sequence). John Caughie argues that the close-up in *Edge of Darkness* (1985) – a political/police thriller in which fantastical, uncanny elements increasingly permeated the narrative – represents a way of conveying significance and intensity without spelling out what is actually going on (Caughie 2007: 95). By contrast, though *Life on Mars* makes some use of Sam Tyler's perplexed reaction shots in (extreme) close-up, it makes much greater use of sweeping, spiralling camera. Not only featured as Tyler first stands in 1973, a variant sweep also accompanies his decision in episode 1.1 to 'walk until I can't think up any more faces or streets'. As The Who's 'Baba O'Riley' is brought up on the soundtrack, the camera spins round a bustling 1973 Manchester street scene. This partly winks at the audience, saying 'Look how well the production team can do period detail', but it also indicates that Sam is immersed in a seamlessly constructed narrative world. Spiralling and whirling the camera around Sam Tyler also stresses how that world is literally and dynamically centred on him.

If the notion of audience immersion in a hyperdiegetic, expansive world is refracted through Sam's story (and styles of camera movement), then so too are discourses of interactivity such as personalised 'me-media' structured into *Life on Mars*. Sam's uncanny attempts to connect with the OU lecturer, and his witnessing of the sentient test card girl, are not only indications of monstrous, interstitial television. They also carry cultural fantasies of interactive media, and of television extending beyond and out of the box in the corner. Series two makes this set of connotations clearer, beginning with a scenario in which criminal Tony Crane (Marc Warren) can seemingly attack Sam in 2006 and affect his existence in 1973. Likewise, Sam discovers that he can interact with the telephone voice calling from Hyde 2612. These diegetic reconfigurations allow the series to move towards its conclusion, shifting the show's format up a gear, and further exaggerating possible interactions between 1973 and 2006. The pre-credits sequence to episode 2.1 shows a blurred 1970s police car on a modern medical monitor, while the as-then-unidentified Crane whistles a tune linked to seventies' comedy double-act Eric Morecambe and Ernie Wise, 'Bring Me Sunshine'. Later in the episode, Crane's indistinct figure seems to appear on a television set out in the street, with a reverse shot from Sam's point of view revealing this form as belonging to a rag and bone man. The 1970s appears to be bleeding into Sam's present-day existence and vice versa, but in a more tangible way than before, given that Crane has the power to physically hurt Sam Tyler. What Sam sees on his television has become more extensively interactive, threatening to permeate his world (for good and ill), though much like series one, this apparent media content remains targeted at him; a parody of so-called 'me-media' and personalised media consumption.

Interactivity is also referenced in an uncanny moment in episode 2.5. Here, Sam watches his colleagues investigate a case on television, sitting and gazing at Annie (Liz White). He reaches out to touch her, caressing the surface of the television screen, and we cut to Annie seeming to register the touch, reacting with puzzlement and mild concern. The touch-screen instant is a minor detail in the episode, not operating as part of any major narrative twist or development, but it does connote the noughties' high-tech whilst denoting yet another magical, strange extension of the televisual image within the show's diegesis. Violating classical diegetic space – as does the test card girl's switch-off at the end of 2.8 – this sequence does not, however, seem to be interpretable as an in-joke in the way that Matthew Graham has sought to contextualise the show's very final moments. Rather, it is readable as a textual incorporation of 'new media' discourses, using television diegetically as more than just a backward-looking, nostalgic apparatus (as does series two's citing of Eric and Ernie, along with the OU lecturer from series one and the test card girl). Metaphorically appropriating contemporary television discourses of hyperdiegetic immersion and interactivity, *Life on Mars* responds to 'convergence anxiety' by connoting new media technologies while denoting seventies televisual nostalgia. As such, its media depictions are no less complicated than its interrogation of seventies versus noughties policing (see Willis in this volume). Just as it invites a 'complex seeing' of the pros and cons of different eras of police work (Nelson 2007: 178–9), so *Life on Mars* provokes audience comparisons between seventies television and current industry discourses of immersion and interactivity. Locating telly within a historical period enables the series to convincingly portray it as an 'uncanny' technology; following the work of Jeffrey Sconce it can be argued that contemporary television tends to be culturally 'less than frightening or even fantastic' (2000: 126). *Life on Mars* both denotes now-historical fears of the medium-as-monster at the same time as connoting more positive, present-day fantasies of immersive television.

Ultimately, the series' resolution validates the messages that are passed to Sam via various media conduits, especially television. Though television may be recurrently interstitial in the show, crossing time zones and featuring figures that move across diegetic 'text' and 'reality', the medium is finally revealed not to be the monster (Carroll 1990), but rather the message that Sam Tyler heeds in order to attain a state of happiness, belonging and sheer aliveness. The promise of Sam's better, brighter life 'on mars', inside a real-seeming and sometimes *Sweeney*-esque fantasy of 1973, discursively corresponds to the promise that audiences can experience heightened emotion and aliveness through immersion in popular, quality television drama. Implicitly responding to 'convergence anxiety' (McPherson 2008), *Life on Mars* has its protagonist choose his own, immersive and interactive narrative world over life itself. The final message could not be any starker: ultimately, *Life on Mars* shifts from denotative representations of uncanny television to connotative discourses of contemporary television's value, affect and world-building brio.

REFERENCES

Adams, G. and Thompson, L. (2006). *Life on Mars: The Official Companion*, New York and London, Pocket Books.

Barthes, R. (1977). *Image–Music–Text*, London, Fontana Press.

Belam, M. (2007). 'The tardis and multiplatform', *currybetdotnet* [website], *http://www.currybet.net/cbet_blog/2007/09/the_tardis_and_multiplatform.php*, accessed 18 December 2008.

Carroll, N. (1990). *The Philosophy of Horror*, New York and London, Routledge.

Caughie, J. (2007). *BFI TV Classics: Edge of Darkness*, London, BFI Publishing.

Freud, S. (1990 [1919]). 'The uncanny', in *The Penguin Freud Library 14: Art and Literature*, London, Penguin, pp. 335–76.

Graham, M. (2007). '*Life on Mars*: the answers', *Manchester Evening News*, 11 April 2007 [online news resource], *http://blogs.manchesterevening news.co.uk/ianwylie/2007/04/life_on_mars_the_answers.html*, accessed 18 December 2008.

Hills, M. (2005). *The Pleasures of Horror*, London and New York, Continuum.

Jenkins, H. (2006). *Convergence Culture: Where Old and New Media Collide*, New York and London, New York University Press.

Johnson, C. (2005). *Telefantasy*, London, BFI Publishing.

Johnson, D. (2007). 'Inviting audiences in: the spatial reorganization of production and consumption in "TV III"', *New Review of Film and Television Studies*, 5, 1, 61–80.

McPherson, T. (2008). '"The end of TV as we know it": convergence anxiety, generic innovation, and the case of *24*', in Robert Kolker (ed.), *The Oxford Handbook of Film and Media Studies*, Oxford, Oxford University Press, pp. 306–26.

Nelson, R. (2007). *State of Play: Contemporary 'High-End' TV Drama*, Manchester and New York, Manchester University Press.

Sconce, J. (2000). *Haunted Media: Electronic Presence from Telegraphy to Television*, Durham, NC and London, Duke University Press.

Wheatley, H. (2006). *Gothic Television*, Manchester and New York, Manchester University Press.

9 CONSUMING RETROSEXUALITIES

THE PAST LIVE ON SCREEN, ONLINE NOW

Ruth McElroy

THIS ESSAY EXPLORES the interrelationship of gender, feminism and nostalgia in *Life on Mars*, paying particular attention to its online fans and their cultural practices. In doing so, it situates the drama within the context of UK popular culture and the contradictions that shape postfeminist media representations within it. The concept of retrosexuality holds particular purchase in this context because it ties together on-screen representations with both cultural practices and interpretative frameworks for comprehending the considerable changes to have taken place in gender relations since the seventies, when *Life on Mars* is (mostly) set.

Published four years after *Life on Mars* first aired, the following *Daily Telegraph* polemic on students' post-feminist sensibilities exemplifies how the programme has become shorthand for retrosexuality in contemporary British culture:

> The week's most depressing story has surely been that of The Tab, a Cambridge University student website, parading features on Cantabrian bra sizes and a 'Tab Totty' section in which undergraduates disport themselves in states of banally stereotypical disarray . . . Viewing these images, it is as if the world has regressed *Life on Mars*-style to a time when garages were littered with images of women posing on sports cars.

If journalists want to summarise the strange past of seventies Britain, a reference to *Life on Mars* does the job. Such references function as ways of speaking without specifying, since authors rarely name precisely which elements of this ironised past are being referred to, and which are being lamented for their passing. Moreover, the show's self-conscious invocation of the seventies – its ironic revisitation, best personified by the macho Gene Hunt – itself elicits an ironic discourse from reviewers and journalists. How is it that writing about a drama suffused with such heterosexual masculine swagger seems then to be so difficult to do straight? And what exactly is the appeal of retrosexuality on screen in a post-feminist media culture?

We may turn to two bodies of literature to help us find an answer. The first entails analyses of men's magazines and their relationship to changing masculinities. Critics have sought to unpick the relationship between such periodicals' representational strategies, their cultural politics and their reception by male readers (Jackson et al. 2001). The soft-porn photographic style common to lad magazines such as *Loaded* has drawn popular and academic criticism but some scholars have argued that:

> [w]ith its slippery ability to disclaim allegiances to particular political or critical positions, it functions to render identity ambiguous, and indeed, to retreat from the formation of stable meanings at the level of discourse. Irony is therefore a key player in the construction of the evasive magazine male. (Benwell 2004: 7)

Emerging in the nineties, such titles have been in the vanguard of irony's rise to prominence in popular culture. The ironist's agile sidestepping of political positions has thus been read as follows:

> [as] a self-conscious, adaptive strategy that keeps in place the status quo in the face of threats to masculine power from the consumerist imperative (e.g. the exhortation to men to 'feminize' themselves through the purchasing of grooming products) and the political values of feminism, which seek to radically deconstruct patriarchal versions of gender relations. (ibid.: 17)

It is this ironic mode of speech, littered with evasive phrases and invisible quotation marks, which links *Loaded* with Gene Hunt (Philip Glenister); as Glenister, 'recalls with a laugh, "Gene Hunt sees Alex Drake, thinks he wants to shag her brains out, but knows he never will"' (Glenister 2008).

The second body of work that helps situate these cultural trends is that undertaken by feminist scholars concerned to analyse the specific histories and rhetorics of post-feminism (McRobbie 2004, 2009; Gill 2007; Gillis et al. 2004; Whelehan 2000). Whilst women's magazines are prominent objects of study here too, so are other commercial forms including advertising (Gill 2008), television (Akass and McCabe 2004; Arthurs 2003; Lotz 2001; Moseley and Read 2002), marketing aimed at girls and children in general (Lamb and Brown 2006) and the broader sexualisation of culture that many critics, both academic and popular, see happening in contemporary consumer culture (Attwood 2009; McNair 2002; McRobbie 2009). Still, the term 'post-feminism' remains contested, especially in its relation to feminism. McRobbie argues that:

> Post-feminism refers to an active process whereby feminist gains of the 1970s and 1980s come to be undermined . . . [it] draws on and invokes feminism as that which can be taken into account, to suggest that equality is achieved, in order to install a whole new repertoire of meanings which emphasise it is no longer needed, it is a spent force. (2004: 255)

It is worth pausing to recall just how recent feminist gains have been in the UK and how much that is now taken for granted was established in the 1970s, including the Equal Pay Act (1970), the Sex Discrimination Act (1975) and the Domestic Violence Act (1976). It was just a year before Margaret Thatcher was elected the first female leader of the Conservative Party in 1975 that free contraception became available to women. However, listing such achievements risks concealing enduring inequalties and areas of feminist concern. For example, in 2009 the overall gender pay gap remained high at 22 per cent, and the inequality between the average incomes of women and men remains a core determinant of female poverty in the UK. Whilst access to contraception may be free, women in the UK, in contrast to many in Europe, have no legal right to abortion. Recognising that the sexual landscape has changed enormously, it is such realities which make the view that feminism's challenge has been resolved seem sociologically naive and ideologically bizarre.

FEMINIST ACCOUNTS

Both *Life on Mars* and *Ashes to Ashes* take feminism into account. Think, for example, of the advocacy on behalf of WPC Annie Cartwright (Liz White) by Sam Tyler (John Simm) in the face of Gene's Hunt's sexist hostility to her doing more than making cups of tea, or, in *Ashes to Ashes* episode 1.3, the fury of Alex Drake (Keeley Hawes) at Gene's insensitive treatment of Trixie (Claire Rushbrook), an alleged rape victim and a prostitute:

Gene: Raped? Who's she trying to kid?
Alex: Well they say it's difficult for rape victims to be believed!
  I wonder why?
Gene: She gets paid for having sex
Alex: It's not about sex, is it? It's about control, and power, and revenge.

Life on Mars and *Ashes to Ashes* both dramatise sexism, mainly by giving voice to it through the male characters. Rather than deny the realities of sexism, the series actively seek to re-animate the discourse of sexism and render it paradoxically both heroic and passé. In this, the audience is invited to share with a mix of horrified reaction and a wry, nostalgic smile. In general, it would appear that the series' writers share the conviction of lads' mags that sexism – and feminism – is a thing of the past, something to be recalled from the safe distance of an improved, if sanitised, present. It is important to emphasise this modality of remembering because it so obviously stands counter to contemporary realities. For example, if we look at contemporary debates on policing and prosecuting rape, we find a continuing pattern of patriarchal assumptions about women's sexual conduct, which may go some way towards explaining the poor conviction rates of this crime, 6.5 per cent in 2007–8, compared with 34 per cent for crime in general. Indeed, Alex's own disbelief in the world of 1981 – 'Where's the rape suite?', she asks Gene ahead of interviewing Trixie, '[i]s that with or without a mini bar?' he replies, dismissing the very notion of designated facilities and treatment protocols – finds its contemporary echo in the 2007 report by Her Majesty's Chief Inspectorate and Her Majesty's Crown Prosecution Service Inspectorate. This report found that many officers dealing with rape victims had 'very little training in responding to rape cases' and a 'lack of awareness' of the need to follow the relevant guidance' (Afua Hirsch, 'Rape conviction rates still very low', *Guardian*, 13 March 2009). The consequences of male violence are not a feminist issue done and dusted, but a live problem for contemporary British society and its police forces.

Women's police dramas have played a part in mainstreaming such feminist concerns. Deborah Jermyn's analysis of Lynda La Plante's work examines how '*Prime Suspect* takes up and interrogates motifs from the media's dissemination of "real-life" sex crime' (2003: 48). In their examination of *Silent Witness*, Heather Nunn and Anita Biressi argue that 'since the inception of television women have been frequently and voyeuristically presented as either the sexualised victims or perpetrators of crime' (2003: 193). They go on to note how during the eighties new series 'gradually altered the gendered terrain of representation' by introducing 'a variety of uniformed and plain-clothes women police officers whose lives operated in dialogue with contemporary isses including feminism, chauvinism, childcare, and the division between the public and private spheres of work and home, professional and emotional work' (2003: 194). Despite *Life on Mars*'s and *Ashes to Ashes*'s selective memory of seventies and eighties sexual politics, DI Drake was not alone as a TV female detective in the eighties. Indeed had Alex ever managed a quiet night in she might have watched one of several police dramas with women in the lead role. We might think here, for example, of Annie's namesake, the actress Anna Carteret, who took the lead as police inspector Kate Longton in the BBC's *Juliet Bravo* (1980–5), a series devised by the same man – Ian Kennedy Martin – who had created *The Sweeney*. Or we might consider DI Maggie Forbes (Jill Gascoine) in LWT's *The Gentle Touch* (1980–4) before later appearing in *C.A.T.S. Eyes* (TVS, 1985–7). Or from the USA, CBS's landmark *Cagney and Lacey* (1982–8) which placed a professional, female partnership at the heart of a prime-time television drama for the first time in that nation's television history, despite considerable initial network opposition to doing so. Much of *Cagney and Lacey*'s 'initial script material was modeled on the concerns of the early liberal women's movement in America, especially equal pay and sexual harassment at work' (D'Acci 1992: 171). Hence, whilst references to *The Sweeney* (ITV/Euston Films, 1975–8), *Miami Vice* (NBC, 1984–9) and *Moonlighting* (ABC, 1985–9) repeatedly appear in press reviews and DVD extras of *Life on Mars* and *Ashes to Ashes*, the history of women and of feminism in the female detective drama of the 1980s all but disappears. Contemporary feminism is thus made to seem not only redundant and anachronistic; it is itself denied a screen past. Alex Drake, unlike Sam Tyler, is a detective who is not only out of time but is outside television history.

RETROSEXUALITY: MASCULINE IRONIES AND POST-FEMINIST SENSIBILITIES

Retrosexuality acknowledges gender as a social category of difference, but it rarely deploys notions of justice and inequality as part of a coherent political force for change. Recent press coverage of the retrosexual almost consistently reads the term as a name for a male subject, most commonly figured as the opposite of the metrosexual icon of the late nineties, himself an inheritor of the eighties New Man. The retrosexual entails a disavowal of modern technology, a rejection of reflexive analysis of the self, a renewal of traits deemed traditionally masculine and a disavowal, when adopted by men, of those traits and practices deemed feminine. *The Sun*'s Derek Brown ('Are you a retrosexual?', 19 August 2008) puts it in characteristically jovial terms when he explains the retrosexual, 'never cries in public and thinks foreplay is a Coldplay tribute band. It's about shrugging off the nancy-boy image and getting back to being real men.'

Though less common, the term 'retrosexual' is also in use to describe women who adopt a retro femininity, embodied perhaps in the figures of British television cook, Nigella Lawson in her incarnation as the *Domestic Goddess*, or Bree Van der Kamp in *Desperate Housewives* (ABC, 2004–); as one poster to an online debating forum wrote:

> A retrosexual is (in the female case) that woman who eschews the sexual-revolution plank of feminism in favor of more-traditional values. Perhaps even 1950s values (this is not to say she goes as far as the cone-bra). A little burlesque, a little Betty Crocker, the retrosexual woman has new-fangled spunk and old-fashioned values . . . She may be, well, Sexless in the City, but only 'cause she chooses to be. (Anna Broadway, *http://www. urbandictionary.com/define.php?defid=873143&term=retrosexual*)

This online version is broader in its definition than the tabloid one above, but again entails the disavowal of the emphasis upon self-reflexivity (especially through the use of consumer goods); an emphasis upon normalising heterosexual relations as the basis for gender relations more broadly and a paradoxical relationship to the fifties, seventies and eighties (note the sixties do not figure). We can see here many of the post-feminist attributes that have been outlined by both Rosalind Gill (2007) and Angela McRobbie (2009).

They include an emphasis upon *choice* as the operation of a free and active subject unconstrained by limitations – either her own or those imposed by society; the nod to and rapid disavowal of feminism, here eschewed as an unappealing option in the ideas marketplace in favour of the 'do-it-yourself' stylisation of burlesque and Betty Crocker; a lifestylisation of the self articulated as a narrative of aesthetic and performative choices that all individuals are free, but obliged, to make. As Gill explains, this grammar of individualism insists on understanding women as 'entirely free agents' who in pleasing themselves, just happen to produce a resulting valued '"look" [that] is so similar – hairless body, slim waist, firm buttocks etc.' (2007: 154). In this infatuation with the self as a chosen assemblage, the social realm is relegated to a surmountable limitation of the past, of limits that may once have existed but are now passé.

This is not to say, however, that the past is dead and buried in contemporary sexual cultures. On the contrary, retrosexuality is a form of nostalgia that entails the playing out of fantasises of the past, often centred on ideas of tradition and the traditional. These are fantasies that focus upon gendered performances articulated through an aesthetic sensibility characteristic of contemporary consumer culture. In both the tabloid and online versions cited above, the communality and sociability of retrosexuality – its need for an audience of the like-minded re-memberers – is especially striking. Retrosexuality is one manifestation of post-feminism but it should be understood more broadly through its ambivalent, paradoxical relationship to the recent past. Retrosexuality is a self-conscious set of discourses, simultaneously aware, often melancholically so, of its distance from the past yet able to perform an intimate familiarity with its contours, its aesthetics and sensibility. In this, retrosexuality seems a clear-cut example of nostalgia; it possesses the nostalgic's sentimental longing for the lost past and, like nostalgia, may be seen as what Pickering and Keightley describe as 'a distorted public version of a historical period' (2006: 922). There are dangers in sweeping aside nostalgia as mere sentiment, overlooking how its specific contemporary manifestation may be understood as part of a wider shift in the uses of the past. Moreover, as Susannah Radstone argues, approaches based on denigrating nostalgia 'run the risk of overlooking the real or felt losses to which nostalgia may respond . . . as well as avoiding any analysis of the pleasures of nostalgia' (2007: 115).

One of the main ways in which the retrosexual text enters the world of *Life on Mars*'s and *Ashes to Ashes*'s viewers' discourse is through its ironic mode. Such texts not only rely upon but also elicit and sanction ironic discourse. This is evident in press coverage of the saga of *Life on Mars*'s American remake. Here's an example, by New York-based David Usborne, writing in the *Independent on Sunday* in May 2008:

In one memorable exchange, Simm's character calls Hunt an 'overweight, over-the-hill, nicotine-stained, borderline alcoholic homophobe with a superiority complex and an unhealthy obsession with male bonding'. Hunt responds: 'You make that sound like a bad thing.'

But will the US writers hold their nerve, and give Meaney all those socially insensitive lines? This is a country, after all, that only last week saw Barack Obama apologising for calling a female reporter 'sweetie'.

Outlining Gene's lack of restraint works well to highlight US writers' potential constraints (see Mills in this volume), yet Usborne implicitly dismisses naming a journalist 'sweetie' as an obvious over-reaction; no space is allowed for dissent. Time and again, the supposed constraints of contemporary 'innocent' speech are contrasted, implicitly and explicitly, with those of the liberated past personified by what the reviewer describes as the programme's 'gloriously politically incorrect one-liners'. Usbourne's own ironic discourse reinforces the view that words, and their political signification, should not be taken too seriously, an unlikely position for a print journalist to take, especially in the context of a black Democrat presidential candidate running against a former First Lady in a bid for the first non-white male White House.

Ashes to Ashes might have been the perfect opportunity to examine more fully the sexism of eighties society and the Met itself. However, often when this is undertaken, it looks remarkably like the soft porn images of the earlier decade. This may not seem like promising material for a female fan base. However, the remainder of this essay examines how these dramas' restrosexualties are created both materially and performatively by audience members watching together online.

THE 'ASHES 2 ASHES WRAP PARTY': POST-FEMINISM AND MEDIATED NOSTALGIA

The 'Ashes 2 Ashes Wrap Party – from 7 p.m. onwards until late' was an online (*Digital Spy*) gathering of 'all us Gene Genies' to mark the end of the second series in the UK in March 2008. The party organiser, Torchwood08, uses the discourse of offline or real-life parties, in creating the online invitation, including the following guidance to guests:

Dress Code: In the words of Gene; 'dress slutty':D
Alcohol: Red table wine, whiskey, as long as theres an alcohol proof

Intertextuality and irony are dominant discursive modes, as the post nods to the textual conventions of party invites and to the language and consumer conventions of the eighties as conjured by *Ashes to Ashes* on screen and in the minds and memories of its viewers. The analysis of fans' online message boards offers scholars a route into understanding how those invested in television programmes negotiate, establish and debate the show's meanings and value from within the parameters of everyday life (see Klein and Wardle 2008; Jenkins 2006; Mills, this volume). This is not to deny the textual nature of such postings, for as Hills (2002) argues, the Internet is not a 'transparent form of mediation', nor does it simply hold the 'essence [of fandom] up to the academic gaze' (175). In exploring the 'Ashes 2 Ashes Wrap Party', this essay seeks to understand how posters engage with the show's sexual politics in ways that traverse the cognitive, affective and performative aspect of television consumption. More broadly, the aim is to consider what post-feminist media culture, including the specific discourse of retorsexuality, demands and offers its participants, recognising, however, that this culture is never solely the product of dominant media institutions but is itself the product of a dynamic, often contradictory interaction between viewers, journalists, producers and other social actors.

At a time when there is a deal of speculation about television's future in a digital era and where it is anticipated that fewer and fewer people will watch television live on the box, it is strikingly television's liveness that endures here, albeit in a remediated online form. The relationship between television, as a mass medium, and liveness, as both a technological and ideological experience, has long been recognised as a key element in the history of how television became a domestic form with a privileged relationship to the spectator, and in particular women. This history helps situate current dressing for television when we consider how it was that television producers and advertisers sought to sell television as a distinct form. Magazines such as *House Beautiful* (1948) encouraged its female readership that 'looking at a television program is much like going to a movie', whilst advertisers commonly spoke of it as a 'family theater', 'a video theatre' or a 'chairside theatre' (Spigel 1992a: 12). Television was an occasion at home. Indeed, as Lynn Spigel argues, 'where film allowed spectators imaginatively to project themselves *into a scene*, television would give people the sense of being *on the scene* – it would simulate the entire experience of being at the theatre' (Spigel 1992b: 139).

One of the most striking aspects of the wrap party is the effort seemingly made by the online fans to dress for the occasion. For example:

> I will be here with my bright blue eyeshadow which I'm going to try tomorrow in honour of Alex :D. After the episode we should all blast the album and sing along :D' (Bubbles101, 26 March 2008, 8.47 p.m.)
>
> Yeah sounds great, I got my off the shoulder top in the washing machine now ready for tomorrow :D' (Torchwood 08, 26 March 2008, 8.48 p.m.)

Such a concern with dressing or, more accurately, costuming, for the final episode and for the online party vividly demonstrates how fans may participate in transforming television into a media ritual (see Couldry 2003) via the resources, both technological and cultural, of their own fandom. The notion of making something of what you're given suggested by the posters' creative uptake of costume design (whether or not dressmaking is literally undertaken, which we can never know) seems central not only to the performative pleasures of the occasion, but also to the nostalgia which suffuses the fans' interaction with the show. Adopting the garb of the eighties is a striking example of mediated nostalgia in the production and performance of contemporary social selves. The posts evidence significant performative effort in making a future event (the final episode) deliver the sensory and emotional pleasures of the past, for example, by offering the chance to wear old clothes and listen to old music. In her work on dressmaking in the fifties and sixties, Rachel Moseley interviewed women who exhibited 'pleasure of remembering the original desire and excitement which cherished garments provoked' (2001: 3). The capacity for fashion's materiality to elicit nostalgic feeling for a lost past is evident in the description of dressing the actors by *Life on Mars*'s costume designer, Emma Rosenthal:

> Fashion was expensive then. You didn't just pop down to New Look for a new outfit . . . I had three cousins and the clothes would pass down through them to my sister and then on to me. We wouldn't dream of doing that now. Everything's much more disposable. I have to say, though, I have developed a taste for the clothes . . . The amount of times I've said to my mates, 'I love that dress!' They just look at me like I'm bonkers. (Adams and Thompson 2006: 66)

Posters collaboratively and performatively engender their own media event through rituals of self-presentation (make-up and dress) more commonly found in 'real' social occasions. Will Brooker argues that 'some form of preparation ritual is not uncommon among media fans, and this often seems to approach an act of communion, a symbolic activity that removes the participant from the everyday and brings him or her closer to the fiction' (2007: 155). Memory, and its pleasures, suffuses these moments as posters, preparing for the future end-of-season episode, finding themselves looking back to detail their own past costumes, as well as their desires for and attempts to access them in the present:

> I used to have a lovely bat wing jumper, back in the days. I wore it whilst wearing orange eyeshadow from my Toyh [*sic*] make-up kit! (Yes, such a thing existed, and I had it for Xmas). My sister had a Gray Numan [*sic*] silver trilby, and a lovely Alex style perm. Would have be [*sic*] perfect for the party! (indecisive-one, 26 March 2008, 9.47 p.m.)

Such posts exemplify how 'intensive nostalgia-oriented documentation not only makes a past moment available in the future: it also . . . increases performativity, and turns the present into a process of direction and production of future-nostalgia' (Schwarz 2009: 359).

Part of the pleasure afforded by *Ashes to Ashes*'s retrosexuality thus appears to be intimately bound up with the pleasure of self-recollection as a dressed girl. In a post-feminist media culture, where the figure of the empowered, sexually active young woman looms large, this recollection of girlhood seems more innocent and self-contained. In *Ashes to Ashes*, however, the mother/daughter relationship is always highly charged. For example, in the first-series episode discussed above, the pre-title sequence includes the scene of Alex with her bottom in the air asking to be stamped by her Met colleagues, only to cut to an emotional exchange between Alex and her mother, who exclaims, 'Thank God the only thing my daughter shares with you is her name. I'd be ashamed if she grew up like you.' The feminist activist eighties mother here acts dramatically to repudiate her noughties post-feminist daughter. This dismissal of the daughter finds an echo in posters' own comments as when Shizuku responds to knickersofbolly's rhetorical question, 'How is Alex gonna get home to Molly now?' with the less than romantic, 'pfft, Molly can look after herself :p'. Given licence to cast the daughter's cumbersome needs to one side, knickersofbolly agrees, 'yes. Ide:ly Moly [*sic*] (little brat says nonchalantly, of I got a blackberry for my birthday ooh boo ho, spolied [*sic*] little missy!) and Evan can carry on while Alex stays in 1981 with the Lion.' The fans' attachment to the heterosexual romance of Alex's time travel is sufficiently strong to outweigh the maternal love Alex may have for her daughter. Moreover, it also contrasts with some posters' present realities and their adoptive heroic personae:

> I will be here, with my red wine! I won't be abl to dress slutty tho, as i will probably be covered n baby food and stuff! (D.I. Drake, 26 March 2008, 9.47 p.m.)

Alex's present homelife loses out to fans' fantasies for her *and* their romantic past with Gene. Rather than seeing this poster's reinvention as DI Drake and her present domestic realities simply as evidence of 'escape', such paradoxes seem to be the very reflexive material that constitutes the nostalgic pleasure of retrosexuality – and its critique. Certainly, fans share their critical recollections of the past and its representation on screen. For example:

> Funny, though, the men didn't seem much like Gene Hunt back in my bat-wing days though! (I was 14 in '81 and was old enough to notice them!). Oh if only, if only . . . he's what we'd have called a 'hunk' back then! Ha ha! (indecisive-one, 26 March 2008, 9.55 p.m.)

> Bak then I'd like one in this present time as well, probbaly [*sic*] why I'm lusting so much over Phil right now:D But I have always had a thing for older men (Torchwood08, 26 March 2008, 9.56 p.m.)

Ironic discourse of this kind is normally well received and seems to cement the fans' discursive community. However, there is one very striking instance in which such harmony breaks down. Whilst disagreements are well-documented aspects of fan cultures (see Hills 2002), what is striking here is that it is irony itself that provides the grounds for generational disagreement.

Debating the episode's ending, jen0607 writes:

> I do wonder if Scar-whathisface (rsh's character) will turn out to be like Frank Morgan though. Gene seems to think that he wants to close him down. Of course, Morgan wanted to get rid of him as well, and ultimately was able to return Sam to 2006 . . . just a thought!

For jen0607, Lord Scarman is purely a character in a televison fiction whose actions can be hypothesised over by fans eager to work out the next series' plot.

A few minutes later, the presumably ironically named fannymottquim replies, 'HAHAAHHAHAHAHAHAHAH – this is a joke yes?' Unlike jen0607, fannymottquim recognises Scarman as a historical figure, and reads his presence in the diegesis as evidence of the show's intertextual relationship with the past. Their misunderstanding continues when jen0607 edgily replies that her comments are not a joke, as she reads Scarman, and fannymottquim's comments, straight:

> No . . . the rest of the plotline is relatively similar. Therefore perhaps Geoffrey Rush's character (I really can't remember his name) will be similar to Frank Morgan and help her 'get rid of Hunt'. Just a thought. Glad I provided amusement though!

In response, fannymottquim responds:

> I guess you are probably quite young? Sorry to Laugh, I thought you were being ironic. – Lord Scarman is a real person – did some enquiries into policing in the early 80s after Brixton Riots or what not.

Whilst the posters at the party share a performative and cognitive pleasure in *Ashes to Ashes*'s nostalgic rendition of the eighties, the past that is commonly experienced is not commonly understood. Because so much of the fans' exchange is geared around the emotional, sensual and erotic pleasures of entering fantastically into the world of the show's diegesis, these differences seem often not to matter or even to surface at all. Indeed, the retrosexual pleasures of the eighties lie outside some posters' personal recollections: 'I want him him!!! I want him!!! Jeezo . . . I want her, I want her! I want it to be 1981!! Even though I was only 4!!!!', writes knickersofbolly, whilst Virtuous-dream posts back, 'I want 1981 and I didn't even exist then :D'. Retrosexual nostalgia need not be reducible to actual personal experience; fans' narcissism, understood as their use of media to project the self into the public realm (Ruddock 2007), can instead circumvent the limits of their own biography. However, without the cultural capital of eighties politics, jen0607 is temporarily lost, unable to get the joke from the inside. When the politics is extracted, what is left? Is it not revealing of *Ashes to Ashes*'s narrative limitations that such an ironic revisitation of the past can be so easily missed by an otherwise astute and careful viewer? Despite initial appearances, it seems that part of the pleasure of retrosexuality lies in the forgetting and the not-knowing the past. Such contradictory impulses to remember and forget, to re-create and to not know, might themselves be indicative of the very problem of history in post-feminist media culture.

REFERENCES

Adams, G. and Thompson, L. (2006). *Life on Mars: The Official Companion*, New York and London, Pocket Books.

Akass, K. and McCabe, J. (2004). *Reading Sex and the City*, London, I. B. Tauris.

Arthurs, J. (2003). '*Sex and the City* and consumer culture: remediating post-feminist drama', *Feminist Media Studies*, 3, 1, 83–98.

Attwood, F. (ed.) (2009). *Mainstreaming Sex: The Sexualization of Western Culture*, London, I. B. Tauris.

Benwell, B. (2004). 'Ironic discourse: masculinity in men's lifestyle magazines', *Men and Masculinities*, 7, 1, 3–21.

Brooker, W. (2007). 'A sort of homecoming: fan viewing and symbolic pilgrimage', in J. Gray, C. Sandvoss and C. L. Harrington (eds), *Fandom: Identities and Communities in a Mediated World*, New York: New York University Press, pp. 149–64.

Couldry, N. (2003). *Media Rituals: A Critical Approach*, London, Routledge.

D'Acci, J. (1992). 'Defining women: the case of *Cagney and Lacey*', in L. Spigel and D. Mann (eds), *Private Screenings: Television and the Female Consumer*, Minneapolis, University of Minnesota Press, pp. 169–201.

Gill, R. (2007). 'Postfeminist media culture: elements of a sensibility', *European Journal of Cultural Studies*, 10, 2, 147–66.

Gill, R. (2008). 'Empowerment/sexism: figuring female sexual agency in contemporary advertising', *Feminism & Psychology*, 18, 1, 35–60.

Gillis, S., Howie, G. and Munford, R. (eds) (2004). *Third Wave Feminism: A Critical Exploration*, London, Palgrave Macmillan.

Glenister, Philip, cited in C. McLean, '*Ashes to Ashes*: hot fuzz', *Daily Telegraph*, 26 January 2008 [online news resource], *http://www.telegraph.co.uk/culture/tvandradio/3670760/Ashes-to-Ashes-Hot-fuzz.html*, accessed 30 June 2010.

Hills, M. (2002). *Fan Cultures*, London, Routledge.

Hollows, J. (2003). 'Feeling like a domestic goddess: postfeminism and cooking', *European Journal of Cultural Studies*, 6, 2, 179–202.

Jackson, P., Stevenson, N. and Brooks, K. (2001). *Making Sense of Men's Magazines*, Cambridge, Polity.

Jenkins, H. (2006). *Fans, Bloggers and Gamers: Exploring Participatory Culture*, New York, New York University Press.

Jermyn, D. (2003). 'Women with a mission: Lynda La Plante, DCI Jane Tennison and the reconfiguration of TV crime drama', *International Journal of Cultural Studies*, 6, 1, 46–63.

Klein, B. and Wardle, C. (2008). '"These two are speaking Welsh on Channel 4!" Welsh representations and cultural tensions on Big Brother 7', *Television and New Media*, 9, 6, 514–30.

Lamb, S. and Brown, L. M. (2006). *Packaging Girlhood: Rescuing our Daughters from Marketers' Schemes*, New York, St Martin's Press.

Lotz, A. (2001). 'Postfeminist television criticism: rehabilitating critical terms and identifying postfeminist attributes', *Feminist Media Studies*, 1, 1, 105–21.

McNair, B. (2002). *Striptease Culture: Sex, Media and the Democratisation of Desire*, London, Routledge.

McRobbie, A. (2004). 'Post-feminism and popular culture', *Feminist Media Studies*, 4, 3, 255–64.

McRobbie, A. (2009). *The Aftermath of Feminism: Gender, Culture and Social Change*, London, Sage.

Moseley, R. (2001). 'Respectability sewn up: dressmaking and film star style in the fifties and sixties', *European Journal of Cultural Studies*, 4, 4, 473–90.

Moseley, R. and Read, J. (2002). 'Having it *Ally*: popular television and postfeminism', *Feminist Media Studies*, 2, 2, 231–50.

Nunn, H. and Biressi, A. (2003). '*Silent Witness*: detection, femininity and the post-mortem body', *Feminist Media Studies*, 3, 2, 193–206.

Pickering, M. and Keightley, E. (2006). 'The modalities of nostalgia', *Current Sociology*, 54, 6, 919–41.

Radstone, S. (2007). *The Sexual Politics of Time: Confession, Nostalgia, Memory*, London, Routledge.

Ruddock, A. (2007). *Investigating Audiences*, London: Sage.

Schwarz, O. (2009). 'Good young nostalgia: camera phones and technologies of self among Israeli youths', *Journal of Consumer Culture*, 9, 3, 348–76.

Spigel, L. (1992a). 'Installing the television set: popular discourses on television and domestic space, 1948–1955', in L. Spigel and D. Mann (eds), *Private Screenings: Television and the Female Consumer*, Minneapolis, University of Minnesota Press, pp. 3–39.

Spigel, L. (1992b). *Make Room for TV: Televison and the Family Ideal in Postwar America*, Chicago, University of Chicago Press.

Usborne, D. (2008). 'The Gene Genie gets a LA makeover', *Independent on Sunday*, 18 May 2008 [online news resource], *http://www.independent.co.uk/news/world/americas/the-gene-genie-gets-an-la-makeover-830371.html*, accessed 30 June 2010.

Whelehan, I. (2000). *Overloaded: Popular Culure and the Future of Feminism*, London, The Women's Press.

PART IV *LIFE ON MARS*
AS INTERNATIONAL TELEVISION

10 'AMERICAN REMAKE – SHUDDER'

ONLINE DEBATES ABOUT *LIFE ON MARS* AND 'BRITISH-NESS'

Brett Mills

THE AMERICAN REMAKE OF *Life on Mars* (ABC, 2008–9) offers an interesting case study for debates about the global marketplace for television and the ways in which texts adapt to the cultural surroundings which produce them. Such remakes demonstrate that there is an assumed relationship between culture and the society that produces it, and that that relationship is one based on the nation. That is, for it to be deemed worthwhile to produce a remake of *Life on Mars* for an American audience, it must be assumed that the British original will not, in some way, be read and enjoyed as much as a geographically specific version. Despite recent technological advances that foreground the international nature of media consumption (Hart 2004), and the growth of transnational productions (Chalaby 2005), the systems of television remain national, and remakes suggest that audiences define themselves and their consumption in this way too. The question can be asked, then: 'What needs to be done to the remake of *Life on Mars* for it to *become* American?'

This chapter examines such cultural specificity through the analysis of debates concerning the production of the remake on the discussion board of the *Life on Mars* and *Ashes to Ashes* (BBC 1, 2008–) fan website, *The Railway Arms*.[1] This forum has nearly 7,000 members, and contains more than 180,000 posts on over 4,000 topics. The section on *Life on Mars* is divided into four categories, with one devoted to the American remake. In this section the largest strand by far is called 'American remake – shudder',[2] which was begun on 4 April 2006 in response to the announcement that David E. Kelley had been put in charge of the proposed adaptation. The opening posting is from George_42 who, referring to the remake, asks, 'Is it just me or is this very wrong?' (7.08 p.m.). This posting, plus the thread's title, demonstrates the community's concern about the project, and the majority of the subsequent contributions query the rationale of the American version, worrying how it will affect the original version of which they are fans. This demonstrates how '[o]rganized fandom is, perhaps first and foremost, an institution of theory and criticism' (Jenkins 1992: 86). This chapter uses this thread in order to explore the discourses within which this debate exists, and the assumptions about national broadcasting systems employed to support arguments that are presented. In doing so, it aims to show how national specificity remains a key component of viewers' understanding of television programmes, as well as examining how such specificity is defined. The posts analysed here cover the period *before* the ABC version was broadcast, and therefore they show the *assumptions* fans and viewers bring to a series before seeing it, which, in turn, demonstrates the cultural categories through which this particular television series is understood by such viewers.

'IT IS VERY BRITISH'

The key component in posters' understanding of *Life on Mars* is its perceived representation of 'British-ness'. For these viewers one of the programme's pleasures is the ways in which it constructs a televisual version of Britain which is not only enjoyable but also convincing. This British-ness, as will be shown, rests on a number of the programme's representational strategies, and these are significant for they demonstrate not only how the British nation is understood, but the conventions that exist for representations of it. Tellingly, there is no dissent on the website concerning these ideas of British-ness; that is, while many historians and sociologists might repeatedly outline the complexities and contradictions that complicate a straightforward understanding of the British national identity (see, among others, Dalyell 1977; Nairn 1981; Ware 2007), for these posters this concept was one that was concrete and apparent. Indeed, it could be argued that, in order to enjoy *Life on Mars*, such an approach to British national identity needs to be adopted as the series draws on the tropes of British social realism that have been at the heart of national culture for decades (Lacey 1995; Caughie 2000). The coherence of understandings of British-ness is shown by this posting:

> It is VERY British, with a whole level, I think, that only works through a kind of cultural nostalgia which you can't hope to grasp if you're not British. Then there's a lot of surface stuff – the English police ranks, the slang, the music, the references – that might just be off-putting to a lot of American viewers. (Kata, 4 June 2007, 4.37 a.m.)

The 'cultural nostalgia' necessary to understand the programme is not outlined here, and is instead assumed. While Kata does not suggest that all British people would understand such cultural signifiers in the same way, it is telling that alternative understandings of British-ness are not acknowledged. Furthermore, the idea that the British *will* have the requisite cultural references to make sense of *Life on Mars* is demonstrated through the assumption that overseas viewers (in this case, American viewers) will *not* have such access. That is, a distinction between American cultural and national identity and its British counterpart is maintained, and an insistence on the *differences* between nations is central to the coherence of the national project.

The particular definition of British-ness on display here is concerned not solely with a 'cultural nostalgia', but also with location. As the poster Sydney argues, 'these shows . . . especially British cop shows . . . thrive precisely because of their setting' (26 April 2006, 1.24 a.m.). The word 'thrive' is telling in this instance, for it implies the programme has a representational strategy that is more than purely functional, and is instead a contributory factor towards the programme's meaning-making processes. For Sydney, the significance of location to police series is 'especially' important for British ones, which is telling considering American series such as the *CSI* franchise (CBS, 2000) foreground their location in their titles (Miami, New York). The significance applied by Sydney to location shows how it is possible to read programmes via their place or setting, and posters imply clearly that this is one of the intentions of *Life on Mars*. While the connotations and meanings of 'Manchester' are likely to differ between viewers, both within and outside the UK, it is clear that there is an assumption here that place is significant. That said, the majority of American posters acknowledged the British-ness of the series via its content and historical location, seeing British-ness as constructed through criteria less reliant on the specifics of Manchester, showing how location works within a complex regime of representations and cultural knowledge.

There is a telling relationship here between the regional and the national. As has often been noted, '[r]egional television drama' (Cooke 2005: 186) has been apparent in British culture since the inception of the medium, and was placed at the core of television output when ITV, and its regional structure, began in 1955 (Johnson and Turnock 2005). Yet the idea of 'the regional' is one with specific geographical peculiarities, in which 'the north', however defined, becomes synonymous with 'the regions'. For Caughie, British culture of the fifties and sixties foregrounded '"up North", where reality seemed to reside' (2000: 66), demonstrating the representational link that was forged between certain parts of the country and realism. Such links are, of course, highly problematic, for they not only sever any possible ties between social realism and other parts of the UK (the Midlands, the south-west and East Anglia, for example) but also work from an assumed norm which is south-eastern and London-centric in nature. The fact that the BBC's new production centre in Salford, which by 2012 will house its sport and children's departments, is named 'BBC North' shows how being outside of London must be geographically marked, for those centres based in London are referred to simply as 'the BBC' and not, as might seem appropriate, 'BBC South'. The north, therefore, has had a long-standing representational role in British culture, and it is one with a clear link to social realism and working-class representations (Russell 2004). The difficulties in offering such representations in a southern setting are shown by the outcry over *Ashes to Ashes* which, by being based in London, was seen not only to be incapable of offering the realist pleasures of *Life on Mars*, but seemed another indicator that 'the "national culture" [of the UK], in terms of both the mentalities and the institutions that form them, has always been largely constructed from within London' (Russell 2004: 8). Concern over the programme's shift to London is seen in the discussion thread 'Setting a Mistake?',[3] which contains a range of responses to the change; that said, the fact that the location of the series is deemed worthy of debate – and in need of justification – shows the extent to which viewers see setting as central to these programmes as a whole.

This centrality is also shown by the recurring debates in the postings concerning the setting of the American version of the series. For Loosefur, for example,

> Chicago would be a great place to set it. It's a great city and really reminded me of Manchester when I visited. It's got the same industrial heritage and subsequent decline, the same working class roots, huge musical influence and Chi-towners have the same friendliness and a great sense of humour that you find in Mancunians. Even architecturally there are similarities though Chicago goes one better than Manchester – it also has beaches! (26 April 2006, 2.40 p.m.)

The similarities between Manchester and Chicago are outlined here through a number of factors, which draw on the history, class, culture, industry and look of the two locations. For this poster the personality of these cities and the people who live there are a consequence of their histories, and this draws on the assumption that characters are 'affected or determined by *environment*' (Williams 1983 [1976]: 217) which, as Williams shows, is often at the heart of cultural forms which strive to be read as 'naturalistic', a term often viewed as 'interchangeable' (259) with realism. This idea is expressed clearly in the following posting, which argues that choosing the 'wrong' location necessarily destroys the ways in which the original series made the characters make 'sense':

> They've also *already* missed the point of the original by setting the US version in New York (like every other cop show, pretty much). Certainly part of the appeal for me of the British series was its Manchester setting. The setting also gives the character of Gene Hunt much of his foundation. I still think one of Hunt's most revealing speeches in the entire series came in only the second episode, where he says to Sam 'I love this city . . . the rest of the country doesn't give a thrupenny bit . . . ' (Hope I spelled that right). But what I'm getting at is, if you change the location to a huge major city you also change Gene. And that changes the show – significantly. (Creativemind, 15 April 2007, 8.29 p.m.)

In other postings, the relationship between the location, the programme's conceit and the characters' 'authenticity' are found within other
aspects of the series, such as the music (Smartypants, 17 August 2006,
3.32 a.m.) and, significantly, its evocation of previous British police series,
such as *The Sweeney* (ITV/Euston Films, 1975–8) (Mr Gerbil, 1 June 2006,
10.10 p.m.). Such factors draw on ideas of realism, making links between *Life
on Mars* and the wider cultural contexts of the period. The fact that such
depictions are presented by the series as historical ones mirrors the ways
in which, Russell argues, 'Much of the power of the northern, working-class
variant of Englishness is that it harks back to a supposedly safer, more certain,
less complex world and an unchanging North has its attractions' (2004: 269).
These postings suggest that such attractions become impossible once the programme moves from that northern English setting, as comparable ones are
assumed not to exist for contemporary American television.

'ANOTHER EXAMPLE OF US CULTURAL IMPERIALISM'

For many posters, the decision to make an American version of *Life on Mars*
is indicative of a lack of respect towards the specificity of culture, and this is
seen to have a number of negative consequences. The first of these concerned
America's perceived domination of the global cultural sphere, for:

> This is another example of US cultural imperialism that constantly wants
> to globalize the world and different cultures so everything is the same.
> (TonyW, 17 May 2008, 3.20 a.m.)

In postings such as these, the international trade in television programmes
and formats is seen as part of a wider process of cultural domination, one in
which America reigns supreme. After all, in none of the postings was there
evidence that anyone saw the selling of the *Life on Mars* format to American broadcasters as evidence either of the success of the British television
industry (Steemers 2004) or of cultural imperialism *from* Britain *to* America.
In these ways, the changes assumed to be wrought by the reworking of the
programme for an American market are seen to be of more significance, and
more powerful, than the British format which remains at the heart of the
series. Such statements can be seen as indicative of an ongoing contemporary
discourse in which the economic, political and cultural power of America is
repeatedly assumed to be of concern, and which equates globalisation with
Americanisation and cultural imperialism (McKay 1997; Campbell et al. 2004;
Tinic 2009). Such statements run throughout postings by British members
of the site, but take on an interesting inflection when American posters link
their national identity to these debates: 'I am proud to be an American but
I have to tell you ABC will butcher *Life On Mars*' (Kandykara, 4 June 2008,
6.19 a.m.). In linking together national identity and the television system that

will 'butcher' the programme, Kandykara places such remakes within the context of national identity, even though these could be perceived to be separate. That is, worrying about what ABC will do to *Life on Mars* need not necessarily require invoking a national context; instead the problems could be blamed on institutional or economic factors alone. The concerns such posters have over the remake are not purely about the differences between the UK and the USA; it is clearly also assumed that there's something about 'American-ness' which is itself in conflict with what it is that defines *Life on Mars* for these posters.

A recurring worry in the postings is that the realism associated with the British series will be lost because of the ways in which American television is assumed to represent characters:

> What makes LoM so special is that it feels so real, the characters are believable because they are ordinary. What worries me most is the casting. There is too much emphasis on the image of a show – by that I mean, casting impossibly beautiful people. Hollywood is image obsessed – there is no-one who looks normal – a lot of the women are stick thin, the men are buffed to perfection. *Life On Mars* is gritty and realistic – I would hate to see someone who looks like Brad Pitt or Paris Hilton cast in the re-make – it would destroy all credibility. (V23474, 22 August 2006, 10.30 a.m.)

It is worth noting the specificity of the term 'image' here. As noted above, the 'look' of the series, especially in terms of its northern English setting, is seen to be highly important to the meaning of the series; in maligning 'too much emphasis on the image of the show', V23474 is presumably referring to a notion of glossy, expensive, good-looking television which has been commonly referred to as 'quality television' (Jancovich and Lyons 2003; McCabe and Akass 2007). Such 'quality' television is associated in particular with American broadcasting, and is seen here as emblematic of the differences between British television and that in the USA. In this way an emphasis on imagery returns to notions of realism which, as noted earlier, are central to the pleasures of *Life on Mars*. Like V23474, Drunk Lawyer valorises 'ordinary people' because it gives the programme a 'human touch' (12 June 2008, 6.31 p.m.); this means that 'ordinary', 'human' and 'realistic' are placed in opposition to 'impossible' beauty, positioning such depictions as unrealistic precisely because they are unattainable by 'ordinary' people. Of course, recent American television series, such as *The Sopranos* (HBO, 1999–2007) and *Deadwood* (HBO, 2004–6), have deliberately not cast actors who conform to the standard definitions of televisual beauty, and have consequently been lauded for their 'realism'. Yet such production processes are ignored here, and instead American television is understood to be an industry obsessed with the beauty of its cast. Indeed, posters' initial responses to Jason O'Mara's casting as Sam Tyler in the American version of *Life on Mars* criticised him for being 'too physically imposing' (inustar, 28 June 2008, 1.12 a.m.) and 'simply too big' (Drunk Lawyer, 21 June 2008, 11.50 a.m.), suggesting one of the attractions of John Simm as an actor is that he does not conform to the physical norms of actors in leading roles in television, and O'Mara suitability is therefore measured against the Simm original.

Similar generalisations about American television run throughout the postings, and demonstrate the assumptions viewers bring to texts before they encounter them. As Caughie notes, British television exists within 'a hierarchy of values in which art and quality were made in Europe and entertainment was American' (2000: 71), even though this now coexists alongside American 'Quality Television' commonly associated with HBO (Leverette, Ott and Buckley 2008). It is therefore unsurprising that Tarkers advises viewers to 'Expect 20 minute long shootouts/car chases with plenty of explosions' (12 April 2007, 10.55 p.m.) and moves on to express concern about whether the ending of the American version will match the bleakness of the British one. Indeed, for many posters American network television appears to be a place in which standards of decency and the prevalence of the 'happy ending' are assumed, and this is seen to have significant consequences for the tone and content of the programme as a whole. A number of posters insist that American values such as optimism and personal development run counter to the atmosphere of the programme, and DCI Haskins expresses this clearly in his prediction of the American version of the opening title's voiceover:

> I have this nightmare vision of him saying: 'My name is Sam Tyler, I had an accident and I woke up in 1973. Am I mad, in a coma or back in time? . . . But whatever I'm finding it a really positive experience and I'm growing as a person because of it'. The thought of a happy clappy Sam in 1973 actually makes me feel physically sick! In other words, all the angst and pathos that for me, as a morose Brit, made the show so touching and special will disappear . . . and that just wouldn't be *Life On Mars*. (10 August 2007, 9.39 a.m.)

That said, a number of posters did argue that the cultural politics so central to the British version of *Life on Mars* could easily be translated to America, and that therefore the programme could still fulfil the same cross-generational analysis that lies at the heart of the series. For Sandiesg, 'The American LOM might very well and will hopefully reflect the real spirit of the time' (12 August 2007, 7.49 p.m.) through contrasting the contemporary George Bush era with issues such as the Vietnam war, race riots, and the assassinations of Robert Kennedy and Martin Luther King, to explore social and cultural changes in a manner parallel to that in the original series.

Such descriptions of the American series demonstrate that while Britishness and American-ness are seen to be different in terms of representational strategies and television conventions, the ways in which each society has changed over the last three decades means that it is seen that it will be possible to adapt one of the key narrative components of the programme. It is through the exploration of events such as Watergate and the Vietnam war, and the shot of the World Trade Center in the opening episode, that the American version can be seen to be truly American; that is, more than simply a remake of the British original. In that sense, such posters remain wedded to the notion of national specificity, for they insist that the only way in which the American version can be valuable is if it manages to exploit its American-ness in order to examine and explore those things particular to American history.

It should also be noted, however, that there was some resistance to the notion of national identity being presented on the site. After a number of postings criticising American television and American culture, Sydney responds with,

> There's a distinct difference between America and Hollywood; the latter just happens to be located within the former. As a cousin, I'd appreciate it if folks would keep those distinctions in mind. 'America' didn't do a remake of 'Wicker Man'. Hollywood did. 'America' isn't planning a remake of *Life on Mars*. Hollywood is. (17 November 2006, 8.51 p.m.)

In such a statement we see a more complex notion of national identity, and a viewer seemingly at odds with the cultural industries that are associated with his country. For this poster, the culture which is made by 'Hollywood' is itself not representative of the majority of the American population, and must be understood as the product of a particular community with specific aims. Such resistance to the overarching discourse of nation is rare, however, and, in acknowledging the distinction between 'Hollywood' and 'America', still assumes that there is something meaningful which can be termed 'America'. This means that while these postings outline the difficulties in defining 'America', 'British-ness', conversely, remains relatively unexplored, precisely because *Life on Mars* is assumed to express that cultural specificity so well.

'WHAT'S TO LOSE?'

Such debates over the ways in which national characteristics can be understood demonstrate the social role played by television, and the ways in which viewers understand their own identities through the television which is made for them. That is, concerns over the loss of 'British-ness' in the American remake of *Life on Mars* are predicated on notions of cultural identity as much as they are on issues of aesthetics and quality. After all, the 'original' series will still exist no matter how much the American remake differs from it, which begs the question as to why it is that these posters become so irate over differences between the two. In relating these to issues of globalisation, some posters clearly see such changes as indicative of a loss of other kinds of culture; that is, a dilution of the 'British-ness' perceived to be at the heart of the pleasures offered by the original. Running through such postings, then, are expressions of these viewers' relationship with the programme, which are meaningful and heartfelt. Changes that might exist within the American remake are, then, not of concern solely because this affects the text; they also reiterate issues of ownership over the programme, in which the industrial nature of broadcasting is inevitably more powerful than the 'powerless elite' (Tulloch and Jenkins 1995: 55) whose 'viewer mastery' (Jenkins 2006: 115) is ignored by the programme makers. Hills places fan activity as negotiating between 'consumerism and "resistance"' (2002: 27), and this example shows how any joy at the continued production of a fan's object of desire is mitigated by this activity's demonstration of the fan's lack of power.

Some of the posters acknowledge that their responses to a remake will be negative regardless of the quality of the programme, precisely because of their relationship to the British series. As Kata notes:

> Even if it's a good adaptation I very much doubt any of our loyalties will transfer because we already think so highly of the original – it would be impossible for the American version to beat that on its own ground. But if its [*sic*] good there'll be some people who didn't like the original who DO like the new version – Americans maybe who didn't get past the Mancunian-ness of the original, or people who prefer the American scale of storytelling, or who find it more interesting or exciting . . . I really hope we get another good show. What's to lose? (28 February 2008, 3.43 a.m.)

In a similar vein, Acquitaine 33 states that 'The more we adore LOM the less we are comfortable with a copy' (16 May 2008, 10.01 p.m.), making clear the presumed link between originality and authenticity. Such self-awareness of the discourses of fan behaviour is the opposite of the majority of the postings, which conform to what Hills calls the 'strikingly *self-absent*' (2002: 7, italics in original) approaches adopted in many fan discourses. While this absence is normally thought about in terms of the fan's relationship to the text, this chapter has shown that broader social and cultural contexts also need to be taken into account. Difficulties in defining 'British-ness' are sidestepped, suggesting that *Life on Mars* is highly successful in adopting the realist representational strategies which such viewers see as emblematic of British television, especially in comparison to its American counterpart. Anderson suggests nations are 'imagined communities' (1983) whose membership is limited and defined, even though those members must imagine their coherence because the size of nations means that no one will ever know the majority of their fellow citizens. Fan forums, such as *The Railway Arms*, offer similarly imagined communities, whose members similarly never meet, even if they are able to communicate with one another. And just as nations rest on assumptions about ways of living, rights and wrongs, and a sense of national identity, so fan communities similarly draw on assumed discourses whose power rests precisely on them remaining unsaid.

Some of the posters here do see beyond national boundaries; Joaniedutch, for example, argues that 'The beauty of LOM is that it has brought together all nationalities. I have met some fab people from the UK, US and Europe' (11 June 2008, 4.46 p.m.). While it might be churlish to point out that the three continents mentioned here certainly don't include 'all nationalities', the major point is that the fan community remains inflected through a national prism, even if it has the possibility of demonstrating what such nations have in common rather than what divides them. The American remake of *Life on Mars* remains a useful case study, then, for demonstrating how television remains understood within national contexts, against all the odds of globalisation. The place where television is made, as well as what it is seen to say about that place, continue to be central to the meanings and pleasures on offer from broadcasting, and viewers appear to define themselves in relation to this. Yet this is also complicated by the ways in which fans situate themselves in relation to 'their' texts and the pleasures which can be gained from displeasure and disgust at 'wrong' production decisions that are being made. This means that *The Railway Arms* remains a place in which fans acknowledge their freedom to complain about the American version of the programme; indeed, that seems to be one of the reasons for the forum to exist, and a role that some of the posters take delight in playing out. The thread analysed here is one with the word 'shudder' in the title, and it is telling how often posters use that word, or others which signal a physical response of displeasure and disgust; that is, such posters are keen to demonstrate that a 'bad' version of *Life on Mars* is something which *affects* them, causing harm in ways that are manifested physically. Yet how much of this is play, a revelling in a 'performance' (Hills 2002: 41) of fandom? This posting from Ducky One helpfully shows that while fans may be shuddering at the horrors of *Life on Mars US*, there is fun, and superiority, and capital to be had in joining in the criticism:

> No, no, a thousand times no. Shudder is the exact feeling that comes over me whenever I think of this. Please don't make me give up my contempt for the remake. The American version will have its own fans and it's [*sic*] own websites. If we can't feel superior here, where can we? (9 July 2007, 1.07 a.m.)

NOTES

1   *http://domeofstars.com/forum/*.
2   *http://domeofstars.com/forum/index.php?topic=2892.0.*
3   *http://domeofstars.com/forum/index.php?topic=2601.0.*

REFERENCES

Anderson, B. (1983). *Imagined Communities: Reflections on the Origin and Spread of Nationalism*, London and New York, Verso.

Campbell, N., Davies, J. and McKay, G. (eds) (2004). *Issues in Americanization and Culture*, Edinburgh, Edinburgh University Press.

Caughie, J. (2000). *Television Drama: Realism, Modernism, and British Culture*, Oxford, Oxford University Press.

Chalaby, J. K. (ed.) (2005). *Transnational Television Worldwide: Towards a New Media Order*, London, I.B. Tauris.

Cooke, L. (2005). 'The new social realism of *Clocking Off*', in J. Bignell and S. Lacey (eds), *Popular Television Drama: Critical Perspectives*, Manchester, Manchester University Press, pp. 183–97.

Dalyell, T. (1977). *Devolution: the End of Britain?*, London, Cape.

Hart, J. A. (2004). *Technology, Television and Competition: The Politics of Digital TV*, Cambridge, Cambridge University Press.

Hills, M. (2002). *Fan Cultures*, London and New York, Routledge.

Jancovich, M. and Lyons, J. (eds) (2003). *Quality Popular Television: Cult TV, the Industry and the Fans*, London, British Film Institute.

Jenkins, H. (1992). *Textual Poachers: Television Fans and Participatory Culture*, New York and London, Routledge.

Jenkins, H. (2006). *Fans, Bloggers and Gamers: Exploring Participatory Culture*, New York and London, New York University Press.

Johnson, C. and Turnock, R. (eds) (2005). *ITV Cultures: Independent Television over Fifty Years*, Maidenhead, Open University Press.

Lacey, S. (1995). *British Realist Theatre: The New Wave in its Context, 1956–1965*, London and New York, Routledge.

Leverette, M., Ott, B. L. and Buckley, C. L. (eds) (2008). *It's Not TV: Watching HBO in the Post-television Era*, New York and London, Routledge.

McCabe, J. and Akass, K. (eds) (2007). *Quality TV: Contemporary American Television and Beyond*, London, I. B. Tauris.

McKay, G. (ed.) (1997). *Yankee Go Home (and Take Me With U): Americanization and Popular Culture*, Sheffield, Sheffield Academic Press.

Nairn, T. (1981). *The Break-up of Britain: Crisis and Neo-nationalism*, London, Verso.

Russell, D. (2004). *Looking North: Northern England and the National Imagination*, Manchester, Manchester University Press.

Steemers, J. (2004). *Selling Television: British Television in the Global Marketplace*, London, British Film Institute.

Tinic, S. (2009). '*Life on Mars* as seen from the United States: the cultural politics of imports and adaptations', *FlowTV* [website], *http://flowtv.org/?p=3241*, accessed 24 May 2010.

Tulloch, J. and Jenkins, H. (1995). *Science Fiction Audiences: Watching Doctor Who and Star Trek*, London, Routledge.

Various (2006). *The Railway Arms: Life on Mars/Ashes to Ashes Forums* [web forum], *http://domeofstars.com/forum/*, accessed 10 June 2010.

Ware, V. (2007). *Who Cares About Britishness?: A Global View of the National Identity Debate*, London, Arcadia.

Williams, R. (1983 [1976]). *Keywords: A Vocabulary of Culture and Society*, London, Fontana.

11 | THE EMIGRATION OF *LIFE ON MARS*
SAM AND GENE DO AMERICA

David Lavery

> We were part of what felt like a very special show, a different show,
> kinda mad, a bit groundbreaking, a bit different, a bit science fiction,
> a gritty drama, you know, something different.
> (Glenister 2007)

JUST BEFORE THE AMERICAN VERSION of *Life on Mars* returned to ABC after a two-month turn-of-the-year hiatus on 28 January 2009 (an episode entitled 'Take a Look at the Lawman', episode 1.9), relocated to Wednesday nights, newly paired with *Lost* (ABC, 2004–10), the network aired an ad that sought to make a connection between the two inscrutable series. Both, we were told, are about being 'lost' on a mysterious island, and indeed Manhattan is inexplicable for Sam Tyler, enigmatically time-displaced there in 1973 from his customary 2008. The hope was that the success of *Lost* would help support the US version of *Life on Mars*. The linkage failed. *Life on Mars US* would lose a sizeable chunk of the *Lost*-earned audience.

Lost and *Life on Mars US*'s mysteries were, of course, hardly comparable. At the end of season four, *Lost*'s inexplicable South Pacific island had been moved, not by network suits hoping to find a more conducive time slot for a problematic show, but by turning a 'Frozen Donkey Wheel', drawing on the time-dislocating power of 'exotic matter' to unseat its temporal location. Sure of itself with a two-year commitment from ABC and a May 2010 end date locked down, *Lost* had, brazenly, confidently, come out of the science fiction closet.

Life on Mars US, on the other hand, seemed utterly uncertain about its identity, beyond being a cop show set in the seventies with a confused hero from our own day. *Life on Mars*, of course, had encouraged speculation about its generic allegiances, inviting its substantial viewership to join its hero in getting to the bottom of his central mystery and, in the end, for the most part resolving it: he had been in a coma in the present. Why, exactly, he ended up back with Gene, Annie, Ray and Chris post-suicide, embarking, as the last shot seemed to suggest, on more adventures (never to be televised), at least until the test card girl turned off the set – that remained unfathomable. The ultimate fate of the US version of *Life on Mars* was out of the hands of its creative team. In a time of 'desperate networks' (Carter 2006), it would be ABC, not a mysterious televisual entity who runs the streets of an afterlife Manchester, that would pull the plug, cancelling the series in early March 2009, announcing that the final episode, its seventeenth, would air on April Fool's Day. The decision surprised no one. Signs of brain activity had been minimal for some time.

In an essay about *Lost* written for an MIT Press book about 'vast narratives', I began my reflections by considering, by way of contrast, *Life on Mars* and, in particular, a pivotal scene in the pilot episode:

> Strolling alongside 'CID Girl' Annie Cartwright, the only one in the past to whom he has confessed his 'true' situation, Sam insists that a 'mind can only invent so much detail' and announces his intention to walk – following the 'Yellow Brick Road' – until he 'can't think up any more faces or streets,' until he escapes the 'madness' in which he finds himself. (Lavery 2009: 313)

Sam never did walk out of the cave, as I went on to explain, though he did jump to his death off the roof of the Manchester police department. His existence 'in a world of the past that, as the opening voiceover of each episode tells us, might as well be "another planet"', was, I noted 'full of cracks – the Test Card Girl's performances, the many messages from radios and televisions [and telephones] that bombard him from his supposed future, his uncanny encounters with his mother, his father, and himself as a child – through which he [could] glimpse the nature of his delusion' (ibid.).

Comparing *Life on Mars* UK to *Lost*, I found both series 'richly intertextual, open-ended, serialized, enigmatic myster[ies] that may or may not be science fiction',[1] but noted that the original *Life on Mars* would never be a vast narrative: 'The narrative skein, the "yellow brick road," of *Life on Mars* will not be long enough for Sam to outpace illusion or, in what amounts to the same perturbation, for the writing team of Matthew Graham, Ashley Pharoah, and Tony Jordan to exhaust their powers of invention' (ibid.). When I wrote those words I had no idea, of course, that *Life on Mars* would make the Atlantic crossing, emigrating from Manchester (and BBC Wales) to New York (and ABC).

The pre-production of the American re-imagining – new creative team, new cast members, relocation to New York – smelled like failure before it aired. It's not called 'development hell' without reason. Series that undergo dislocations in place, setting and creative teams seldom turn out well. The pilot turned out well enough though. When *Life on Mars US* debuted on 9 September 2008, it achieved viewing figures of over 11 million. Irish actor Jason O'Mara was just fine as Sam Tyler (though John Simm's original is impossible to surpass). Jonathan Murphy's Chris Skelton was a bit sweeter, and a lot more handsome, than Marshall Lancaster's, and Ray Carling – Michael Imperioli (*The Sopranos*'s (HBO, 1999–2007) Christopher Moltisanti) – was a smarter and sharper, though still repulsively sexist, nemesis for Sam than Dean Andrews's dim bulb. Gretchen Mol's Annie – now blonde, sexy and Norris rather than brunette, adorable and Cartwright – brought about a noticeable alteration in the Sam/Liz White/Annie dynamic but was certainly an acceptable alternative. Harvey Keitel as Gene Hunt was the biggest disappointment. He was supposed to be a casting coup: a major movie actor in his first series television role, but he was old, tired, anything-but-larger than life, and the pilot's weakest link, a pale imitation of the unforgettable 'Gene Genie' Philip Glenister, not half as clever and with little physical presence. It was almost as if Manchester Gene was a quarter of a century younger than New York Gene.

From the opening sequence – complete with the franchise signature spinning wheel cover shot – to Sam's attempt to outwalk his illusions, the episode frequently re-enacted *Life on Mars*'s UK maiden voyage. The musical choices and the period look both worked well. Especially memorable: Sam's gobsmacked reaction when, just after he wakes up in 1973, he turns to see the towers of the World Trade Center still standing. As the series progressed in the weeks to follow, the ratings declined, and the initial optimism – US fans of the BBC version wanted to root for the show – came to be seen increasingly as wishful thinking.

Writing for the Onion TV Club, one of a variety of 'snarky' (that is, snide and cynical) fan-scholar sites now providing intelligent television commentary on the web,[2] *Life on Mars US*'s chronicler Zach Handlin had the following to say about 'Let all the Children Boogie' (1.10), an episode in which Sam investigates a missing glam rock enthusiast who may have been abducted by a flying saucer in New Jersey's Meadowlands:

> Boo, I say. And boo I say again. There was no point to any of this; the Case Of The Disappearing Groupie never rose above mild diversion levels (turns out the 'UFO' was an experimental helicopter whose thrust actually pushed [the victim] down into the muck, where she drowned; so there's no aliens and no murderer), and we didn't even get *those scant hand-ful of weird moments that I try and cling to keep myself interested* . . .
> (Handlin 2009a, my italics)

All perfectly justifiable complaints about a lame, utterly forgettable hour, especially the observation that *Life on Mars US* seemed increasingly to have given up on its mythos/mystery – Handlin's enticing 'weird moments' – in favour of attention to the world of 1973. As Handlin goes on to say: 'Hell, they've even gotten lazy about the nature of Sam's reality; we spent lengthy time with both Chris and Annie outside of Sam's presence, which means if this is a hallucination, it's got a long reach.'

Back when *Life on Mars*'s US pilot originally aired, the observant Handlin had already identified a core distinction in the narratological approach of the two series: 'Everything feels rushed, scenes and actors arriving at conclusions without bothering to think through them first . . . Right now, everybody seems to be running for the end credits.' Ironic, is it not, that the American version, with an extended duration of narrative time at its disposal, at least potentially, operated in haste, while *Life on Mars* UK, its days numbered from day one, advanced deliberately, systematically towards its end?

That *Life on Mars US* lost its way may not have been solely due to its creative team. We know from a *Futon Critic* interview with decidedly profane executive producer Josh Appelbaum, who insists he knows exactly where his show is going and even the series' final moments, that the American version was supposed to have a very different mythology – one more conducive to the duration of an American series:

> In the BBC version he was always in a coma and you pretty much knew that from [the beginning] and that was sort of, the audience could be playing around with different theories, [but] it was relatively clear that that's what it was. They were doing 16 episodes, that's what it was. Our mythology is completely different with the kind blessing of the BBC people. They encouraged us to change the mythology. It's great for episodes, it's not so great for 116 episodes – that the whole thing is a dream sequence.[3] (Sullivan, 2008b)

With ratings down in the first new season after the strike by the Writers Guild of America, with American network television still trying to find its way in a multi-platform 'convergence culture' (Jenkins 2006), top-down micromanagement of shows evidently become standard operating procedure, especially in the case of the new and still-unproven. In its first year, ABC had sought to curtail *Lost*'s sci-finess, afraid that esoteric weirdness might prematurely kill their exoteric, mainstream cash cow (Porter and Lavery 2007: 28–31). Will we eventually learn that after seeking out and taking on a high-concept British series with proven appeal that ABC had sought to rein in its very uniqueness?

Whatever the reason, *Life on Mars US* never succeeded in balancing Sam's dual existence in the twentieth and twenty-first centuries. It gave us a somewhat interesting, reasonably believable 1973 and a likeable 2008 hero entrapped there, but it did not move narratively back and forth between the two with any degree of conviction or imagination. If the fantastic aspects of

Life on Mars UK's narratives were not properly foregrounded, neither was its memorable non-PCness. *Life on Mars US* gave us severed heads, grisly crime scenes, some sex, and a lot of male chauvinism (Annie's in-house nickname, thanks to Ray is 'No Nuts'), but the 'in-your-face, true-to-the-era' sexism and racism of the original was toned down. (The series offered substantially tamer challenges to political correctness than its contemporary basic cable time-travel show *Mad Men* (AMC, 2007–), set in the early sixties.) Nor was its humour as profane as that of the UK original. In the fourth episode of the after-the-watershed *Life on Mars* UK, Gene and Sam force their way into the office of Manchester mobster Stephen Warren, where they find him fellating a young man. 'How dare you come in here!' Warren growls angrily. 'You could have said that to the boy', Gene replies. We never heard such an obscenely witty double entendre on *Life on Mars US*, even though network standards would likely, obliviously, have let it pass.

In February, two-thirds of the way through *Life on Mars US*'s run, the episode entitled 'Home is Where You Hang Your Holster' (1.11) seemed to indicate that the series might not be brain dead after all. The Annie/Ray gender clash and the introduction of Ray's wife were exceptionally well done, showing a significant deepening of Annie's character and revealing Ray to be even more of a creep than we had believed. Annie gets the last word, challenging her sexist pig colleague with the telling question: 'Why are you so afraid of me?' Most interesting of all, however, was the revelation – in the teaser no less – that someone else in 1973 New York, a quite progressive city councilman, claims to be from the present – from Barack Obama's America. ('He won?' Sam responds to the news from 2009, his time trip having begun in 2008 of course.) Councilman Green has more of an idea how, after a blow to the head, he ended up in the past than Sam or the audience does, but he is murdered before Sam can find out what he means.[4] Was the introduction of this new mystery a hint of the totally different mythos *Life on Mars US*'s makers claimed to be governed by?

Two weeks later ABC cancelled *Life on Mars US*, and the only suspense left was the question of how Appelbaum and company would resolve the mystery of Sam Tyler. Alas, 'Life is a Rock' (1.17) may well go down as one of the worst series finales of all time. In its last five minutes, we learn that Sam has in fact been an astronaut in suspended animation on a mission to Mars in 2035 (the 'creative team' having taken the title a bit too literally) during which he has been subject to a Philip K. Dick-tye neural stimulation programme that had him dreaming he was a 1970s cop (after something has gone haywire with the 2008 cop programme). His crewmates are, of course, Ray, Chris and Annie. Windy – his hippie neighbour in the series – was, in reality, the spaceship's computer. ('And you were there, and you, and you!') The mission they are on is research into DNA – a 'gene hunt' so to speak – and the Keitel Gene Hunt turns out to be . . . Sam's father, aka 'Major Tom'! Now awake as they approach Mars, 'Tom' and Sam, father and son, decide they don't want to fight any more.

The already sceptical Zach Handlin spoke for many when he wrote of the finale: 'I didn't think it was possible, but the *Mars* people managed to somehow find whatever small speck of investment I had in the series and beat it to death in about ten minutes.' He continued: '[t]oo unconventional to attract a mainstream audience, too heavy-handed and clichéd to earn much of a cult following' (Handlin 2009b), *Life on Mars US* was over, having reduced its creative narrative to a highly unimaginative, literal one. It would have been better, much better, never to have begun.

Writing in *Variety* early in the Obama era, Brian Lowry wondered if the time is not ripe for 'change' to come to TV as well (2009: np). He presents a convincing case for why American small-screen programming should abandon, once and for all, the 100-episode paradigm, an increasingly out-of-date model for series longevity tied to the promise of syndication after a show has ended. Television revenue streams like DVD sales and international distribution, Lowry notes, can be lucrative with significantly fewer episodes per year (and, indeed, audiences abroad – in the UK for instance – are already accustomed to shorter series). More importantly, 'producing a smaller number of episodes could be an act of creative self-preservation', for the complexities of the average narratologically ambitious television series these days, '22 episodes a year [the American television series standard since the last century] has often become a bridge too far'.[5] After all, alternative models – from British television and premium channels like HBO and Showtime – are available, and they are likely to appeal to everyone involved, networks, fans and 'creatives'. Lowry quotes *Lost* co-creator Damon Lindelof: 'Creatives will definitely forgo richer deals in the spirit of [producing] fewer episodes and gaining more creative latitude' (Lowry 2009: np). As Lindelof admitted in a National Public Radio interview, 'tap dancing' – running in place in order to prolong a narrative of indefinite length – can be fun to watch, but not for long (Ashbrook 2007).

Unsurprisingly, *Life on Mars* springs to mind as a test case of the dilemma Lowry identifies: 'Despite a promising start, the U.S. reboot could be hard-pressed to sustain the mystery before viewers grow itchy' (ibid.). Whatever the good intentions of Appelbaum and *Life on Mars US*'s creatives, the series would appear to be hoofing big time. In yet another irony, ABC's retro-in-subject-matter reincarnation may have been doomed from the start because it arrived at the end of an era. It seems unlikely anyone will remember *Life on Mars US* in a fashion similar to Glenister's description of the experience of being on the original as 'kinda mad, a bit groundbreaking, a bit different, a bit science fiction, a gritty drama, you know, something different' (Glenister 2007). *Life on Mars US* only succeeded in offering us 'the same kind of different' (Lavery 1994: 13–14).

NOTES

1 For more on the problematic nature of *Lost*'s SF, see Lavery (2008).
2 The motto of the best known of these, Television Without Pity, a dot.com start-up now owned by Bravo, is appropriately 'Spare the snark, spoil the network'.
3 In *Life on Mars US*'s second episode, Sam lists the following possible explanations for his predicament on a blackboard (with the '?' standing for everything he hasn't thought of yet): Coma, Drug-Trip, Time Travel, Different Planet, Extra-Terrestrial, Mind Experiment, Heaven, Insanity, Brain Tumor, Virtual Reality, Multi-Dimensional Travel, ?
4 Annie discovers, by the way, that the victim had a blackboard with a list almost identical to Sam's.
5 For Lowry (2009), *Lost* is Exhibit A in the virtues of going shorter: 'the genius of announcing a far-in-advance end date for *Lost* in 2010 – while reducing its annual output to 17 installments' was a win/win, offering the network 'security' while placing limits on the need for 'viewers to suspend their curiosity indefinitely'.

REFERENCES

Ashbrook, T. (2007). 'ABC's *Lost* TV drama', *On Point with Tom Ashbrook* [online radio resource], 28 March 2007, *http://www.onpointradio.org/shows/2007/03/abcs-lost-tv-drama/*, accessed 24 May 2010.

Carter, B. (2006). *Desperate Networks*, New York, Broadway Books.

Glenister, P. (2007). 'The return of *Life on Mars*', Disc 1, Bonus Features, *Life on Mars: The Complete Series Two*, Contender Home Entertainment.

Handlin, Z. (2008). 'Out here in the fields', *Onion TV Club* [website], *http://www.avclub.com/articles/out-here-in-the-fields,13245/*, accessed 24 May 2010.

Handlin, Z. (2009a). 'Let all the children boogie', *Onion TV Club* [website], *http://www.avclub.com/articles/let-all-the-children-boogie,23732/*, accessed 24 May 2010.

Handlin, Z. (2009b). 'Life is a rock', *Onion TV Club* [website], *http://www.avclub.com/articles/life-is-a-rock,26085/*, accessed 24 May 2010.

Jenkins, H. (2006). *Convergence Culture: Where Old and New Media Collide*, New York, New York University Press.

Lavery, D. (1994). *Full of Secrets: Critical Approaches to* Twin Peaks, Detroit, Wayne State University Press.

Lavery, D. (2008). 'The island's greatest mystery: is *Lost* science fiction?', in J. P. Telotte (ed.), *The Essential Science Fiction TV Reader*, Lexington, University Press of Kentucky, pp. 283–98.

Lavery, D. (2009). '*Lost* and long term television narrative', in P. Harrigan and N. Wardrip-Fruin (eds), *Third Person: Authoring and Exploring Vast Narratives*, Cambridge, MA, MIT Press, pp. 313–22.

Lowry, B. (2009). 'A creative cure for TV: less is more', *Variety* [website], 30 January 2009, *http://www.variety.com/index.asp?layout=print_story&articleid=VR1117999370&categoryid=14*, accessed 24 May 2010.

Porter, L. and D. Lavery (2007). *Unlocking the Meaning of* Lost, Napierville, IL, Sourcebooks.

Sullivan, B. F. (2008a). 'On the futon with *Life on Mars* executive producer Josh Appelbaum', part 1, *The Futon Critic* [website], 10 March 2008, *http://www.thefutoncritic.com/rant.aspx?id=20081003_lifeonmars*, accessed 24 May 2010.

Sullivan, B. F. (2008a). 'On the futon with *Life on Mars* executive producer Josh Appelbaum', part 2, *The Futon Critic* [website], 6 October 2008, *http://www.thefutoncritic.com/rant.aspx?id=20081006_lifeonmars*, accessed 24 May 2010.

LOCATING GENERATIONAL AND CULTURAL CLASHES IN THE TRANSFER OF SUCCESSFUL FORMATS BETWEEN THE UNITED KINGDOM, SPAIN AND THE UNITED STATES

12

THE CASE OF *LIFE ON MARS*

Joseba Bonaut and Teresa Ojer

I N 2009, THE SPANISH CHANNEL Antena 3 broadcast a Spanish version of *Life on Mars* set in 1978, five years later than the original. This meant that the general problems of adapting the series for a new national context – the question of how the social history of the United Kingdom in the 1970s could be 'nationalised' – were compounded by a shift in cultural reference points. Of particular importance was the role that British popular music played in shaping the dramatic tone of the series, marking not only the time of the action but also the emotional landscape of the characters, especially that of the protagonist, Sam Tyler (John Simm). The changes that the series made to the score were controversial and symptomatic of a wider problem; one of the main purposes of this chapter will be to show how the Antena 3 re-imagining of *Life on Mars* drew attention to some of the crucial cultural determinants of the series, and focused some of its key elements in a new national and temporal context. In addition, the chapter will highlight the importance of media structure in a programme's success or failure and will contribute to debates about quality television. It will also examine the ABC reworking of the series in the USA, drawing attention to the differences and similarities between the ways in which some of the key themes and motifs were translated from the UK context. In particular, the Spanish and US versions renegotiate the ambiguous question of whether the policeman has been killed, is in a deep coma, mad or has travelled in time, in a way that provokes a reflection on the UK original.

Recent decades have seen a significant increase in competition between different television stations, which has led the television industry into a fierce struggle for the highest possible audience share and maximum profitability (with even the public television stations being dragged into the process). The television channels need programmes that attract the highest number of viewers as well as the certainty that their programming is suitable for achieving their financial and audience targets. As a result, in recent years television companies have purchased and adapted standardised television formats that have proven successful in other countries (hence the growing importance of international television markets, such as Cannes), prompted by global formulae and a theoretical absence of geographical borders. The risk posed by this phenomenon is the difficulty of 'nationalising' certain television ideas with clearly local cultural and social nuances. In a global society, the clash with the notion of 'the national' is often cited as the reason behind the failure of television programmes.

In the current politics of TV formats, fiction content reigns supreme in prime-time slots, making it a highly prized genre in the trend of adapting successful programmes. The transfer of successful fictional formats between markets is not a new phenomenon, however. The most obvious case is the historical transfer between two major television industries: the British and the US. There have also been American versions of British programmes such as *The Office* (BBC, 2001–3; NBC, 2005–), *Little Britain* (BBC, 2003–6; HBO, 2008) or, conversely, *Law and Order* (NBC, 1990–) and its British version *Law and Order: UK* (ITV, 2009–), and co-productions between stations (particularly between HBO and the BBC) such as *Rome* (HBO, 2005–7), *Extras* (HBO and BBC, 2005–7), *The Passion* (HBO, 2008), *House of Saddam* (HBO, 2008), *Five Days* (HBO, 2007), *Into the Storm* (HBO, 2009), or the *Song of Ice and Fire* series (HBO, 2010).

The model is not limited to these two countries, however. Other markets have copied it, adapting successful formats to their national standards, either through remakes or through free adaptation. In this context, the Spanish television market has been very active. Thanks to a robust television production structure, especially during the nineties, the private Spanish television networks have sourced successful formulae from foreign markets (mainly the USA and the UK). As a result, there has been a noticeable increase in remakes such as *Doctor Mateo* (Antena 3, 2009–), based on the British programme *Doc Martin* (ITV, 2004–), or free adaptations such as *Hospital Central* (*Central Hospital*) (Telecinco, 2000–), based on the celebrated US series *ER* (NBC, 1994–2009), or *Física o química* (*Physics or Chemistry*) (Antena 3, 2008–), a free adaptation of the hit British teen drama series *Skins* (Channel 4, 2007–). Clearly television companies face difficulties in adapting fiction formats to their national contexts, and the extent to which the characteristics of their own particular markets affect the success or failure of new programmes. It is also critically important to ask whether this format adaptation process contributes to the concept of 'quality TV' or whether, on the contrary, it reinforces a sense that the television market lacks new ideas.

Life on Mars and its Spanish adaption *La chica de ayer* (*The Yesterday Girl*) provides a very useful case study through which to explore these issues. The UK version is characterised by a marked local flavour in terms of cultural and social references, besides being framed within a complex genre hybridisation between police drama and science fiction. The series was also adapted by the US television station ABC as *Life on Mars US* (2009). Neither the US nor the Spanish version has managed to achieve the success of the original series in terms of ratings or content, and neither has continued into a second season. How might such difficult challenges be overcome? What are the barriers faced by the television stations in format adaptation? To what extent does format adaptation contribute quality content to television programming?

LIFE ON MARS (UK): A LOOK AT THE SEVENTIES BETWEEN LIFE AND DEATH

How can the success of *Life on Mars* be explained? First of all, we need to take a close look at the characteristics of the market in which it is framed (British) and the television network broadcasting it (the BBC). Only a television channel with the patience and interest in quality drama such as the BBC could make a firm commitment to a series with an unusual mix of genres and clear hints of science fiction, following hot on the heels of the success of *Doctor Who* (BBC, 2005–). The structure and characteristics of the British audiovisual market determine the content of the programmes broadcast in the UK. All terrestrial television operators have the obligation to contribute towards public service broadcasting, in particular the BBC, but also the advertising-financed television stations: ITV, Channel 4 and Five (Ofcom 2005: 3). This requirement forces the above four companies to ensure the maintenance of the cultural and social aspects of British citizenship in the public domain. Thus, the system aims to ensure that television programmes reflect, to a larger extent than in other countries, the values and tastes of a broad spectrum of the community (Peacock 2004: 58–63). Another peculiarity of the British television industry is that 25 per cent of broadcasting time by free-to-air television stations must be sourced from independent production companies, as stipulated by the Broadcasting Act 1990. This provision contrasts with the European Television without Frontiers Directive of 1989 (Art. 5), which requires a quota of only 10 per cent. The British stipulation has led to a proliferation of independent television producers in the UK who collaborate with the major national broadcasters, thus promoting a plurality of TV programmes, both informative and fictional. In addition, the BBC is working towards raising this percentage; hence in 2006, 35 per cent of broadcasting time was sourced from independent production companies, and 37 per cent in 2007. Particularly significant is the BBC's annual investment of £1.2 billion in the last three years (2006–8) in the so-called creative economy (BBC 2009: 18).

Kudos Film & Television, the independent production company that was commissioned to make *Life on Mars*, has been an important partner of the BBC, and is linked with high-profile success (for example, *Spooks* (BBC, 2001–11)). The corporation also has agreements with other independent production companies such as Tiger Aspect Productions, Endemol and Hat Trick Television. Claire Parker, the producer of *Life on Mars* for Kudos Film

& Television, is cited in the *BBC Annual Report and Accounts 2007–2008* as saying that the value of TV drama series is based on their reflection of the people's different voices and opinions. These are aspects in which television operators are exceedingly interested. This is why both the television stations and production companies pay particular attention to their mutual relationships (BBC 2008: 13).

As the major UK public broadcaster, the BBC stands out: a television network with a long broadcasting history (more than eighty years) and worldwide reputation for creative and innovative programming and impartiality, the corporation, it is argued, contributes to the democratic character of British society and sets it apart from its competitors. The BBC is also a very large organisation, with more than 23,000 employees and a budget that reached £4.414 million during the 2007–8 financial year. It should be emphasised that, unlike the majority of other European public broadcasters, the BBC does not accept advertising on any of its channels, including BBC Three and BBC Four. Therefore, BBC programmes can be watched without any interruption and they are longer than audiences in other countries are used to. For example, the episodes of *Life on Mars* aired in the UK had a duration of sixty minutes, while the same series broadcast for an international audience was cut by ten minutes.

The BBC would also seem to be popular with both audiences and television professionals. Recently, the members of the British Film Institute chose the 100 greatest British TV programmes of the last century. Of the top twenty highest-ranked programmes, seventeen were made by the BBC. Many of them have continued to air for several seasons, with some of them such as *Doctor Who* and *Blue Peter*, still being broadcast after several decades (BFI 2007). The experts' verdict of quality receives the backing of the audience. For example, in 2009, the BBC channels (BBC 1 and BBC 2) drew 29.6 per cent of the total British television audience, in a context where the viewing figure for the combined satellite, cable and digital terrestrial TV channels was 38.8 per cent. ITV, the BBC's main terrestrial competitor, was the third most popular channel with an 18.4 per cent share of the audience. In recent years, the BBC has placed special emphasis on popular drama series, broadcasting *Jane Eyre* (BBC, 2006), *Torchwood* (BBC, 2006–), *Life on Mars* or its sequel series *Ashes to Ashes* (BBC, 2008–10). This has been a risky move, as the drama genre is the most expensive to produce. According to a recent BBC report (2007: 73), the production cost per hour of drama programmes is £472,800, whereas the production cost per hour of news and weather programmes is just £25,900. However, BBC audience surveys highlighted that audiences demanded a larger proportion of this type of content (ibid.: 84).[1]

Life on Mars, broadcast over two seasons each consisting of eight episodes, enjoyed major audience success. In the UK the first series achieved an average audience figure of 6 million viewers who tuned in each week to accompany police detective Sam Tyler in his attempts at solving cases. The final episode, in which Tyler finally finds an answer to his question 'Am I mad, in a coma or back in time?', was watched by 7 million viewers, a 28 per cent audience share, despite strong competition from a UEFA Champions League football game between Manchester United and Roma on ITV (Holmwood 2007). The show received extremely positive reviews from media with a range of ideological stances, and won national and international awards, including an Emmy and a BAFTA for best drama series on British television in 2006 (see the Introduction to this volume).

The success of the series was matched in the other countries where it was broadcast: the United States, Canada, New Zealand, Australia, Ireland, Sweden, the Netherlands, Germany, France, Spain, Israel, Serbia, Norway and Hong Kong, whilst the United States and Spain showed interest in adapting the format for their respective audiences. This suggests that a commitment to quality can be profitable, since the sale of broadcasting rights and format brings the BBC a benefit that will be reinvested in the station's public service programming for its national audience. Moreover, the international sale and broadcasting of its quality programmes contributes to the increasing prestige of the BBC in the global television market.

The second feature that helps us understand the success of the series is its distinctive narrative structure, which mixes the genres of both sci-fi fantasy and police procedural against a 'travel-back-in-time' backdrop that goes beyond the simply novel. The narrative structure of sixty-minute programmes, favoured by the absence of advertising, allows each episode to explore the psychological profile of the characters, in particular the protagonist. The entire series is built around two worlds, 1973 Manchester and 2006 Manchester – one of them present (physically) and the other, with the exception of sequences in the first and last episodes, suggested (almost always by technological elements such as telephones, radios, televisions). The ambiguity of Tyler's predicament, and the interplay between reality, madness and science fiction, feeds the audience's interest in the protagonist and informs his relationship with the other characters. The clash between different historical eras transforms into an abrupt collision between Sam's and Gene's (Philip Glenister) outlook on life and their profession, as well as those of the other police officers at the police station, with special attention paid to the relationship with the women in the series (and, in particular, with that of WPC Annie Cartwright (Liz White)). In this respect, the programme engages skilfully in subplots depicting relationships between characters that strengthen and provide depth to the narrative: examples include the romantic relationship between Annie and Sam as well as the confrontations between Sam and Detective Sergeant Ray Carling (Dean Andrews) or a number of other police officers.

What is most remarkable, however, is that the 'game' played between the two worlds allows the series to explore the internal conflicts of the characters, and this makes the programme especially appealing. *Life on Mars* puts aside a mere interest in a particular plot (What happens to Sam Tyler? How will he get out of there?), focusing instead on more profound, universal themes that unfold throughout the two seasons (with the format lending itself to adaptation): the father–son relationship and the torment of a troubled childhood, the past that haunts the characters (for example, in the case of 'Gene Genie'), abandonment of the home, the impossibility of doing justice and the moral dilemma brought about by the transgression of established rules (especially those concerning police procedures). In the end, the success of the adapted series depended on the treatment given to these themes and to a lesser extent on the literal adaptation of the plot. Achieving this, however, requires time (the duration of episodes and the time needed to write and produce them), which translates ultimately into fewer episodes per season.

Finally, let us not omit one of the key elements that has enabled *Life on Mars* to become a success: the representation of established and familiar national sociocultural patterns which seem to appeal to British audiences. Most significantly, this was not solely an exercise in nostalgia. The series' depiction of British society in the seventies is a critical analysis of the foundations of that country and of its contradictions and historical issues. Cinematographic, television and literary references are interwoven with the treatment of basic themes of British society at this time, such as the strength of trade unions, urban transformation, football and its implicit violence, racial integration, the social role of war veterans and heroism, the media and the role of women. These themes are seamlessly intertwined in the central plot, rather than being mere decorative motifs; they influence the configuration of the internal conflicts of the characters as well as the external social and cultural clashes.

Finally, attention should be drawn to the vital role played by music in the creation of the private world of the characters in the series (see Smith elsewhere in this volume). Music is not used as an accessory, as an artificial adornment bearing witness to an era in a generalised way, but is rather an essential means to convey the desperation of a character who is trapped in a turbulent past ('Life on Mars' by David Bowie – Sam Tyler), the larger-than-life character and leadership of an old-school cop ('The Jean Genie' by David Bowie – Gene Hunt), or the constant game between life and death suggested by the coma into which the main character has fallen ('Live and Let Die' by Wings). This is a complex game of cultural cross-referencing which makes the story of *Life on Mars* something unique and difficult to imitate or adapt.

LA CHICA DE AYER (THE YESTERDAY GIRL) (SPAIN): AN UNUSUAL LOOK AT THE NEW-FOUND SPANISH DEMOCRACY

In order to explain the possible reasons for the failure of the Spanish adaptation of the series, this chapter will examine not only the differences in the narrative approach between the British and Spanish versions, but also the structure of the television market in Spain and the characteristics of the television station Antena 3, as these are aspects that affect the content and quality of television formats.

The first television station to operate in Spain was a public service broadcaster, which began in 1956. The principal function of the new service was to entertain, pushing into the background the mission to educate and inform: a characteristic that was typical of the Spanish system. Through its two channels, La 1 and La 2, the Spanish Radio and Television Corporation (RTVE) had a monopoly on broadcasting for more than thirty years, until the enactment in 1988 of Act 10/1988 of 3 May on Private Television, which permitted the running of the television public service through private companies. This act led to the creation of three new television stations: the pay television channel Canal +, and the advertising-funded companies Telecinco and Antena 3, which further strengthened the entertainment function of television. This structure stayed in place for fifteen years until 2005, when new legislation[2] approved the creation of two new advertising-funded general interest television stations, Cuatro and La Sexta.

In the years since then the increase in the number of general interest television operators in the Spanish market has led manifestly to a growth in competition for the main source of financing, advertising; this is even more the case if we take into account that until now RTVE had also competed for advertising revenue.[3] Adding to this competition has been the development of cable and satellite television companies and the boost for digital terrestrial television. This overall television landscape reflects an industry driven by the need for profitability, in which only programmes that strike a balance between audience ratings, advertising revenue and production costs manage to survive. These objectives are shared by the private station Antena 3, which, in contrast to the BBC, is unable to keep on air formats that fail to meet minimum audience targets as these would not prove profitable.

Antena 3 was the first Spanish television network to be funded through advertising and began broadcasting regularly on 25 January 1990. Throughout its existence, Antena 3 has been characterised by a number of changes in its shareholders' structure, which have also been reflected in the content of its television programming. Some programmes have been criticised for their excessive tabloid style, such as *El diario de* (*The Diary of*) (2001–). The company is also best known for its legendary programmes for the Spanish audience, being the first television station to launch Spanish-produced family sitcoms. These programmes, including *Farmacia de Guardia* (*Duty Chemist*) (1991–5) and *Aquí no hay quien viva* (*There is nobody who lives here*) (2003–6), proved very successful. The Antena 3 network is a favourite with Spanish viewers (achieving a 16 per cent audience share in 2008); however, in recent years it has been overtaken by its main competitor, Telecinco (18.1 per cent in 2008). During the same period RTVE (the Spanish public broadcaster) has become the second-favourite option among Spanish viewers, with 16.9 per cent of the audience share (TNS 2009). Yet, according to television programme image studies conducted by GECA, Antena 3 is the highest-rated television station among Spaniards.

The need to maximise audiences, and the financial risk involved in the production of fictional TV series, has driven Antena 3 to adopt a strategy of buying in successful foreign formats which should, to some extent, guarantee ratings success. For example, as mentioned earlier, in 2008 Antena 3 had embarked on the production of *Física o Química* (*Physics or Chemistry*), steering away from its main target audience (families) in an effort to reach out to new audiences (teens). Despite the risks taken by the television station in producing a series that dealt with controversial themes, including alcohol, sex, homosexuality and suicide, the series was a huge success, dominating Monday and later Wednesday prime-time slots.

In the wake of the success of this show, Antena 3 decided to look to the increasingly fertile British television market and opted for the nationalisation of another two hit series targeted at a family audience: *Doc Martin* (ITV, 2004–) and *Life on Mars* (BBC, 2006–7). *Life on Mars* was the most interesting option due to the social dimension of the series in the UK, and the challenge of adapting a series that engaged directly with the social reality of a particular country. This was to prove very challenging after the massive success in Spain of *Cúentame cómo paso* (*Tell me how it happened*) (TVE, 2001–), a television series that recounts the experiences of a Spanish middle-class family during the last years of Francoist rule. This was the same historical period as that covered by *Life on Mars*, so the producers and screenwriters felt it necessary to locate the Spanish version in the year 1977 (referencing different problems and issues than had been covered in *Cuéntame cómo pasó*). Despite the risks involved, Antena 3 bought the remake rights to *Life on Mars* in 2008 for its debut in April 2009. For weeks, Antena 3 heavily promoted the BBC-endorsed show, generating expectations among the channel's viewers. As a result, the first episode of the series attracted more than 3.7 million viewers, leading the day's prime-time figures with a 19.7 per cent audience share. However, the viewing figures declined steadily throughout the eight episodes of the first and only series of the Spanish adaptation. The final episode was watched by 2.7 million people (an audience share of 15.7 per cent) and Antena 3 decided not to renew the series for a second season (Fórmula TV 2009). The need to respond to the demands of the television market and the narrative difficulties caused, among other things, by the need to include several commercial breaks, have hindered the adaptation of a quality format from a public television network to a commercial television station such as Antena 3.

So what are the reasons for the failure of the Spanish adaptation of *Life on Mars*? To begin with, there are major differences between *La chica de ayer* and its British counterpart. First, *La chica de ayer* focuses on the police procedural genre, leaving aside any references to science fiction; for example, the flashback references and the game between the past and the present played by technological devices (such as the TV and the radio) were reduced to the minimum. The sci-fi aspect is present only in a surprising final episode in which Samuel Santos (Ernesto Alterio) is trapped in the past through a peculiar time tunnel. In Spanish television, sci-fi has not proved to be a popular genre with audiences seeming to prefer love stories, comedy or drama. As a result of these differences, the ambivalence between genres, the winning formula behind the success of *Life on Mars*, is somewhat diluted. *La chica de ayer* then descends to the ordinary to become more of a police drama series, only set in the past with nostalgic appeal.

The overall length of the episodes also differs from the original series. Initially, the episodes were sixty minutes long, and then went on to run for ninety minutes with the purpose of covering the entire prime-time slot. The interruption of commercial breaks marked the narrative structure of the series in Spain, in contrast to the UK, and would also prove damaging for the US version. This is a key aspect that caused the storyline to stretch unnecessarily, creating a significant dependence on dialogue, which is too often banal. This characteristic, typical of Spanish series that usually extend the length of the formats to earn higher advertising revenue, forced *La chica de ayer* to use repetitive narration and created unnecessary subplots which weakened the real theme of the show: the fate of Sam Tyler.

The fact that *La chica de ayer* draws on fewer genres is reflected in the configuration and definition of the main character – regarded as a rather poor performance from the lead actor – which is particularly weak. As with the US protagonist, the greatest concern of the Spanish detective Samuel Santos (Ernesto Alterio) is to find a way back home to 2009. Some characteristics of the British Sam Tyler, who is tormented and challenged and subject to a strong internal conflict, have been excluded from the Spanish adaptation. The conflict becomes external, the context social and interpersonal relationships more important, thus detracting from the strength of the gradual discovery that the viewer makes of Sam Tyler's past in *Life on Mars*. This is why the relationships between Samuel Santos and the other characters are essential. The romantic plot between Samuel and Ana (Manuela Velasco) (Annie in the British version) is reinforced, creating a significant sexual tension between them, as also occurs in the US adaptation. The choice of this theme takes *La chica de ayer* away from the spirit of *Life on Mars*, in which the suggestion and impossibility of love is justified by a world that is rendered senseless by an unresolved past. At the same time, the personality conflict between Samuel and 'Quin' (Antonio Garrido) (the 'Gene Genie' character in *Life on Mars*) is absent, not only because of the lack of chemistry between them but because they are depicted as stereotypes and their internal conflicts remain unexplored. Again, the Spanish adaptation literally transfers archetypal characters, dialogues and dramatic situations yet fails to give them a meaningful role within the story: an adaptation must be close to the viewer and the viewer should be able to identify with it (without internal conflict, viewers do not easily recognise themselves in the story).

The social and historical contexts also have an adverse effect on the adaptation. As observed previously, the adventures of the Spanish characters take place in the year 1977, while in *Life on Mars* (in both the UK and the US versions) the year is 1973. Interestingly, like in the US version, the historical context serves as an excuse to let the story unfold without having to reflect on the change in attitude among Spanish citizens towards the major themes that shaped the life of the country (this, however, is skilfully achieved in *Cuéntame cómo pasó*). Social references are mere storyline excuses, which do not allow the viewer to reflect upon the passage of time (like the football references in *Life on Mars* and their connection with future events). It is rather disappointing that the opportunity has been missed to portray one of the most relevant historical moments in Spanish history, the transition to a newfound democracy that Spaniards were learning to live in. It does not work as a historical portrayal of the time and thus it fails to attract the interest of the audience towards the pressing, contemporary issues facing Spanish citizens.

Finally, the musical dimension of the Spanish series (of especial relevance in the UK version of *Life on Mars*) is of as little interest as in the US adaptation. This represents yet another missed opportunity, since the show's title, *La chica de ayer*, is a reference to a well-known song by Antonio Vega, a singer-songwriter who inspired an entire generation of young Spanish people; however, it has nothing to do with the series' protagonist. The UK series uses the David Bowie song to show Sam Tyler's confusion and also to suggest the importance of music throughout the episodes. Once again, as in the US adaptation, music in the Spanish series is opportunistic and does not echo the dramatic sense of the plots or of the characters.

Evidence of the failure of the Spanish version to understand the complex way in which music is used in the UK *Life on Mars* can be found in the scene of Samuel Santos's accident in episode 1.1. The scene recreates the same dramatic situation as in the other two versions, however the music played is the Queen track *Bohemian Rhapsody*, a 1975 song that has no relevance to the year in which the story is set, and which has no relation to the main character. All of this begs the question: why wasn't the song of the show's title, *La chica de ayer*, used in this case? There is no obvious explanation, even though the result was very clear for the viewers: a series format cannot be transferred literally from one country to another unless it is brought closer to its intended audience.

LIFE ON MARS (US): THE PROBLEMS OF LITERAL ADAPTATION

Some of the difficulties encountered by Spanish television companies when adapting the UK series were mirrored in the US adaptation. First, the purely commercial nature of the US television market (with fierce competition among national television stations) and its dependence on advertising shaped the adaptation produced by the television network ABC (the American Broadcasting Company). ABC decided to place its bets on the adaptation of *Life on Mars* after the series' success in the UK, and as part of its programming strategy of deploying drama series in prime time: other examples included *Grey's Anatomy* (ABC, 2005–), *Lost* (ABC, 2004–10) and *Desperate Housewives* (ABC, 2004–). Once again, the adaptation of a successful format was considered a safer bet in terms of ratings success. The US adaptation, however, faced many of the same problems as those faced by the Spanish series. The storyline had to be cut down and compressed to fit the forty-two-minute length of each episode due to the introduction of five commercial breaks. In addition, the genre hybrid (science fiction and police procedural) was watered down with a simplification of the plot. In theory this should have been more likely to reach the viewer, yet it eliminated some key elements of the British series, such as Sam Tyler's internal conflict and the great 'universal' themes that allow viewers to identify with the show (for example, father–son relationships and childhood trauma).

The decision to introduce these changes had a radical influence on the choice of actors. In the US series Sam Tyler is played by Jason O'Mara, an actor of imposing physical appearance and tremendous inner and outer strength who displays nothing of John Simm's vulnerability. This is also a vital trait in his relationship with the other characters, which is limited to a purely narrative bond, the clash regarding his outlook on his profession and Sam's desire to return to 'his reality'. Even though the cast includes well-known names such as Harvey Keitel and Michael Imperioli, their roles lack depth and strength in terms of their connection with the viewer. The lesser-known actors in the British series managed to have more appeal than some of Hollywood's leading performers.

Even so, the importance of the US version's achievements (like those in the case of *La chica de ayer*) should not be underplayed. These include, for example, the development of a romantic plot between Sam and Annie, underpinned by a significant sexual tension. Not only is Sam portrayed as a stronger character, but Annie takes on an increasingly powerful, decision-making role – although often more in line with a more contemporary behavioural pattern far removed from the reality of the time.

Lastly, the sociocultural patterns reflected in the US version are only weakly present, being reduced to a mere photographic representation of New York in the 1970s, as shown in the scene in which Sam discovers the Twin Towers (episode 1.1). The social conflicts of the time are portrayed in the hippie community, the role of women, the homosexual world, the power of the media (in this case the radio rather than the press as is the case in the original British version) and interracial fighting in the ghettos between African Americans and Puerto Ricans. However, these are always a complement to the main plot, never an element that serves to shape the internal conflict of a character who is only focused on his way back home and on his love affair. Similarly, music is often shoehorned into the show, especially the titular 'Life on Mars'.

Translating British sociocultural patterns into a US context was not difficult in itself; however, the decisive step was ensuring that they made dramatic sense, and that is where the series failed.

All of these circumstances combine to explain the relative failure of the series and the network's final decision not to broadcast a second season and cut the first down to seventeen episodes. The programme achieved an audience of just 5.5 million viewers despite being scheduled after the hit series *Grey's Anatomy* (Schneider 2009). In this case, the adaptation of a successful drama format failed because it could not reproduce the key elements that should be present in any good television programme that deals with human conflict.

NOTES

1   The BBC pays close attention to the comments and opinions of its audience through audience research and BARB data.
2   Act 10/2005 of 14 June on Urgent Measures for the Promotion of Digital Terrestrial Television, Liberalisation of Cable TV, and Promotion of Media Pluralism.
3   This changed on 1 January 2010, following the approval of the new funding model for public service broadcasting which prohibits advertising.

REFERENCES

BBC (2004a). 'BBC boss details 3,000 job cuts', *BBC News* [online news resource], *http://news.bbc.co.uk/1/hi/entertainment/tv_and_radio/4073571.stm*, accessed 9 March 2009.

BBC (2004b). 'Building public value: renewing the BBC for a digital world', *BBC* [website], *http://www.bbc.co.uk/thefuture/pdfs/bbc_bpv.pdf*, accessed 9 March 2009.

BBC (2007). *BBC Annual Report and Accounts 2006–2007*. London, BBC.

BBC (2008). *BBC Annual Report and Accounts 2007–2008*. London, BBC.

BBC (2009). *BBC Annual Report and Accounts 2008–2009*. London, BBC.

BFI (2007). *The BFI TV 100* [website], *http://www.bfi.org.uk/features/tv/100/list/list.php*, accessed 9 March 2009.

Bielby, D. (2008). *Global TV. Exporting Television and Culture in Global Market*, New York, New York University Press.

Broadcasters Audience Research Board (2009). 'Annual % shares of viewing (individuals) 1981–2008', *BARB* [website], *http://www.barb.co.uk/facts/annual ShareOfViewing?_s=4*, accessed 17 November 2009.

Carson, B. and Llewellyn-Jones, M. (eds) (2000). *Frames and Fictions on Television: The Politics of Identity within Drama*, Exeter, Intellect.

Dowell, B. (2006). 'BBC chiefs welcome White Paper', *Guardian.co.uk* [online news resource], *http://media.guardian.co.uk/broadcast/story/0,,1730801,00.html*, accessed 9 March 2009.

European Directive (89/552/EC) (1989). 'Television without frontiers', *European Directive* [website], *http://www.europa.eu.int/scadplus/leg/en/lvb/l24101.htm*, accessed 9 March 2009.

Fórmula TV (2009). *'La chica de ayer* se despecide de la audiencia con una media cercana al 15%', *Fórmula TV* [website], *http://www.formulatv.com/1,20090611,11705,1.html*, accessed 5 July 2010.

Holmwood, L. (2007). 'Plenty of life on Mars', *Guardian.co.uk* [online news resource], *http://www.guardian.co.uk/media/2007/apr/11/overnights*, accessed 13 March 2009.

Medina, M. (1998). *Valoración publicitaria de los programas de television (Advertising value of television programmes)*, Pamplona, Eunsa.

Moran, A. (2006). *Understanding the Global TV Format*, London, Intellect Ltd.

Moran, A. (2010). *TV Formats Worldwide: Localizing Global Programs*, Bristol, Intellect Ltd.

O'Brien, S. (2006). *SFX Magazine*, 139, January, 58.

Ofcom (2005). *Ofcom Review of Public Service Television Broadcasting. Phase 3, Competition for Quality*, London, Ofcom.

Office of Public Sector Information (1990). 'Broadcasting Act 1990', OPSI [website], *http://www.opsi.gov.uk/acts/acts1990/Ukpga_19900042_en_1.htm*, accessed 9 March 2009.

Peacock, A. (2004). *Public Service Broadcasting without the BBC?*, London, The Institute of Economic Affairs.

Pérez-Lanzac, C. (2009). 'El gran bazar de los formatos (The great format bazaar)', *El Pais Edition Impresa* [online news resource], *http://www.elpais.com/articulo/Pantallas/gran/bazar/formatos/elpepirtv/20090222elpepirtv_1/Tes*, accessed 13 March 2009.

Schneider, M. (2009). 'ABC cancels *Life on Mars*', *Variety* [website], *http://www.variety.com/article/VR1118000748.html?categoryid=14&cs=1&query=life+on+mars*, accessed 12 March 2009.

TNS (2009). 'Histórico de audiencias. España', *Fórmula TV* [website], *http://www.formulatv.com/audiencias/ver/historico/*, accessed 5 July 2010.

PART V

DEBATING PRODUCTION

JULIE GARDNER
13 AND CLAIRE PARKER

IN CONVERSATION

THE FOLLOWING IS AN EDITED TRANSCRIPT of an interview, with subsequent discussion, conducted at a symposium on *Life on Mars* held at the Cardiff School of Creative and Cultural Industries (University of Glamorgan) on 18 November 2007. The interview was chaired by Professor David Lavery and featured Julie Gardner, executive producer of the series for BBC Cymru Wales, and Claire Parker, producer for Kudos, the independent production company that won the commission to make both *Life on Mars* and *Ashes to Ashes*.

Key
DL: David Lavery;
CP: Claire Parker;
JG: Julie Gardner;
Q. . .: Questions from the audience.

DL: We are honoured today to have two of the people responsible for having made this amazing television show possible, Claire Parker, who is a producer at Kudos, and Julie Gardner of BBC Wales.

I want to start with what I'm calling 'Origin myths'; I've become fascinated recently with how stories get told about how a show gets made . . . And the origin myths of this show are kind of intriguing, a weekend of debauchery in Blackpool?

CP: Well, I mean neither Julie nor I were actually there! I think it was about seven years before the show eventually got commissioned, and the then sole managing director of Kudos, Steven Garret, sent Matthew, Ashley and Tony, the three writers, off to Blackpool and they came up with a load of ideas; most of them made a lot more sense than *Life on Mars*, but *Life on Mars* was one of them. It sat in a drawer for a long time but Jane Featherstone and I became involved and we developed the idea with Channel 4 initially, and Julie wasn't involved at that time.

JG: No, still not invited!

(Laughter from audience)

CP: It was developed for a number of years at Channel 4, two years I think, and then was turned down by them. And at that point, happily, Julie *did* get involved.

JG: I was invited, finally! Yeah, I had breakfast with Jane Featherstone, who is Kudos, and she said: 'I'm going to send you something and I'm not actually going to tell you anything about it – absolutely nothing.' I started reading, and I can't remember what page it was, but I thought: 'Okay, it's a cop show, and it could turn into a kind of *Prime Suspect* thing, and his girlfriend has kind of been kidnapped; I can see where this is going and it's nicely written' – and then I turned the page, and it was like: 'Okay, it's not that, he's now in the seventies!' And I phoned Jane up and said: 'You are just horrible to me, you've only sent it to me because you know I make *Doctor Who* and you think someone will understand sci-fi', and, of course, *Life on Mars* isn't sci-fi, but you know that was my joke with her. I continued reading it and I abso-lutely loved it, because it felt like a very clear concept, even though from that point on we had to work phenomenally hard at the clarity of the storytelling, and every single script, it was one of the hardest things I think to develop. We had to be so rigorous with the format and the character point of view, but to me it felt like a great opportunity of, on one hand, doing a police show – and doing a police show in a very kind of different way, and it felt like doing a big concept show as well, that would say something about the world; it wouldn't just be a straight investigation. But if we got it right, it would play to two very distinct audiences, the audience that want a story of the week that is reward-ing, where you see how the crime story pans out, but then another audience, and of course they are not completely separate, but another audience that would want to be nostalgic about the seventies, that would want to think about the world they live in, that would want to compare policing in the sev-enties with present day and look at it from that point of view. And then the added layer, of course: was he in a coma, or was he not in a coma. So it was a great thing to read.

DL: May I just clarify, did you say it is *not* sci-fi.

JG: I think it's not solely sci-fi.

CP: I don't think it's sci-fi at all.

DL: I want to return to that later on, but can you tell me, had the Blackpool trio worked together before, and were they known to you?

CP: Basically, they had worked together on *Eastenders* and, I think, *City Central* at that point, maybe not all of them . . .

JG: *City Central* was a cop show set in Manchester; we should mention John Yorke.

CP: Yes.

JG: John Yorke was – at the time of *Life on Mars*'s development – was the commissioner for Drama at Channel 4.

CP: And he had known about the project from its original incarnation seven years previously, but just kind of knew of it because he knew Matthew, Ashley and Tony and when he became Head of Drama at Channel 4, he remembered the project and thought it was potentially interesting for Channel 4. So the three writers had worked together on [other] series, but they hadn't ever come together to co-create before.

DL: Somewhere on the DVD the original title was mentioned; I guess that was fairly well known over here [in the UK], that originally it was called . . .

CP: It was called *Ford Granada* or something.

DL: How did it get from there to *Life on Mars*? At what point did Bowie come in . . . ?

CP: I'm not sure; the script in its original form was always called *Life on Mars*, and I wasn't involved at the time, but when I was given the original draft by Matthew, it was always called *Life on Mars*.

JG: There was a lot of anxiety by calling it *Life on Mars*. Before we transmitted, there was a lot of discussion about what would it say to the audience about what it was, was it too clever, was it . . .

DL: It certainly suggests science fiction.

JG: What were we saying that the show was, and on a show where we were constantly having the debates about: it is not sci-fi, well, it's kind of a bit, or the heightened concept, it's a cop show, it's a character show, it's seventies, you know, all of those debates, were kind of also encapsulated in the discussion about what should we call it, but I don't think we ever had a valuable alternative.

CP: Yeah, there was never an alternative. Jane Featherstone, who was the executive producer on the first series had just produced *Spooks*, which had suffered, she felt, from people thinking it was a ghost show, before they understood that it was a spy show, so she was very anxious that the same thing might happen with *Life on Mars*.

DL: Matthew Graham and Ashley Pharoah say that they thought that you, Julie, were the perfect person, because you already had time travel, but they also acknowledged that this was going to be hard for you to commission two time-travel shows.

JG: Oh, from my point of view, it was one of the easiest things I ever was involved with commissioning, because it just hit the BBC at the right time. Often projects sit on commissioners' desks for a long, long time, not because we're lazy and sitting in spas, but because we're looking at a whole map of a year of TV and we're looking at what writers, what companies are delivering, what projects, what companies miss a delivery deadline, it's an endless jigsaw puzzle to put together. It was very fortunate that, I think, if Jane sent me the script on a Tuesday I literally think it was green-lit on the Friday, something like that, which was completely mad; I read it immediately, because she'd kind of tantalised me with 'I'm not going to tell you about it, but it's great, just go with it', and I gave it to the commissioner, Jane Tranter, and she knew that we needed a cop show. We knew that we had a gap for a series. We knew, I don't know how, but instinctively we knew that it was worth a risk because it felt very bold, and even if the anxiety was that it would divide the audience, between those two groups of the cop-loving audience and the audience that wants more serious drama, it felt like a very bold and easy commission.

CP: And that, from my point of view, is amazing, because we'd just had a huge blow with it having been developed for two years with Channel 4 and then having been turned down, when we were quite far down the road in terms of getting it off the ground for production.

JG: We can't talk about why Channel 4 turned it down, I wasn't in the room, but I heard anecdotally that an anxiety was that it would be silly. That seems slightly mad now, but it could've been silly, it could've been a bit frivolous and a bit fanciful.

DL: It was occasionally silly; I mean, there were moments when it was silly, in a good way. I'm intrigued by this, because I know numerous cases in American television where a show has gotten bottlenecked, was rejected by one network, and then became a big hit, afterwards. Philip Glenister said that he knew it was a very special show from when they first started shooting. What is it that makes you know?

CP: I don't think we knew. I think there was a strong feeling on the series, because at every stage we were getting great responses; so the scripts when we sent them out for casting got great responses, but I was a first-time producer, so for me, I didn't know if this is what actors always said when they came in for casting. And then people started seeing the rushes and saying 'There's something great here.' Obviously I was trying to give everyone a sense of confidence and a sense of 'This was gonna be a great show', but it's easier to say that in hindsight than it is to say it at the time, because it was a risk, you know, we were trying to do something different and we weren't sure if it was going to work.

JG: You absolutely never know. You never even know when you're making a second series of something. Maybe that's because you need to be frightened all the time to make yourself work as hard as you can, but you never know.

DL: But you were very confident about the show because the second series was commissioned before the first series even aired.

JG: Only because we had to!

DL: Because you had to?

JG: That's right, isn't it?

CP: I don't think you needed to commission it as quickly . . .

JG: Oh, really we loved it, we knew, we knew!

(Laughter from audience)

JG: Sometimes you do have to commission a second series before the first series is aired, because you're locked into windows of filming with your actors, so financially, sometimes you have to.

CP: We would have had to make a decision, I think, before we'd aired, but I think it was still made before that point.

DL: Glenister says on the DVD something to the effect of even if it had been a ratings disaster, he still thought they would've made a second series.

JG: I think that is *partly* true. Because, you are making me remember, that when the recommission happened with Jane Tranter, it was about, we're not judging this solely on ratings, which actually the BBC doesn't because it's a public service broadcaster and there's so many other things to consider; we were able to look at so many episodes, and we knew that there was a quality, so that's a difference, you're judging a recommission based on the quality of the work, rather than trying to second guess what an audience is going to connect to or accept.

DL: Turning to casting; this was not the kind of show that John Simm would've normally done. Do you want to talk a little bit about that?

CP: John was genuinely my first choice, but obviously he was on a list of other people, because we didn't think he would do it. We met with him, and I think it was just one of those happy timing things; he wanted to do something that would move him to a different audience from the audience that he was reaching and this was a kind of show that, with Kudos's record, he felt that he could potentially trust us to do something that was hopefully going to be more mainstream than some of the stuff he'd done, but still be of a good level of quality. That was his decision, really.

DL: Matthew Graham says on the DVD that 'We didn't think Simm would slum it down with us in series TV.'

CP: Well, he had done some series TV before, but not for a long time, so . . .

JG: He'd done *The Lakes*; I mean, series work is so different to anything else, the endless pressure of the schedules, it's not for everyone.

DL: Especially in this case, because he's on screen in virtually every frame.

JG: His point of view all the way through season 1; it was ferocious, his schedule.

JG: I really sympathise with actors, it's very hard; you have a great actor like that who has endless opportunities and essentially we're asking him to commit to two years of work, to eight episodes in the first run, on the basis of one script; I mean there's an enormous amount of trust in that moment, when you say every single script we promise will be of the quality of episode 1, we'll cast it properly, we'll get good directors, it will be fine. Every single series I do, there's this moment where they have to trust us, it's huge.

[. . .]

DL: There's been some talk this morning about the influences and *The Sweeney* was often mentioned; *Get Carter* was talked about. How conscious is that? How does it inform the making of the show?

CP: In terms of the script development, it didn't really inform it a huge amount, because at that point it was just about storytelling and the rules and getting the world right. When it did start to inform it was when the first director, Bharat Nalluri, came on board. He really drew on those kind of seventies films like *Get Carter* and *The Long Good Friday* and those kind of things. He would talk about that with the set designer and the costume designer; then everybody watched those films to see the material he was referring to.

JG: I think those films are influential in maintaining a tone for the show. So rather than trying to steal a look or a particular sensibility, it's about trying to maintain a consistent tone. When you are dealing with so many elements of cop show or sci-fi or fantasy or human drama, the comedy, the when it's tough, the how far should Gene Hunt be a racist, be a misogynist, be those things; he's a heightened character, but he's also a real character, so all the time, whenever in meetings we would refer to *The Sweeney* or something, it was about how robust is the storytelling of the cop show, what is it like for them as policemen versus, I don't know, a discussion about Mark Twain in one meeting; so all the time you're trying to find a way through, tonally, an episode.

DL: Was *Life on* Mars sold as a nostalgic show?

JG: It wasn't sold to us as a broadcaster that way, it was sold as, 'The drama will have added depth because we're gonna look at how we live versus how we lived in the seventies'. When we talked about *Life on Mars* as set in the seventies, it really felt like an alien planet. It's only thirty-five years ago, but it felt so different, everyone's attitudes, so we knew we were really on to something in that regard.

CP: A lot of people have memories of the seventies, and that's why people liked it, but I don't have any memories of that period, so I had to do a lot of research about it and that threw up things that we hadn't remembered or things that were surprising. So it wasn't nostalgia, exactly, but it was a chance to look at the past in relation to the present.

JG: And we're never trying to say one period is better than the other; actually, we never try and answer that question; that's for the audience.

DL: I wanted to turn now to questions related to the actual making of the show. Could you tell me how long the shoot was for a given episode?

CP: We shoot basically two episodes at a time in a block, and each block takes five weeks, so twenty-five days of filming.

DL: Twenty-five days for an episode?

CP: For two episodes.

DL: For two episodes, as opposed to the American standard of eight days for an episode.

JG: Yeah, we're slower, much slower than you.

DL: As I mentioned earlier, there was a question all along about trying to give John Simm a break, because he was so overwhelmed, and if I understand correctly the *Camberwick Green* episode was in a way born out of an attempt to give him some time off?

CP: It was. It was a practical concern, trying to help John, but also, by the time we got to series two, we did quite like the idea of is there a way in which we can play with the form of an episode? We did talk about whether there would be an entire episode that he wouldn't be in, whether there'd be elements in each episode that he might not be in. In the end, it fell on to the *Camberwick Green* episode and we felt that was an interesting way to tell a story, but also a practical way to give him a bit of a break.

DL: It's striking to me how often some of the great decisions made in television series are made out of necessity. The director of the first episode, Bharat Nalluri, had worked for your production company on *Spooks* and *Hustle*, both, so he was a fairly natural choice to be the director of the first episode.

CP: He was.

DL: Can you talk a little bit about how directors are chosen? Because by the time you were done, how many people had directed an episode of *Life on Mars*?

CP: Probably about six.

DL: And when you came to the end, to arguably the most important episode, it was S. J. Clarkson that you chose to be the one you wanted to be in charge. How did those decisions happen?

CP: They were fairly organic, really, the same as when you're commissioning writers. You sort of look at who is the best person for the job, whether they're available, whether they want to do it, past collaborations; and, in terms of directors, the key thing is how well they're going to get on with the actors. The choice of S.J. to do the final episode was because she had a huge investment in the series; she had come on board as quite a new director on series one and she was incredibly passionate about the show and she's a strong storyteller. We therefore invited her back to open the second series, and

I wanted her to be involved in the storylining process as well, which is not unheard of, but quite unusual for a director to be involved in that stage, because I really valued her opinions. So she was very invested in the series and I just knew she would be the right person to close the series.

JG: You're thinking about really practical things, can they shoot the schedule, can they work within budget, because you can't have one block of two episodes going off the rails, because the implications for the whole series are just simply too damaging, so it's about the whole creative process and what creativity a director would bring, but within a framework of what is a series, that is defined by the producer and the lead director. So it's a very kind of specific thing you're looking for. One of the things that was brilliant about S.J. was that she was so immensely collaborative. She's a creative force in her own right, but then what I adored about Sam on the roof in that last episode, was how it mirrored his arrival in the seventies in term of the camera shots. That felt like she wasn't going to be precious, wanting her own shot there, she was going to honour episode one, because that's the right thing to do for the whole show.

DL: Even though she didn't make that first episode.

CP: She'd watched it, obviously, incredibly carefully and thought about why Bharat had chosen that particular shot and then thought about how well that could work as the final shot.

DL: In the States, the number of women directors working in film is very rare, and there's many more in television, it seems. Do you think it's easier for a woman director to break into television here in the UK, than in film?

JG: I don't think so. I think there's just more TV, more opportunities; there's just simply more hours of TV, so your chances are that much greater.

CP: And potentially you could work your way up, in a way, but that's the same with any director, male or female, getting their break.

DL: Another topic that's been raised often at this symposium is the political correctness. No matter how many horrible things they put into Gene Hunt's mouth, the people just seem to love him more, and if I'm remembering correctly, someone said they were a bit troubled by that. Was it an issue for you at all?

JG: Not really. It was something that we were vigilant about, that we would talk about; I wouldn't say it was an issue. The primary thing you're trying to achieve is a character that is faithful to himself and the world in which he exists. Gene Hunt, all the time we were looking at not going too broad with him, because he's a seventies figure, because he is occasionally sexist and racist and homophobic. It has to be truthful about him, and you see these terribly outdated, awful views, you also need to flip that and see the morality of the man and what he does stand for. I think all the time you're looking at a balance of that. Where it's tricky is if you're doing a story that is about race, because what you then don't want, in my view, is for all the characters in that story to be horribly racist, which is a kind of turn-off to watch. I want to go into that world, I want the issues to be raised, but I don't want to spend the time, particularly, in that world in a BBC 1 prime-time show.

CP: That's probably why, in the first series, we tried to avoid any of the episodes being about something that you could define as some sort of issue, whereas in the second series, we felt like we really wanted to explore all those things. We had a bit more space and confidence to do that.

JG: There were a few times where Sam would make jokes about . . . What political jokes does he make?

CP: There were a couple of references to Margaret Thatcher and all that. We tried not to be too overtly political, because I don't think Sam would've been and Gene would've been; they're just doing their thing, really.

DL: I mentioned I wanted to come back to sci-fi. Why is it that so many people wanted to read it as science fiction?

JG: I got confused by this debate, to be honest, because of how we opened episode one of season one, which was very clearly: he's in the present day, he's knocked out, it's very clear to me that he's in a coma. So from that point on, I was kind of bewildered by 'Is he in a coma? No!' I mean, did anyone see the first five minutes of episode one? Did they not see that? What I do understand, though, because it's also about an investment; it's fascinating, it's the curiosity of the viewer; they want to look for things, they want to ferret things out, and explore it and think about it. That's a great thing and I think, in that way, I would say, it's sci-fi: the discussion, and all those discussions about 'Maybe Gene Hunt is actually existing in the present day, and he's actually, Gene Hunt's the doctor'; that's quite good, why didn't we think of that? It's the discourse, I think, that sci-fi offers.

CP: The reason that I never wanted to think of it as sci-fi is that I wanted it always to be real. Sam's a real character, and whatever has happened to him, his world needs to be completely real. For me, sometimes, sci-fi has the air of being even more heightened than *Life on Mars* is, being in a world that doesn't really exist. We wanted to feel like, he doesn't know what's happened to him, but whatever's happened to him, he has to deal with it, he has to deal with it in a real way.

DL: I've been intrigued, particularly towards the end of series two, by the emphasis on metaphor. We think of metaphor as something more literary, that film and TV do not necessarily pull off all that well, and yet, the end of *Life on Mars*, in narrative and in theme, really made use of metaphor in a lot of ways. How much were you trying to be metaphoric, and do you think it worked?

JG: I don't think we were trying specifically to be metaphoric; I think you're looking for symbols that people will identify and recognise and I think the tunnel, in a show where a man is in a coma, where he is living in his mind, where he is a moment from death, a tunnel is something everyone will understand. For me the end of series two is immeasurably romantic, and I think Sam is immeasurably heroic on that roof, the choice he makes, essentially, to die in order to live, to live a fantasy life, is incredibly romantic, and brave, and is a very kind of poetic literature, almost.

DL: It was rumoured, but I couldn't tell from interviews, that an alternate ending was ever shot.

CP: We made it up.

JG: Yeah, we lied, essentially.

DL: To what end?

JG: To protect the stories. Everyone's constantly going on 'we shot five endings, which one is it going to be?' On a TV budget, you don't really have the time to shoot five endings, but you're desperately, ferociously, trying to protect the way your season two ends.

CP: The press, you know, they were . . .

JG: They were all over us!

CP: All sorts of tricks to try and get people to give away the ending, so we started the rumour for that reason.

DL: Just one last thing; one of the people on the DVD talks about how the finale was actually changed, not just in shooting, but in post-production, that there were things that happened in 2.8, and I believe it was in regard to sound?

CP: There was always quite a lot that we added in sound.

DL: Clues, suggestions, thematic?

CP: Exactly, and that for me crystallised the collaborative nature of the show, because everyone who worked on it was so enthusiastic, even by the time we got to the sound. We'd have new ideas, and then something would come up and we would play around with stuff. All the way through the series, there were extra levels and quite a few hidden things in there that we played around with in the edit and that no one would even notice, just small details.

DL: Well, that's the end of my questions. Does anyone in the audience have any?

Q1: Just to jump back to the casting, Annie, who kind of emotionally is the centre of the show, but physically is probably as far away from a *FHM*-friendly babe as you could get.[1] Was that a conscious decision early on, before the casting even happened, or was that Liz White coming in . . . ?

JG: I think it was Liz White coming in. She's an extraordinary actor, and as soon as we saw her, it was about, she's girl-next-door. If Sam is in a completely alien world, you want a girl-next-door, you want a touchstone, you want an anchor. Maybe she's a nostalgic character, to use that word, in his mind he's creating these characters, it makes sense to me that Sam would create Liz White.

CP: Liz can look different in many different roles, but we were sure she'd be convincing as a 1970s woman.

Q2: I wonder if you both might talk about your own personal roles within the show, and what you think about the idea of the 'creative producer'.

JG: I love it; I applaud it.

CP: I think the thing is that on a series, the producer is the only person, really, who is across every single decision and the writers are hugely instrumental, but they can't be across every single decision, and neither can the directors, because we had lots of different directors . . . So I don't really see that there is any other way; there has to be someone having that role on a show and it naturally falls to the producer.

JG: I think there are two distinctions I would make. Specifically for *Life on Mars*, I am one removed, because it's an independent show making it for me as the BBC exec, so specifically for *Life on Mars* my job is to be a cheerleader, come in when everyone's exhausted or come in when there's a script that they want me to read, so I'm not reading every single draft of every script. I'm not viewing the rushes as fast as that team; I can delay, I can watch every few days. I'm watching the fine-cut when they invite me in; I'm not watching every single fine-cut. When I'm exec-ing my in-house shows, I'm watching the rushes every single day, I'm watching every edit, I'm going to every single script meeting, I am the link across the whole series, so that's the first thing. The second thing is that for the creative producer as you call it, personally I think it sometimes depends on what format of show you're making, because occasionally, if I make a single drama, I don't quite mean, this is too black and white, but I'm there to support the director's vision. On a series, of course I'm still there to support the director's vision, but it's what Claire says, I'm the one left standing nine months into a run; the first director is long gone and on their third job by that point. In that world, I'm the person that defines the tone, or helps define, maintain the consistency of the tone.

Q3: Kudos Productions has developed a reputation for quality dramas. I was wondering if you're actually conscious of a specific identity creating shows like *Hustle*, like *Life on Mars*, which are cinematic, breaking conventions of television and using more kind of cinema stylistic elements. Can you talk about the identity of the company, of the kind of drama it produces; and the relation with BBC?

CP: I think, we just try to make programmes we know we would watch, that we would like, try to always be ambitious with them and never fall into patterns.

JG: I'd give you two examples, specifically about Kudos. I was working for ITV when *Spooks* was about to air and there was this brilliant conversation where I said 'Oh my God, that's such a good idea, I'd love to do a spy show, Christ, we should've thought of that.' The person I was talking to said 'It will be terrible; it's for the BBC, it will be so wordy, it will all be about the Cold War and oh God, it will just be so wordy and dull.' Maybe . . . And then episode one saw a head in a chip-fat-fryer . . . Okay, it's not wordy, then, it's not 1950s Cold War, we're not doing 'state of the nation'. That is one of the things they did, they brought really robust entertainment – very well written, very bold, very clear storytelling – to series. I think the other thing, that's not just Kudos, I'm speaking in very broad industry terms, I think at that point, shall we say seven years ago [c.2001], I think that show really made series TV in the UK exciting again, because, I think, as a nation, a lot of our work is defined by playwrights and theatre, which is fantastic in many ways, but I think they made TV series start to feel sexy, start to feel quite American, in the good ways that kind of pace the wit of the story-telling, the clear definition of a genre, and I think at that point we needed that.

[. . .]

Q4: It seems that in every episode there was a song from 1973, or maybe around there, that was very pronounced; there was Thin Lizzy, there was Free, there was David Bowie, obviously. How important was this particular kind of popular music element for the show?

CP: Firstly, it was about setting the scene and using songs like we use in the design or the costumes to create the world. Obviously, in terms of the emotional impact of the storytelling, there were certain songs that were chosen for the impact. What we wanted to do, as well, was to make a clear distinction between 1973 tracks and the incidental music which Edmund Butt wrote, which he really felt strongly – and it was part of a discussion we had – it was not to pastiche the seventies, but to use the seventies songs where we wanted to use the seventies songs. His take on it was that it was a story about a man from the present day and therefore he could use contemporary music to illustrate his story. The music was important, and in a lot of cases was chosen by the director and editor in the edit suite. In some cases, we changed the music for practical reasons or because we just couldn't find the right song and then eventually we did. It was really important, the music.

Q4: Was it part of the script, if it was scripted, which song was to be used?

CP: Sometimes it was, but often the writers would write a song in to show that they wanted a song to play over a certain sequence of scenes, but often it wouldn't work, for whatever reason, or the director would have another particular song that they had in mind, but, still, it was sometimes helpful to just have the kind of song, the idea that they were thinking about in the script.

Q5: We were talking this morning about how British *Life on Mars* and *Ashes to Ashes* seems to many of us. *Life on Mars* has been aired on BBC America. How do you feel about sending it off in that way? And on the American remake of it, what degree of investment or involvement do you have and would you like to have in such a process?

CP: Once it's made, it's kind of out of our control, anyway, whether it's shown for British audiences or American audiences. It's kind of exciting to see the difference in reactions and interpretations.

JG: We initially thought it might not sell abroad as well as it has, because it felt like such an English-centred, British-focused show. Some of the anecdotes, language, references were very, very British. But in having that consideration, we underestimated not just the quality of the show, but that the concept is so universal and I think there's such an appetite for those concepts that can play anywhere, and I think it does, the kind of idea of a man lost, trying to find his way home. It's easy, actually, to sell that away, and for the American remake, I just can't wait! I just can't wait to see what is done with that, and it's actually incredibly liberating not to have any involvement. I know Jane Featherstone does, to some extent, but it's, you kind of want to let it go, you want to kind of see how another country will interpret it, and whether it would work.

[. . .]

Q6: Could you say a little bit about the demographics of the audience, whether you had a sense of strong groups watching or not?

JG: I've got no idea and I really should! People send me bits of paper about it, I go to all these meetings with 'Oh God, no one young is watching, oh God, they're all on YouTube', yeah, I know, it's terrible. I have a vague recollection that a slightly younger student audience was watching as well as . . .

CP: And a slightly more male.

JG: Because a more male audience normally comes to drama because, frankly, the car, I think, the car and Gene; it was a bit more male and a bit younger. Beyond that . . . Over to you, no idea.

CP: I just remember reading that it was above average for the slots, and that's all I can remember.

JG: Which is all you cared about! If she'd read it was below average, we'd know everything!

CP: It's not going to change the way you think about a programme, you just have to only be thinking . . . You can't be worrying, I don't think you can, anyway, you can't be thinking is this going to work better for a younger or an older audience, apart from in very broad terms, but if your main aim is to make a programme for as broad an audience as possible, which I'd have thought is mainly the point of most programmes, then that's the only thing you can do.

JG: I think that's right. Before you go on this crazy enterprise of filming anything, you do think about what your slot is and I think that is where I do my work rather than later, looking at who is watching that slot. A 7 o'clock Saturday slot is a very specific thing that you are thinking in a very specific way about the ages of characters and the kind of mix. It was just obviously very different to 9 o'clock Monday night; and that's where you do your thinking, it's up-front, though I am alone, possibly, in saying this.

[END]

NOTE

1   *FHM* is a UK men's magazine aimed at a twenty-something audience.

LIFE ON MARS AND ASHES TO ASHES

PRODUCTION AND TRANSMISSION DETAILS

Both series of *Life on Mars* were co-created by Matthew Graham, Ashley Pharoah and Tony Jordan. *Ashes to Ashes* was co-created by Graham and Pharoah.

LIFE ON MARS: SERIES 1

All episodes were first transmitted 9.00–10.00 p.m. on BBC 1, and the dates are of first broadcast.
Executive producers: Jane Featherstone (Kudos); Julie Gardner (BBC Wales); Matthew Graham.
Producer/line producer: Claire Parker, Marcus Wilson
Cinematography: Adam Suschitzky (1.1, 1.2); Tim Palmer (1.3, 1.4); Balazs Bolygo (1.5, 1.7); Grant Cameron (1.6, 1.8)
Original music: Edmund Butt

Episode One (1.1)
Writer: Matthew Graham
Director: Bharat Nalluri
Transmission: Monday 9 January 2006

Episode Two (1.2)
Writer: Matthew Graham
Director: Bharat Nalluri
Transmission: Monday 16 January 2006

Episode Three (1.3)
Writer: Matthew Graham
Director: John McKay
Transmission: Monday 23 January 2006

Episode Four (1.4)
Writer: Ashley Pharoah
Director: John McKay
Transmission: Monday 30 January 2006

Episode Five (1.5)
Writer: Tony Jordan
Director: S. J. Clarkson
Transmission: Monday 6 February 2006

Episode Six (1.6)
Writers: Matthew Graham and Ashley Pharoah
Director: John Alexander
Transmission: Monday 13 February 2006

Episode Seven (1.7)
Writer: Chris Chibnall
Director: S. J. Clarkson
Transmission: Monday 20 February 2006

Episode Eight (1.8)
Writer: Matthew Graham
Director: John Alexander
Transmission: Monday 7 February 2006

LIFE ON MARS: SERIES 2

All episodes were first transmitted 9.00–10.00 p.m. on BBC 1 except where noted below. There was a break in transmission on Tuesday 27 February (the series made way for a football match). After this point, the practice of trailing the following week's episode on BBC Four directly after transmission of the current episode was dropped in favour of repeating the previous weeks.
Executive producers: Jane Featherstone (Kudos); Claire Parker (Kudos); Julie Gardner (BBC Wales); Matthew Graham
Producer/line producer: Marcus Wilson, Cameron Roach
Cinematography: Balazs Bolygo (2.1–2.6); Tim Palmer (2.7, 2.8)
Original music: Edmund Butt

Episode 1 (2.1)
Writer: Matthew Graham
Director: S. J. Clarkson
Transmission: Tuesday 13 February 2007

Episode Two (2.2)
Writer: Chris Chibnall
Director: S. J. Clarkson
Transmission: Tuesday 13 February 2007, 10.00–11.00 p.m. on BBC Four and then Tuesday 20 February 9.00–10.00 p.m. on BBC 1.

Episode Three (2.3)
Writer: Julie Rutterford
Director: Richard Clark
Transmission: Tuesday 20 February 2007, 10.00–11.00 p.m. on BBC Four and then Tuesday 6 March 9.00–10.00 p.m. on BBC 1.

Episode Four (2.4)
Writer: Ashley Pharoah
Director: Richard Clark
Transmission: Tuesday 13 March 2007

Episode Five (2.5)
Writer: Matthew Graham
Director: Andrew Gunn
Transmission: Tuesday 20 March 2007

Episode Six (2.6)
Writer: Guy Jenkin
Director: Andrew Gunn
Transmission: Tuesday 27 March 2007.

Episode Seven (2.7)
Writer: Mark Greig
Director: S. J. Clarkson
Transmission: Tuesday 3 April 2007

Episode Eight (2.8)
Writer: Matthew Graham
Director: S. J. Clarkson
Transmission: Tuesday 10 April 2007

ASHES TO ASHES: SERIES 1

All episodes were transmitted 9.00–10.00 p.m. on BBC 1, and the dates are of the first broadcast.
Executive producers: Jane Featherstone (Kudos); Simon Crawford Collins (Kudos); Matthew Graham (Monastic Productions)
Producer/line producer: Beth Willis, Helga Dowie

Cinematography: Julian Court (1.1, 1.2); Nic Lawson (1.3, 1.5); Simon Archer (1.4, 1.6); Tim Palmer (1.7, 1.8)
Original music: Edmund Butt

Episode One (1.1)
Writer: Matthew Graham
Director: Jonny Campbell
Transmission: Thursday 7 February 2008.

Episode Two (1.2)
Writer: Ashley Pharoah
Director: Jonny Campbell
Transmission: Thursday 14 February 2008

Episode Three (1.3)
Writer: Julie Rutterford
Director: Bille Eltringham
Transmission: Thursday 21 February 2008

Episode Four (1.4)
Writer: Mark Greig
Director: Catherine Morshead
Transmission: Thursday 28 February 2008

Episode Five (1.5)
Writer: Mark Greig
Director: Bille Eltringham
Transmission: Thursday 6 March 2008

Episode Six (1.6)
Writer: Mick Ford
Director: Catherine Morshead
Transmission: Thursday 13 March 2008

Episode Seven (1.7)
Writer: Matthew Graham
Director: Jonny Campbell
Transmission: Thursday 20 March 2008

Episode Eight (1.8)
Writer: Ashley Pharoah
Director: Jonny Campbell
Transmission: Thursday 27 March 2008

ASHES TO ASHES: SERIES 2

All episodes were transmitted 9.00–10.00 p.m. on BBC 1, and the dates are of the first broadcast.
Executive producers: Jane Featherstone (Kudos); Simon Crawford Collins (Kudos); Matthew Graham (Monastic Productions); Piers Wenger (BBC Wales)
Producer/line producer: Beth Willis, Patrick Schweitzer
Cinematography: Simon Archer (2.1, 2.2, 2.7, 2.8); Fabian Wagner (2.3, 2.4); Tim Palmer (2.5, 2.6);
Original music: Edmund Butt

Episode One (2.1)
Writer: Ashley Pharoah
Director: Catherine Morshead
Transmission: Monday 20 April 2009

Episode Two (2.2)
Writer: Matthew Graham
Director: Catherine Morshead
Transmission: Monday 27 April 2009

Episode Three (2.3)
Writer: Nicole Taylor
Director: Ben Bolt
Transmission: Monday 4 May 2009

Episode Four (2.4)
Writer: Ashley Pharoah
Director: Ben Bolt
Transmission: Monday 11 May 2009

Episode Five (2.5)
Writer: Julie Rutterford
Director: Philip John
Transmission: Monday 18 May 2009

Episode Six (2.6)
Writer: Jack Lothian
Director: Philip John
Transmission: Monday 25 May 2009

Episode Seven (2.7)
Writer: Mark Greig
Director: Catherine Morshead
Transmission: Monday 1 June 2009

Episode Eight (2.8)
Writer: Matthew Graham
Director: Catherine Morshead
Transmission: Monday 8 June 2009

ASHES TO ASHES: SERIES 3

All episodes were transmitted 9.00–10.00 p.m. on BBC 1, and the dates are of the first broadcast.
Executive producers: Jane Featherstone (Kudos); Simon Crawford Collins (Kudos); Alison Jackson (Kudos); Matthew Graham (Monastic Productions); Piers Wenger (BBC Wales)
Producer/line producer: Howard Burch, Sue Calverley
Cinematography: Adam Sushitzky (3.1–3.4); Balazs Bolygo (3.5–3.8)
Original music: Edmund Butt

Episode One (3.1)
Writer: Matthew Graham
Director: David Drury
Transmission: Friday 2 April 2010

Episode Two (3.2)
Writer: Ashley Pharoah
Director: David Drury
Transmission: Friday 9 April 2010

Episode Three (3.3)
Writer: Julie Rutterford
Director: Alrick Riley
Transmission: Friday 16 April 2010

Episode Four (3.4)
Writer: Jack Lothian
Director: Alrick Riley
Transmission: Friday 23 April 2010

Episode Five (3.5)
Writers: Tom Butterworth and Chris Hurforth
Director: Jamie Payne
Transmission: Friday 30 April 2010

Episode Six (3.6)
Writer: James Payne
Director: Jamie Payne
Transmission: Friday 7 May 2010

Episode Seven (3.7)
Writer: Ashley Pharoah
Director: David Drury
Transmission: Friday 14 May 2010

Episode Eight (3.8)
Writer: Matthew Graham
Director: David Drury
Transmission: Friday 21 May 2010

BIBLIOGRAPHY

'ABC's *Lost* TV drama' (2007), *On Point with Tom Ashbrook* [online radio resource], 28 March 2007, *http://www.onpointradio.org/shows/2007/03/abcs-lost-tv-drama/*, accessed 24 May 2010.

Adams, G. and Thompson, L. (2006). *Life on Mars: The Official Companion*, New York and London, Pocket Books.

Akass, K. and McCabe, J. (2004). *Reading Sex and the City*, London, I. B. Tauris.

Akass, K. and McCabe, J. (eds) (2007). *Quality TV: Contemporary American TV and Beyond*, London, I. B. Tauris.

Altman, R. (1999). *Film/Genre*, London, British Film Institute.

Anderson, B. (1983). *Imagined Communities: Reflections on the Origin and Spread of Nationalism*, London and New York, Verso.

Arthurs, J. (2003). '*Sex and the City* and consumer culture: remediating post-feminist drama', *Feminist Media Studies*, 3, 1, 83–98.

Ash, B. (ed.) (1977). *The Visual Encyclopedia of Science Fiction*, London, Pan Books.

'Ashes to Ashes: cops love Gene Hunt', *Unreality Primetime* [website], *http://primetime.unrealitytv.co.uk/ashes-to-ashes-cops-love-gene-hunt*, accessed 10 June 2010.

Attwood, F. (ed.) (2009). *Mainstreaming Sex: The Sexualization of Western Culture*, London, I. B. Tauris.

Bachelard, G. (1958). *The Poetics of Space*, Boston, MA, Beacon Press.

Barthes, R. (1977). *Image–Music–Text*, London, Fontana Press.

BBC (2004a). 'BBC boss details 3,000 job cuts', *BBC News* [online news resource], *http://news.bbc.co.uk/1/hi/entertainment/tv_and_radio/4073571.stm*, accessed 9 March 2009.

BBC (2004b). 'Building public value: renewing the BBC for a digital world', *BBC* [website], *http://www.bbc.co.uk/thefuture/pdfs/bbc_bpv.pdf*, accessed 9 March 2009.

BBC (2007). *BBC Annual Report and Accounts 2006–2007*, London, BBC.

BBC (2008). *BBC Annual Report and Accounts 2007–2008*, London, BBC.

BBC (2009). *BBC Annual Report and Accounts 2008–2009*, London, BBC.

BBC Press Pack (2005). 'A sign of the times: How the seventies were brought back to life', *BBC* [website], *http://www.bbc.co.uk/pressoffice/pressreleases/ stories/2005/12_december/08/mars_life.shtml*, accessed 23 October 2007.

Benwell, B. (2004). 'Ironic discourse: masculinity in men's lifestyle magazines', *Men and Masculinities* 7, 1, 3–21.

Belam, M. (2007). 'The tardis and multiplatform', *currybetdotnet* [website], *http://www.currybet.net/cbet_blog/2007/09/the_tardis_and_multiplatform. php*, accessed 18 December 2008.

BFI (2007). *The BFI TV 100* [website], *http://www.bfi.org.uk/features/tv/100/list/list. php*, accessed 9 March 2009.

Bielby, D. (2008). *Global TV. Exporting Television and Culture in Global Market*, New York, New York University Press.

Bignell, J. (2007). 'Seeing and knowing: reflexivity and quality', in J. McCabe and K. Akass (eds), *Quality TV: Contemporary American Television and Beyond*, London, I. B. Tauris, pp. 158–70.

Broadcasters Audience Research Board (2009). 'Annual % shares of viewing (individuals) 1981–2008', *BARB* [website], *http://www.barb.co.uk/facts/annualShare OfViewing?_s=4*, accessed 17 November 2009.

Brunsdon, C. (2000). 'The structure of anxiety: recent British television crime fiction', in E. Buscombe (ed.), *British Television: A Reader*, Oxford, Oxford University Press, pp. 195–217.

Butt, E. (2006). 'The music of *Life on Mars*', Disk 2, Bonus Features, *Life on Mars: The Complete Series One*, Contender Home Entertainment.

Campbell, J. (2008). 'Commentary on episode one', Disk 1, Bonus Features, *Ashes to Ashes: The Complete Series One*, Contender Home Entertainment.

Campbell, N., Davies, J. and McKay, G. (eds) (2004). *Issues in Americanization and Culture*, Edinburgh, Edinburgh University Press.

Cardwell, S. (2007). 'Is quality television any good? Generic distinctions, evaluations and the troubling matter of critical judgement', in J. McCabe and K. Akass (eds), *Quality TV: Contemporary American Television and Beyond*, London, I. B. Tauris, pp. 19–34.

Carr, G. (2008). *The Angry Brigade: The Spectacular Rise and Fall of Britain's First Urban Guerrilla Group*, Oakland, PM Press, DVD.

Carroll, N. (1990). *The Philosophy of Horror*, New York and London, Routledge.

Carson, B. and Llewellyn-Jones, M. (eds) (2000). *Frames and Fictions on Television: The Politics of Identity within Drama*, Exeter, Intellect.

Carter, B. (2006). *Desperate Networks*, New York, Broadway Books.

Castells, M. (1998). *End of Millenium: Vol. III: The Information Age – Economy, Society and Culture*, Oxford, Blackwell.

Castells, M. (2000). *The Rise of the Network Society: Vol. 1: The Information Age: Economy, Society and Culture* (second edition), Oxford, Blackwell.

Caughie, J. (2000). *Television Drama: Realism, Modernism, and British Culture*, Oxford, Oxford University Press.

Caughie, J. (2007). *BFI TV Classics: Edge of Darkness*, London, BFI Publishing.

Chalaby, J. K. (ed.) (2005). *Transnational Television Worldwide: Towards a New Media Order*, London, I. B. Tauris.

Clark, A. 'Sweeney, The (1975–78)', *BFI Screenonline* [website], *http://www.screenonline.org.uk/tv/id/473709/index.html*, accessed 24 May 2010.

Clarke, E. F. (1999). *Music Analysis 18/iii*, Oxford, Blackwell, pp. 347–74.

Collins, A. (2003). *Where Did It All Go Right? Growing Up Normal in the 70s*, London, Ebury Press.

Cook, J. and Wright, P. (2006). '"Futures past": an introduction to and brief survey of British science fiction television', in John R. Cook and Peter Wright (eds), *British Science Fiction Television – A Hitchhiker's Guide*, London, I. B. Tauris, pp. 1–20.

Cook, N. (1998). *Analysing Musical Multimedia*, Oxford, Oxford University Press.

Cooke, L. (2005). 'The new social realism of *Clocking Off*', in J. Bignell and S. Lacey (eds), *Popular Television Drama: Critical Perspectives*, Manchester, Manchester University Press, pp. 183–97.

Cooke, L. (2008). 'The crime series', in Glen Creeber (ed.), *The Television Genre Book* (second edition), London, British Film Institute/Palgrave, pp. 29–34.

Cooke, M. (2008). *A History of Film Music*, Cambridge, Cambridge University Press.

Couldry, N. (2003). *Media Rituals: A Critical Approach*, London, Routledge.

D'Acci, J. (1992). 'Defining women: the case of *Cagney and Lacey*', in L. Spigel and D. Mann (eds), *Private Screenings: Television and the Female Consumer*, Minneapolis, University of Minnesota Press, pp. 169–201.

Daily Mail Reporter. 'Philip Glenister: drugs, shoplifting and why he loves cuddling babies', *Mail Online* [online news resource], *www.dailymail.co.uk/femail/article-1168290/Philip-Glenister-Drugs-shoplifting-loves-cuddling-babies.html#ixzz0TpkK7qIy*, accessed 9 October 2009.

Dalyell, T. (1977). *Devolution: The End of Britain?*, London, Jonathan Cape.

Day, C. (2007). *Environment and Children – Passive Lessons from the Everyday Environment*, Oxford, Architectural Press.

Dillon, B. (2005). *In the Dark Room – A Journey in Memory*, Dublin, Penguin Ireland.

Dobson, N. (2009). 'Generic difference and innovation in *CSI: Crime Scene Investigation*', in M. Byers and V. Johnson (eds), *The CSI Effect*, Lanham, MD, Lexington Books.

Dowell, B. (2006). 'BBC chiefs welcome White Paper', *Guardian.co.uk* [online news resource], *http://media.guardian.co.uk/broadcast/story/0,,1730801,00.html*, accessed 9 March 2009.

Dromey, J. and Taylor, G. (1978). *Grunwick: The Workers' Story*, London, Lawrence & Wishart.

Dunleavy, T. (2008). 'Hybridity in TV sitcom: The case of comedy verité', *Flow* Volume 9.04. [website], *http://flowtv.org/?p=2244*, accessed 25 August 2010.

Dyer, R. (1992). *Only Entertainment*, London, Routledge.

Eco, U. (1981). *The Role of the Reader: Explorations in the Semiotics of Texts*, London, Hutchinson.

'Edmund Butt', *Cool Music Ltd* [website], *http://www.coolmusicltd.com/Composers/ Edmund-Butt/Edmund-Butt.html*, accessed 2 February 2009.

European Directive (89/552/EC) (1989). 'Television without frontiers', *European Directive* [website], *http://www.europa.eu.int/scadplus/leg/en/lvb/l24101.htm*, accessed 9 March 2009.

Fiske, J. (1987). *Television Culture*, London and New York, Routledge.

Fórmula TV (2009). *'La chica de ayer* se despecide de la audiencia con una media cercana al 15%', *Fórmula TV* [website], *http://www.formulatv.com/ 1,20090611,11705,1.html*, accessed 5 July 2010.

Freud, S. (1919). *The Uncanny*, London, Penguin Books.

Gill, R. (2007). 'Postfeminist media culture: elements of a sensibility', *European Journal of Cultural Studies*, 10, 2, 147–66.

Gill, R. (2008). 'Empowerment/sexism: figuring female sexual agency in contemporary advertising', *Feminism & Psychology,* 18, 1, 35–60.

Gillis, S., Howie, G. and Munford, R. (eds) (2004). *Third Wave Feminism: A Critical Exploration*, London, Palgrave Macmillan.

Glenister, P. (2007). 'The return of *Life on Mars*', Disc 1, Bonus Features, *Life on Mars: the Complete Series Two,* Contender Home Entertainment.

Glenister, P., cited in McLean, C. *'Ashes to Ashes*: hot fuzz', *Daily Telegraph*, 26 January 2008, [online news resource], *http://www.telegraph.co.uk/culture/ tvandradio/3670760/Ashes-to-Ashes-Hot-fuzz.html*, accessed 30 June 2010.

Graham, M. (2006). 'Take a look at the lawman – the making of *Life on Mars*, Part 1', Disk 1, Bonus Features, *Life on Mars – The Complete Series One*, Contender Home Entertainment.

Graham, M. (2007). *'Life on Mars*: the answers', *Manchester Evening News*, 11 April 2007 [online news resource], *http://blogs.manchestereveningnews. co.uk/ianwylie/2007/04/life_on_mars_the_answers.html*, accessed 18 December 2008.

Graham, M. (2008). 'Backstage: questions: inspiration', *BBC Drama: Life on Mars*, *http://www.bbc.co.uk/lifeonmars/backstage/questions_inspiration.shtml*, accessed 24 May 2010.

Graham, M. (2010). 'Dust to dust', DVD extras on *Ashes to Ashes: Series 3*, BBC Worldwide/Contender Home Entertainment.

Hammond, S. (2006). 'Top cop's race charge', *The Asian News*, 29 June.

Handlin, Z. (2008). 'Out here in the fields', *Onion TV Club* [website], *http://www. avclub.com/articles/out-here-in-the-fields,13245/*, accessed 24 May 2010.

Handlin, Z. (2009a). 'Let all the children boogie', *Onion TV Club* [website], *http://www.avclub.com/articles/let-all-the-children-boogie,23732/*, accessed 24 May 2010.

Handlin, Z. (2009b). 'Life is a rock', *Onion TV Club* [website], *http://www.avclub. com/articles/life-is-a-rock,26085/*, accessed 24 May 2010.

Hart, J. A. (2004). *Technology, Television and Competition: The Politics of Digital TV*, Cambridge, Cambridge University Press.

Harvey, D. (1989). *The Condition of Postmodernity: An Enquiry into the Origins of Cultural Change*, Oxford, Blackwell.

Haslam, D. (2005). *Young Hearts Run Free*, London, Harper Collins.

Hill, J. (1986). *Sex, Class and Realism: British Cinema 1956–1963*, London, British Film Institute.

Hills, M. (2000). *Fan Cultures*, London, Routledge.

Hills, M. (2005). *The Pleasures of Horror*, London and New York, Continuum.

Hockley, L. (2001). 'Science fiction', in G. Creeber (ed.), *The Television Genre Book*, London, British Film Institute.

Hollows, J. (2003). 'Feeling like a domestic goddess: postfeminism and cooking', *European Journal of Cultural Studies*, 6, 2, 179–202.

Holmwood, L. (2007). 'Plenty of life on mars', *Guardian.co.uk* [online news resource], *http://www.guardian.co.uk/media/2007/apr/11/overnights*, accessed 13 March 2009.

Hurd, G. (1981). 'The television presentation of the police', in T. Bennett et al. (eds), *Popular Television and Film*, London, British Film Institute, pp. 53–70.

Jackson, P., Stevenson, N. and Brooks, K. (2001). *Making Sense of Men's Magazines*, Cambridge, Polity Press.

Jancovich, M. and Lyons, J. (eds) (2003). *Quality Popular Television: Cult TV, the Industry and the Fans*, London, British Film Institute.

Jenkins, H. (1992). *Textual Poachers: Television Fans and Participatory Culture*, New York and London, Routledge.

Jenkins, H. (2006). *Convergence Culture: Where Old and New Media Collide*, New York and London, New York University Press.

Jenkins, H. (2006). *Fans, Bloggers and Gamers: Exploring Participatory Culture*, New York, New York University Press.

Jenkins, S. (1984). '*Hill Street Blues*', in Jane Feuer, Paul Kerr and Tish Vahimagi (eds), *MTM 'Quality Television'*, London, British Film Institute.

Jenkins, S. (2006). *Thatcher and Sons: A Revolution in Three Acts*, London, Penguin.

Jermyn, D. (2003). 'Women with a mission: Lynda La Plante, DCI Jane Tennison and the reconfiguration of TV crime drama', *International Journal of Cultural Studies*, 6, 1, 46–63.

Johnson, C. (2001). '*The X-Files*', in G. Creeber (ed.), *The Television Genre Book*, London, British Film Institute.

Johnson, C. (2005). *Telefantasy*, London, British Film Institute.

Johnson, C. and Turnock, R. (eds) (2005). *ITV Cultures: Independent Television over Fifty Years*, Maidenhead, Open University Press.

Johnson, D. (2007). 'Inviting audiences in: the spatial reorganization of production and consumption in "TV III"', *New Review of Film and Television Studies*, 5, 1, 61–80.

King, R. (2006). '*Life on Mars* writers on another planet – top cop', *Manchester Evening News*, 27 February.

Klein, B. and Wardle, C. (2008). '"These two are speaking Welsh on Channel 4!" Welsh representations and cultural tensions on Big Brother 7', *Television and New Media*, 9, 6, 514–30.

Lacey, S. (1995). *British Realist Theatre: The New Wave in its Context, 1956–1965*, London and New York, Routledge.

Lash, S. and Urry, J. (1988). *The End of Organised Capitalism*, Cambridge, Polity Press.

Lash, S. and Urry, J. (1994). *Economies of Signs and Space*, London, Sage.

Laycock, G. (1999). 'Foreword', in T. Newburn, *Understanding and Preventing Police Corruption: Lessons from the Literature*, London, Home Office.

Lamb, S. and Brown, L. M. (2006). *Packaging Girlhood: Rescuing our Daughters from Marketers' Schemes,* New York, St Martin's Press.

Lavery, D. (1994). *Full of Secrets: Critical Approaches to* Twin Peaks, Detroit, Wayne State University Press, pp. 1–23.

Lavery, D. (2008). 'The island's greatest mystery: is *Lost* science fiction?', in J. P. Telotte (ed.), *The Essential Science Fiction TV Reader*, Lexington, University Press of Kentucky, pp. 283–98.

Lavery, D. (2009). '*Lost* and long term television narrative', in P. Harrigan and N. Wardrip-Fruin (eds), *Third Person: Authoring and Exploring Vast Narratives*, Cambridge, MA, Massachusetts Institute of Technology Press, pp. 313–22.

Leverette, M., Ott, B. L. and Buckley, C. L. (eds) (2008). *It's Not TV: Watching HBO in the Post-television Era*, New York and London, Routledge.

'Life on Mars', *BBC Drama* [website], *http://www.bbc.co.uk/lifeonmars/*, accessed 2 February 2009.

Lotz, A. (2001). 'Postfeminist television criticism: rehabilitating critical terms and identifying postfeminist attributes', *Feminist Media Studies*, 1, 1, 105–21.

Lovell, T. (1990). 'Landscape and stories in 1960s British realism', *Screen*, 31, 4, 357–76.

Lowry, B. (2009). 'A creative cure for TV: less is more', *Variety* [website], 30 January 2009, *http://www.variety.com/index.asp?layout=print_story&articleid=VR1117999370&categoryid=14>*, accessed 24 May 2010.

McKay, G. (ed.) (1997). *Yankee Go Home (and Take Me With U): Americanization and Popular Culture*, Sheffield, Sheffield Academic Press.

McNair, B. (2002). *Striptease Culture: Sex, Media and the Democratisation of Desire*, London, Routledge.

McPherson, T. (2008). '"The end of TV as we know it": convergence anxiety, generic innovation, and the case of *24*', in Robert Kolker (ed.), *The Oxford Handbook of Film and Media Studies*, Oxford, Oxford University Press, pp. 306–26.

McRobbie, A. (2004). 'Post-feminism and popular culture', *Feminist Media Studies*, 4, 3, 255–64.

McRobbie, A. (2009). *The Aftermath of Feminism: Gender, Culture and Social Change*, London, Sage.

Massey, D. (2005). *For Space*, London, Sage.

Medina, M. (1998). *Valoración publicitaria de los programas de television (Advertising value of television programmes)*, Pamplona: Eunsa.

Mittell, J. (2004). *Genre and Television: From Cop Shows to Cartoons in American Culture*, New York, Routledge.

Moran, A. (2006). *Understanding the Global TV Format*, Bristol, Intellect.

Moran, A. (2010). *TV Formats Worldwide: Localizing Global Programs*, Bristol, Intellect Ltd.

Moseley, R. and Read, J. (2002). 'Having it Ally: popular television and post-feminism', *Feminist Media Studies*, 2, 2, 231–50.

Nairn, T. (1981). *The Break-up of Britain: Crisis and Neo-nationalism*, London, Verso.

Neale, S. (2000). *Genre and Hollywood*, London, Routledge.

Neal, C. (2006). 'Gangstas, divas, and breaking Tony's balls: musical reference in *The Sopranos*', in D. Lavery (ed.), *Reading the Sopranos: Hit TV from HBO*, London, I. B. Tauris, pp. 121–6.

Nelson, R. (1997). *TV Drama in Transition*, Basingstoke, Macmillan.

Nelson, R. (2007). *State of Play: Contemporary 'High-End' TV Drama*, Manchester, University of Manchester Press.

Nunn, H. and Biressi, A. (2003). 'Silent witness: detection, femininity and the post-mortem body', *Feminist Media Studies*, 3, 2, 193–206.

O'Brien, D. (2000). *SF: UK – How British Science Fiction Changed the World*, Richmond, Reynolds and Hearn.

O'Brien, S. (2006). *SFX Magazine*, 139, January 2006, 58.

Ofcom (2005). *Ofcom Review of Public Service Television Broadcasting. Phase 3, Competition for Quality*, London, Ofcom.

Office of Public Sector Information (1990). *Broadcasting Act 1990*, OPSI [website], *http://www.opsi.gov.uk/acts/acts1990/Ukpga_19900042_en_1.htm*, accessed 9 March 2009.

Orwell, G. (2001[1937]). *The Road to Wigan Pier*, London, Penguin.

Palmer, T. (1977). *All You Need is Love: The Story of Popular Music*, UK DVD, TPDVDBOX1.

Parker, C. (2006). 'Take a look at the lawman – the making of *Life on Mars*, part 1', Disk 1, Bonus Features, *Life on Mars – The Complete Series One*, Contender Home Entertainment.

Peacock, A. (2004). *Public Service Broadcasting without the BBC?*, London, The Institute of Economic Affairs.

Pérez-Lanzac, C. (2009). 'El gran bazar de los formatos' (The great format bazaar), *El Pais Edition Impresa* [online news resource], *http://www.elpais.com/articulo/Pantallas/gran/bazar/formatos/elpepirtv/20090222elpepirtv_1/Tes*, accessed 13 March 2009.

Pickering, M. and Keightley, E. (2006). 'The modalities of nostalgia', *Current Sociology*, 54, 6, 919–41.

Porter, L. and Lavery, D. (2007). *Unlocking the Meaning of* Lost, Napierville, IL, Sourcebooks.

Rabkin, E. S. (ed.) (1983). *Science Fiction: A Historical Anthology*, Oxford, Oxford University Press.

Radstone, S. (2007). *The Sexual Politics of Time: Confession, Nostalgia, Memory*, London, Routledge.

Royle, N. (2003). *The Uncanny: An Introduction*, Manchester, Manchester University Press.

Russell, D. (2004). *Looking North: Northern England and the National Imagination*, Manchester, Manchester University Press.

Schwarz, O. (2009). 'Good young nostalgia: camera phones and technologies of self among Israeli youths', *Journal of Consumer Culture*, 9, 3, 348–76.

Sconce, J. (2005). *Haunted Media: Electronic Presence from Telegraphy to Television*, Durham, NC and London, Duke University Press.

Schneider, M. (2009). 'ABC cancels *Life on Mars*', *Variety* [website], *http://www.variety.com/article/VR1118000748.html?categoryid=14&cs=1&query=life+on+mars*, accessed 12 March 2009.

Spigel, L. (1992a). 'Installing the television set: popular discourses on television and domestic space, 1948–1955', in L. Spigel and D. Mann (eds), *Private Screenings: Television and the Female Consumer*, Minneapolis, University of Minnesota Press, pp. 3–39.

Spigel, L. (1992b). *Make Room for TV: Television and the Family Ideal in Postwar America*, Chicago, University of Chicago Press.

Steemers, J. (2004). *Selling Television: British Television in the Global Marketplace*, London, British Film Institute.

Sullivan, B. F. (2008a). 'On the futon with *Life on Mars* executive producer Josh Appelbaum': part 1, *The Futon Critic* [website], 10 March 2008, *http://www.thefutoncritic.com/rantaspx?id=20081003_lifeonmars*, accessed 24 May 2010.

Sullivan, B. F. (2008b). 'On the futon with *Life on Mars* executive producer Josh Appelbaum': part 2, *The Futon Critic* [website], 6 October 2008, *http://www.thefutoncritic.com/rant.aspx?id=20081006_lifeonmars*, accessed 24 May 2010.

Tagg, P. (2000). *KOJAK Fifty Seconds of Television Music: Towards the Analysis of Effect in Popular Music*, New York, The Mass Media Scholars' Press.

Tagg, P. and Clarida, B. (2003). *Ten Little Title Tunes: Towards a Musicology of the Mass Media*, New York and Montreal, The Mass Media Scholars' Press.

'The Sopranos', *IMDb* [website], *http://www.imdb.com/title/tt0141842/*, accessed 31 March 2009.

Tinic, S. (2009). '*Life on Mars* as seen from the United States: the cultural politics of imports and adaptations', *FlowTV* [website], *http://flowtv.org/?p=3241*, accessed 24 May 2010.

Tiratsoo, N. (ed.) (1997). *From Blitz to Blair: A New History of Britain Since 1939*, London, Weidenfeld & Nicolson.

TNS (2009). 'Histórico de audiencias. España', *Fórmula TV* [website], *http://www.formulatv.com/audiencias/ver/historico/*, accessed 5 July 2010.

Tranter, J. (2004). Interview, *The South Bank Show – TV Drama Stories Part Two*, ITV, 8 February.

Tulloch, J. and Jenkins, H. (1995). *Science Fiction Audiences: Watching Doctor Who and Star Trek*, London, Routledge.

Urry, J. (1995). *Consuming Places*, London, Routledge.

Usborne, D. (2008). 'The Gene Genie gets a LA makeover', *Independent on Sunday*, 18 May 2008 [online news resource], *http://www.independent.co.uk/news/world/americas/the-gene-genie-gets-an-la-makeover-830371.html*, accessed 30 June 2010.

Ware, V. (2007). *Who Cares About Britishness? A Global View of the National Identity Debate*, London, Arcadia.

Warner, M. (2006). *Phantasmagoria – Spirit Visions, Metaphors, and Media into the Twenty-first Century*, Oxford, Oxford University Press.

Westfahl, G. (2000). *Science Fiction, Children's Literature, and Popular Culture – Coming of Age in Fantasyland*, Westport, CT, Greenwood Press.

Whelehan, I. (2000). *Overloaded: Popular Culure and the Future of Feminism*, London, The Women's Press.

Wheatley, H. (2006). *Gothic Television*, Manchester and New York, Manchester University Press.

Williams, R. (1981 [1968]). *Drama from Ibsen to Brecht*, Harmondsworth, Penguin.

Williams, R. (1983 [1976]). *Keywords: A Vocabulary of Culture and Society*, London, Fontana.

Willis, B. (2006). Commentary, bonus features, *Life on Mars – The Complete Series One*, Contender Home Entertainment.

Wylie, I. (2007). '*Life on Mars*: the answers', *Life of Wylie* [website], 11 April 2007, *http://blogs.manchestereveningnews.co.uk/ianwylie/2007/04/life_on_mars_the_answers.html*, accessed 25 August 2010.

Wylie, I. (2010). 'Interview with Matthew Graham', *http://lifeofwylie.com/2010/05/23/ashes-to-ashes-the-answers/*, accessed 8 August 2010.

Zukin, S. (1982). *Loft Living: Culture and Capital in Urban Change*, New Brunswick, NJ, Rutgers University Press.

Zukin, S. (1991). *Landscapes of Power: From Detroit to Disney World*, Berkeley, University of California Press.

ONLINE FAN FORA

Various (2006). *The Railway Arms: Life on Mars/Ashes to Ashes Forums* [web forum], *http://domeofstars.com/forum/*, accessed 10 June 2010.

Various (2007–8). 'Hunt's housewives', *Digital Spy Entertainment Zone Forums* [web forum], *http://www.digitalspy.co.uk/forums/showthread.php?t=765591*, accessed 10 June 2010.

Various (2008). *BFI Film and TV Database* [website], *http://www.bfi.org.uk/filmtvinfo/ftvdb/*, accessed 10 June 2010.

INDEX

Note: references to actors are included for the first point in the text where an actor is specified as playing a character or where the actor is discussed in the text. Other references are listed under the characters' names.